Fever Spores

The Queer Reclamation of William S. Burroughs

Edited by
Brian Alessandro and Tom Cardamone

REBEL SATORI PRESS
New Orleans

Published in the United States of America by

Rebel Satori Press

www.rebelsatoripress.com

Portions of this collection have appeared previously:"The Beats: Pictures of a Legend," Edmund White, originally published in *The New York Review of Books* in July 2010; "The Arrested Evolution of William S. Burroughs," Tom Cardamone, originally published in *The New Engagement* in July 2020;"My Hungry Interzone or: What You Consume," Brian Alessandro, originally published in *Lambda Literary* in February 2021

Hardcover ISBN: 978-1-60864-201-4

Paperback ISBN: 978-1-60864-202-1

Ebook ISBN: 978-1-60864-203-8

Library of Congress Cataloguing In Publication Date: 2022937085

What they are saying about

Fever Spores

"Brian Alessandro and Tom Cardamone's exhilarating *Fever Spores: The Queer Reclamation of William S. Burroughs* takes the already refractory genius of William S. Burroughs and strains it through the prism of dozens of other geniuses, thereby restoring to us one of the most necessary writers of the 20th Century. Transgressive, startling, surreal, and queer as hell, Alessandro and Cardamone's book is itself fully worthy of its subject."—**Matthew Specktor**, author of *Always Crashing in The Same Car: On Art, Crisis, and Los Angeles, California*

"I confess that I'd rather read about Burroughs than read him. This aristocratic scarecrow in seedy suits is far more interesting to me than his experimental fantasies. But Brian Alessandro and Tom Cardamone have put together a lively collection of different voices and points of view that gave me a wonderful place to think about Burroughs, both the man and his work. I learned a lot and came away with new appreciation for him and his place in culture, popular, unpopular, queer and otherwise."—**Christopher Bram**, author of *Gods & Monsters*

"*Fever Spores* is a cornucopia, a total feast: for the Burroughs student, fan, newcomer too: enjoy and be satisfied by this queer writer like none other. Bravo to Alessandro & Cardamone!"—**Kathe Koja**, author of *Cipher, Under the Poppy* and *Dark Factory*

A note from the editors:
in the spirit of William S. Burroughs's Cut-Up philosophy
the writings herein were organized in a random fashion.

Calling all boys of the earth we will teach you the secrets of magic control of wind and rain. Giver of winds is our name. We will teach you to ride the hurricanes bending palm trees to the ground, high tension wires fall on the police car. We will teach you control of animals birds and reptiles how to pass into their bodies and use them like a knife. We will show you the sex magic that turns flesh to light. We will free you forever from the womb.

—*William S. Burroughs,* **Port of Saints**

CONTENTS

INTRODUCTION: THE ARRESTED EVOLUTION OF WILLIAM S. BURROUGHS

TOM CARDAMONE

I consider that immortality is the only goal worth striving for: immortality in Space. Man is an artifact created for the purpose of Space travel. He is not designed to remain in his present state any more than a tadpole is designed to remain a tadpole. But man is in a state of arrested evolution.

Time is that which ends, and Man is in Time.

The transition from Time to Space is quite as drastic as the evolutionary transition from water to land . . . Immortality is something you have to work and fight for . . . The Old Man of the Mountain discovered that immortality is possible in Space, and this is the Western Lands of the Egyptian Book of the Dead.

The Western Lands is a real place. It exists, and we built it, with our hands and our brains. We paid for it, with our blood and our lives. It's ours, and we're going to take it.

1982, Excerpt from Statement on the Final Academy, *William S. Burroughs: Invisible Hombre* Barry Miles

Tallahassee, Florida State University, a pale blue kidney bean-shaped pool of my then-girlfriend's nondescript apartment complex, 1992. Wallowing in the residue of cheap weed and an ever-handy thermos of watery Jack and Cokes, deathly thin, I was soaking up the sun. She and I had met during a post-undergraduate semester in London, where I'd bought so many books around Charing Cross Road that when I packed them for the trip home, the handle came off the suitcase when I attempted to lift it. Stuffed among my prized Philip K. Dick reprints (most of his work was out of print in the states at the time) were pulpy William S. Burroughs paperbacks. I'd scored something from the *Nova Trilogy: The Soft Machine, The Ticket That Exploded,* or *Nova Express.* I wish I could recall which ones; they had this psychedelic cover that insinuated paranoia over strawberry fields. I enjoyed the surreal, cut-up method of the book, the razor sharpness of certain sentences. Whichever books I read, I didn't know they were parts of a trilogy, just that the cut-up method worked. It exposed the fallacies of narrative storytelling while serving up a self-aware con game—I felt the author was an admirable hustler entranced by his own version of Three-card Monte and I wanted to know more. I was desperate to be a writer but afraid to put anything down on paper. I was okay with stalking the darker figures of literature, however, knowing that the entrances I required were in alleyways or underground.

Back in Florida, I read Ted Morgan's *Literary Outlaw: The Life and Times of William S. Burroughs* poolside beneath the withering sun. The drainage pond over my shoulder was a polluted shadow patrolled by a lone, minute alligator, a silent sentinel cutting verdant scum. Satellites of crushed Budweiser cans bounced in his wake. Across from me, an impossibly skinny blonde girl in an American flag bikini would not stop talking to her brunette friend—endless chatter, wiry, white arms tossed across their foreheads. I passed them on the way back to the apartment to refill my thermos. "Anyone who has AIDS deserves to die," the blonde girl spat in my direction. I pretended not to hear this.

Inside was air-conditioning and white stucco walls: bong hits, a quick Marlboro Light to heighten the high—I was at the pool again in fifteen minutes with a fresh thermos of whiskey, nonplussed by the poisoned arrow hurled at me just moments ago. I had all the armor I needed: girlfriend, the daily anesthesia of drugs and alcohol, sleeping twelve hours every day, pouring myself into books. If death slipped the occasional Valentine's Day card under the door, so be it. That was the price to play a heterosexual charade.

A few years later I moved to New York City, where the lingering psychological accoutrements of the closet are unceremoniously stripped from you right there at La Guardia. When I wasn't clubbing or delving into the bar scene, I was nosing around libraries and bookstores, devouring gay literature. I was writing and meeting writers, and as the years progressed, I noticed that Burroughs was divorced from these conversations. Having edited two nonfiction books on gay writing, which required research and readings across the queer spectrum and communications written or in-person with a multitude of professional writers and scholars, I can confirm this: William S. Burroughs was never once mentioned. A gay writer whose most famous and formerly banned novel, *Naked Lunch*, has been certified a classic of American literature and filmed by David Cronenberg, a gay writer whose books are in every Barnes & Noble in the country, a gay man whose image is on the cover of the Beatles' album *Sgt. Pepper's Lonely Hearts Club Band*, a lover and mentor to Allen Ginsberg—he has been sainted by the literary establishment in general but not the gay literati in particular.

One reason is the "gay canon" itself*, an unofficial collection of books that, while often progressive and transgressive, adhere to the more formal structures of the novel and storytelling, falling within the political narratives of coming out or self-discovery. Some books successfully represent the decade in which they were written in a way that allows them to exist under glass, dated but not dated, intricate amphorae depicting discos and cocaine, furtive cruising 'round the Coliseum at night and the like. By and large, these are often great books that have superseded their sexuality to join the ranks of classic works in general.

I'm certainly not declaring that the "gay canon" is restrictive or restrained in general (though I can imagine others more widely read offering additional titles for inclusion, hence the parentheticals) but rather that it *is* to Burroughs in particular. While he can be considered one of the most political writers of the twentieth century, on par with Orwell, if not a less-than-direct descendent, his politics are not those of our beloved Larry Kramer. Additionally, homosexuality is rarely the driver of the characters in the books of his that I have read (many of them dripping with menacing homosexuality, some really insane sex, and vibrant gay characters. Plus, lots of sketchy pirate boys on the make.) Full disclosure: I am not a William S. Burroughs disciple. I have enjoyed and pondered what Burroughs has crossed my path over the years: *Junky, Queer,* two of the cut-up books, *The Place of Dead Roads* trilogy, assorted miscellanea, and two biographies. Even with my limited knowledge, I feel that a question worth asking is worth answering and that a partial answer lies in the previous sentence: the novel *Queer,* a planned sequel to *Junky,* was written between 1951 and 1953 but not published until 1985 well after Burroughs was an established literary celebrity. The book is darkly hilarious, irreverent, and singularly bizarre. The main character (a sidewinder version of Burroughs), Lee's gayness is dealt with in such a disarmingly offhand manner that the casual reader can be excused for getting carried away with Burroughs's noirish free styling and not pick up on how revolutionary this depiction really is. Black humor aside, rare moments of introspection poke through the constant grit and grift of this tight little novel.

"I had a duty to live and to bear my burden proudly for all to see, to conquer prejudice and ignorance and hate with knowledge and sincerity and

love. *Whenever you are threatened by a hostile presence, you emit a thick cloud of love like an octopus squirts ink . . ."*

This from the fifties. Had it debuted alongside Gore Vidal's *The City and the Pillar* (1948), or James Baldwin's *Giovanni's Room* (1956), with decades to cement itself as a groundbreaking classic rather than a curious relic overshadowed by *Naked Lunch* then it's possible that this essay would have been a moot point.

Queer, like much of Burroughs's writing, has dark shifts in narration, and while Lee is obsessed with an easily bored heterosexual boy who only occasionally puts out, the latent driver of the plot is the search for yage, a drug that promotes telepathy. The recreational drug use found in the more daring gay novels of the 80s pale in comparison to Burroughs's informative lifelong addiction to heroin (he was on methadone well into his 70s). As a subculture figurehead, he was romanticized by heterosexual rock musicians (in concert, Lou Reed used to wrap his microphone cord around his arm and mimic shooting up) and gonzo journalists in the 70s and 80s for his transgressive behavior and writings—anathema to a percentage of the modern gay reader. Broadly speaking, our community's current relationship with substance use is defined through the shaming lens of addiction.

However, in the 60s drug use was often viewed as an opportunity for mind expansion; presently harder drugs are gobbled by gays for heightened, prolonged sex. Before that, we had a collective love affair with cocaine, which is synonymous with the narcissism of the 70s. To be blunt, gays are more interested in the riot of self-expression and the dissolution of past trauma that comes with drug-fueled orgies than mediations on time and space, the viral nature of language, and anti-authoritarianism. And that's not a criticism, just a note that we can expand our priorities by mixing up our substances of choice.

After all, Burroughs was a founding member of the Beats, that loose artistic collective dedicated to raising the consciousness of our species.

Gay issues were but a simmering subset of concerns when the burgeoning counterculture was up against the mammoth American war machine and the rigidity of political conservatism. Even then, the Beats's embrace of eastern mysticism and more personal forms of literary self-expression were merely starting points for Burroughs. He went farther and darker into existential territories only ever previously encountered in the prison writings of the Marquis De Sade. Here's the crux: the nihilism in his work is counter to the constant drumbeats of gay life: positivity, perseverance, and consumerism. Really, imagine Burroughs in the back of the convertible with Gilbert Baker, waving to the throngs at that Gay Parade in heaven. It's just not possible.

The most likely reason that Burroughs is not habitually referenced as a founding member of modern gay letters is that his gay book has yet to be *compiled*. Throughout Barry Miles's 1993 biography, *William Burroughs: El Hombre Invisible: A Portrait*, he references that Burroughs felt his works were all one long text. This is confirmed in *The Letters of William S. Burroughs: 1945-1959*, also published in 1993. His letters, predominately to Ginsberg, are profound and profane, gossipy, bitchy, and a record of events, themes, and personas that will inform future books for decades to come. "Maybe the real novel is letters to you." Excerpts of these letters, *Queer* in its entirety, parts of his trilogies, who knows what else—there is a masterwork yet to be assembled. I wonder where Barnes & Noble would shelve it?

Even his heterosexual hagiographers have it wrong. In what I believe was the last original book published in Burroughs's lifetime, *My Education*, a collection of dreams with occasional reminisces, he casually confronts his biographer, Ted Morgan, and his biography's chosen title, *Literary Outlaw*, head-on. "To be an outlaw you must first have a base in law to reject and get out of. I never had such a base. I never had a place I could call home that meant more than a key to a house."

How much of gay literature counteracts repression, serves as a declaration of the right to exist or provides an elegiac record of existence under such repression, where Burroughs exists, thinks, creates fully outside this diametrical opposition? William S. Burroughs was a writer who accidentally killed his wife, spent decades addicted to heroin, was an expatriate's expatriate, and was more involved with Scientology than his acolytes would care to admit, all while generating reams of writing that not only smashed the strictures of fiction but influenced generations of writers. Forget "coming out." With William S. Burroughs, there's no negotiation, no need for acceptance, for escape, for forgiveness or reconciliation.He wanted *us* to advance, wholly, willfully, with immortal intent.

"The transition from Time to Space is quite as drastic as the evolutionary transition from water to land . . ."

If William S. Burroughs were writing this, then that alligator is still there, a stationary emerald set in a pool of shimmering mercury. A potent Egyptian God. I'm there, too. When the skinny girl wishes me dead, I pull a Luger from behind the waistband of my red swimsuit and aim it at her head. She screams as I shoot her friend instead. Blood droplets black as old pennies coat the bottom of the pool.

That's what writers do. We leave witnesses.

Example: The 25 Best LGBT Novels of All Time, The Advocate/ However The Publishing Triangle List of the 100 Best Lesbian and Gay Novels, *compiled in the late 1990s, lists* Naked Lunch *at #52. The judges were Dorothy Allison, David Bergman, Christopher Bram, Michael Bronski, Samuel R. Delany, Lillian Faderman, Anthony Heilbut, M.E. Kerr, Jenifer Levin, John Loughery, Jaime Manrique, Mariana Romo-Carmona, Sarah Schulman, and Barbara Smith.*

"I DON'T GET THE IMPRESSION THAT HE WAS INTERESTED IN GAY LIBERATION": AN INTERVIEW WITH SAMUEL R. DELANY

BRIAN ALESSANDRO

With four Nebula Awards and two Hugo Awards, Samuel R. Delany is one of the most respected and influential science fiction writers in the world. His work, like Burroughs's, blurs the lines between the surreal and the actual, the erotic and the speculative, the satiric and the deadly serious. And like Burroughs, his literature is unabashedly queer. Among his most noted titles are, Nova, The Einstein Intersection, Hogg, Dhalgren, The Mad Man, *and* Babel-17.

Delany discusses his encounter with Burroughs in Kansas, Burroughs's missing finger, their marriages to women, and the intellectual and literary interactions they shared in their writing.

BRIAN ALESSANDRO: Samuel, in your book, *Occasional Views, Volume 1,* you chronicle a dinner between yourself and Burroughs. What were some of the key insights you gleaned from that meeting?

SAMUEL R. DELANY: That he was a serious writer. People were

calling him up with jobs, which is one of the reasons he called me, you know. He called me in to sort of brainstorm about a job that he had just been given, which was in this case to write a film script for William Gibson's *Neuromancer*. I believe it was for a group, two brothers, who used to go by the title The Cabana Boys, and they were kind of like, you know, The Wachowski Brothers, for instance, or the Wachowski *Sisters*, is the case.

ALESSANDRO: Yes.

DELANY: I haven't heard their names in twenty-five years. They were these two guys. They were like Ethan and Joel Cohen.

ALESSANDRO: Sure.

DELANY: Whom I also knew slightly, just personally, but that's another story. Anyway, they asked him if he'd consider doing a proposal for a script of Gibson's *Neuromancer*. I don't believe a movie was ever made of it.

ALESSANDRO: Not to my knowledge, but that would have been really fascinating.

DELANY: Yeah, it would have been. It influenced, I think, a lot of other movies. I don't think a movie like Disney's *Tron* would have been made if it wasn't for *Neuromancer*.

ALESSANDRO: I agree.

DELANY: Bill [Gibson] was, among other things, one of my students at one point.

I knew him sort of personally for a short time when he was at Clarion [an annual science fiction and fantasy writers' workshop]. But anyway, when I met Bill [Burroughs], I knew that Bill—I called him "Bill" … Burroughs! I felt more comfortable calling him "Burroughs," but I mean, since I did go to his house for dinner, for that day he was "Bill." I didn't call him "Mr. Burroughs." James Grauerholz had basically come and picked me up at the University of Kansas where I was staying, which was also in Lawrence, and simply drove me over to Burroughs's home. And I was there for an afternoon into an evening. One of the things that happened is Bill had just gotten a book on lemurs. Among other things, he showed me his gun collection, and I said, "Gee, that's interesting."

(Delany and I laugh.)

DELANY: I'm not a gun person, at all. I mean, you know.

ALESSANDRO: Nor am I.

DELANY: I had a BB gun when I was thirteen that my father got for me. I have never let guns in my house because for a while I had a kid. My superintendent used to carry a gun around. He was named Ashley and I would say, "Ashley, actually don't bring the gun in the house! I have a three-year-old!"

ALESSANDRO: It's dangerous.

DELANY: "You're gonna hang your coat up with a gun in the pocket? You know, I don't want it. You know, I don't think she [Delany's three-year-old daughter at the time] is going to go in the pocket." But we [Burroughs and Delany] had a very nice night, after a very nice afternoon. I came over at about three thirty in the afternoon. And we talked about the film script and what he could do, and different ways to approach the film script. I'm a movie person. I've made a couple of films myself, at that point. And I was talking about, you know, film, film scripts, and what have you. He'd been involved in being in films, but I don't think he'd been involved in making them. I do not remember what I said, quite honestly, and I don't remember very clearly what he said. But I do remember that he had gotten this big coffee table book on lemurs and started talking to me about how enthusiastic he was about lemurs. At one point, I saw something that I don't think anybody ever mentioned. Burroughs was missing the first joint of one of his fingers.

ALESSANDRO: I've never heard that!

DELANY: Like it had been cut off at some point. And so, and I've known two or three people who've had, you know, [lost a finger], and so I sort of said, "Oh, by the way, how did you lose the joint, the finger?" You know, well, he got very, very embarrassed and began to sputter and well, you know, like, it's very clear, it was something he did not want to talk about. I have no idea what it was. And so, I said, "No, I'm sorry, it's none of my business." I backed off and so, we skipped over. But I do know that he was very ... it was something. I'm still curious how he lost the finger.

ALESSANDRO: As am I now. It's very intriguing.

DELANY: Yeah, but I also knew it was not something that he was eager to talk about. You know, I don't know whether people asked him about it all the time. I've had friends, other friends, who were missing a finger and I've asked them, and usually they can say, "Oh, yeah, well, I was working in a machine shop and ..."

(We laugh.)

ALESSANDRO: There's an interesting backstory, usually.

DELANY: Yes, which is what somebody just explained to me about two months ago, on the phone, somebody I met a while ago who was missing a finger. And then I knew another kid who was missing a finger joint, and it was in a motorcycle accident. None of them had problems answering it. But this was something that he really didn't want to go into and that stayed with me.

ALESSANDRO: How did Burroughs connect with you?

DELANY: Grauerholz sent me a postcard. He was Bill's keeper at the time. Jim was an obviously gay man. Burroughs was not. So, you know, like your gaydar did not …

ALESSANDRO: Didn't register?

DELANY: You just saw it. Grauerholz also had a friend at the house. And as well, they had invited an older woman. I think she was older than I was. And one of the things that they mentioned was Debbie Harry. They said, "Oh, yeah, well, Debbie Harry was here just yesterday, last evening." So, I came the day after Debbie Harry had been there. I also got the impression that Debbie was in and out. I was only there that one evening.

ALESSANDRO: She and Chris Stein were close with Burroughs. They spent a lot of time together in New York, in The Bunker.

DELANY: So, we talked about filmmaking and what you have to do, you know, and proposals, and shooting scripts and things like that, and interiors and exteriors. You know, that's what he wanted. I don't know how much he knew about that, at all. Then I stayed for dinner and the dinner was very, very good.Grauerholz prepared it. Tournedos Rossini!

ALESSANDRO: You remember the dinner? That's great.

DELANY: That was very, very nice.

ALESSANDRO: You emerged as a writer in the early 1960s, not long after Burroughs. More than anything for many decades you were contemporaries. How have your writings overlapped or even informed each other?

DELANY: I first knew about Burroughs through *Naked Lunch*, when I was a teenager. And we shared a publisher. Ace Books. His very first novel came out with Ace Books. And my then wife, Marilyn Hacker, her second or third job was with Ace Books. So, she and Carl Solomon, of *Howl* fame (Ginsberg dedicated his poem to Solomon), was down the hall and Carl, whom I never met, I called him, "Solomon," had brought in *Junky*, Burroughs's first novel, which was published under the pseudonym of William Lee. And I used to own an Ace Books copy of *Junky*, but I don't anymore. I just lost a lot of my library not too long ago. I'm just replacing it here and there. I have no idea if anything I ever did informed him, at all. And I don't think anything he wrote particularly influenced me. I enjoyed *Naked Lunch*, but it's not anything like I ever would have thought about writing. A book I much preferred to *Naked Lunch* was Alexander Trocchi's *Cain's Book* (1960), which was also published by Grove Press, and I thought that was a superb novel. He was a Scottish novelist who traveled around and didn't live too terribly long because he was also under the influence of drugs.

ALESSANDRO: I have to say, Samuel, that even though you don't think that you influenced one another, you both do that same brave, rare thing of combining erotica with science fiction and social commentary and queerness, though I realized that you often keep the genres separated, whereas Burroughs kind of mixed them all together. Did you two ever discuss this sort of novel, provocative approach?

DELANY: No, no, no, I hadn't read *Queer*. The only thing I had read was *The Ticket That Exploded*, some of *The Yage Letters*, and I had the whole [City Lights] Pocket Poet series, but Burroughs didn't publish poetry, per se. So, I never had a Pocket Poet volume of his, whereas I had *Howl* and *Gasoline* by [Gregory] Corso, and what have you, and Robert Duncan, and all those things.

ALESSANDRO: Would you describe Burroughs as a science fiction writer?

DELANY: No, not at all. No. No, I think he *likes* science fiction. And I gather that there is an element of that in some of the stories, but I mean, I don't think he was interested. I think in science fiction … *good* science fiction does not violate what is known to be known. Burroughs was a fantasy writer! An interesting fantasy writer. But then I've argued that in this sense, everybody who writes fiction is some kind of a fantasist, more or less. Even writing autobiographical fantasy.

ALESSANDRO: Even the Saul Bellows and the Philip Roths among us take fantastical spins.

(*We both laugh.*)

DELANY: I think, yes, right. Exactly.

ALESSANDRO: Many people do not recognize Burroughs's queerness even though it was central to his books and his life. Why do you think that is?

DELANY: Burroughs did tend to write for people very close to him. He envisioned his audience to be other people, and he moved in a queer circle. From the start, I envisioned my audience to be people who were "out there." And so, there's no touch of anything particularly queer until you get to … well, in *Babel-17* there's a group of people who have a three-way sexual relationship. Now two guys and a woman and they're not the main characters, but the main characters have also had that kind of relationship, although not on stage. So, I would think that's about as close as I get to it. And one of my major interesting relationships was a three-way relationship that inspired that, and I'm very glad I had it and I still remember it as a very, very pleasant time. But I don't know how Burroughs managed, you know, the heterosexuality and homosexuality, and how they worked. One of the things I did not mention, I knew all about the situation with his first wife.

ALESSANDRO: Oh, Joan.

DELANY: I knew that it was public knowledge by that point. But I certainly didn't walk in and say, "Oh, and by the way, how did you shoot your first wife?" I knew enough not to go in and do that. And especially given how not ready to talk about how he lost the joint of a little finger, you know, I'm sure that would have been a problem for him. You know, I've been married, and I knew he had been married. And I think I knew by that time that there was a William Burroughs, Jr. There was a guy in San Francisco … I lived in San Francisco for a couple of years … and there was a guy running around there who claimed to be William Burroughs, Jr, who was in the same circle. And all the circles in San Francisco were much smaller than they were in New York.

ALESSANDRO: Yeah, absolutely.

DELANY: There was as little of an exchange between Burroughs and myself on this matter [Burroughs's identity as a queer writer] because I think that was very much a sociological point. I grew up in New York. As soon as I was interested in it, I had no problem finding gay partners. At least, for casual sex. Thousands and thousands. I once estimated the number of gay partners I had sex with it, and it was in the nature of 57,000.

ALESSANDRO: That's incredible.

DELANY: As opposed to eight women. [*Laughter*] Now that is just an estimate. And that's maybe on the conservative side. One of the reasons for that is because it was so available. There were movie theaters, there were bars, there were parks. And I was a movie theater person. And there were baths! Bathhouses, which I tried. The ones that I liked the most and rewarded my particular kinds of taste were movie theaters. You could go and spend an afternoon and have twelve partners or more. On a good day you could have between twelve and twenty-four partners. If you were a full-time writer, you could do that three times a week and that's a lot of partners per week. At the end of my book, *The Mad Man*, I include a *Lancet* Kingsley-Kalsow-Rinaldo medical study from February 1987, ["Risk Factors for Seroconversion to Human Immunodeficiency Virus Among Male Homosexuals"] and it is still the best study ever done [about oral sex and transmission] and the fact that many, many studies like it were not done is a crime.

ALESSANDRO: Yes, it is.

DELANY: It makes it fairly clear that HIV is not passed on orally. Statistically, there was something like a 0.00000 point something chance of contracting it that way. And that covered mistakes. That's why the way I have and am having sex and I have had lots and lots of sex—and I remain HIV-negative to this day—was probably the best way to do it. My partner and I are both HIV-negative. I once went with someone who insisted on using a condom and he tried to rob me.

(*We both laugh.*)

ALESSANDRO: Rubbers are forever associated with larceny!

DELANY: Yeah, right, exactly! Condoms for me are bad!I was also never interested in anal sex. I'm an oral guy. And am proud to be so. I wear the badge proudly. And it's kept me alive.

ALESSANDRO: You write quite transgressively (*The Mad Man, Hogg*) about gay themes, similarly to Burroughs in that respect. What kind of resistance did you encounter from publishers, critics, and censors over your work?

DELANY: Well, it depends. The people who publish pornography were perfectly happy to publish me. Richard Kasak, who was the second publisher of my pornography, the first was Lancer Books, who did some highly sexual stuff. They changed the title of *Equinox* to *Ties of Lust*, or something, and with me fighting and screaming all the way. Because I said, the name of the book was *Equinox*! I eventually republished it, and, when Kasak republished it, he said you can call it anything you want. His one thing, he said, "You can't have any characters under eighteen." And so, my way of getting around that was very simple. I just added 100 years to everybody's character. I put a little introduction from the publisher that stated, "This is because of our great moral thinking, we do not have any characters under eighteen." And so, I have just gone through the manuscript and added an even 100 years. So, if you have sex with somebody who is fourteen years old, they're 114.

ALESSANDRO: And speaking of *Hogg*, which many consider one of the most seminal transgressive novels of American literature, did Burroughs ever read or comment on the book?

DELANY: I don't, as far as I know, I don't know. I asked Jim [Grauerholz] why does Burroughs want to particularly see me? He says, "Well, he likes science fiction." That is all I knew. He never mentioned any particular work of mine he'd ever read. Just that that I was a science fiction writer. I think I may have mentioned that I knew Gibson. We didn't dwell on it. He never mentioned that he'd read a word of my work other than that he knew I was a science fiction writer, and he wanted to talk with somebody who was an actual science fiction writer. And we ended up talking more about films as I remember, than we did about science fiction.

ALESSANDRO: Which modern day writers do you think carries the mantle for confrontational literature these days? Do we have a living writer on parity with Burroughs?

DELANY: I have no idea. I don't read as much anymore. My reading has gone way down. I am severely dyslexic, and I have a mild cognitive disorder, my doctor tells me, which has made the dyslexia worse. I don't trust my judgement of anything I read anymore. I find the instructions on the back of a box hard to read.

ALESSANDRO: Is Burroughs significant to American culture? And if so, why?

DELANY: Yeah, I think he was. I think the drugs, I think the drug stuff was much more important. I think it was a much more important part of Burroughs's life. And I think it was a much more important part of his writing. I haven't read the work like *Queer* or *The Wild Boys* or *Cities of The Red Night*, which I gather are the ones that talk about sex directly. And gay sex particularly. I don't think he was interested in it at all as from a political point of view. I mean, I don't get the impression that he was interested in, you know, gay liberation or anything like that. I was! I was very, very interested in that. In fact, I was interested in feminism long before I was interested in gay liberation. At the same time, I was never a joiner. You know, I belong to an association. At one point, just when my daughter was an infant, I helped start a group of gay fathers called The Daddies, named by my daughter, that grew to about a group of about forty guys, and I started with a with a music teacher at Columbia, who had two kids who was a gay father and married to a Chase Manhattan Bank vice president. I've lost touch with both of them. As far as I know, Burroughs was never a member of any group at all.

THE WILD BOYS

PAUL RUSSELL

I carry in me at least four different *Wild Boys*, widely separated in time and comprehension. It was the first queer text I ever read, though I don't think I could have had any idea what the phrase *queer text* might even mean back in the early seventies, the wasteland of my high school years, when I came across the Evergreen Black Cat paperback in a bookstore. I've often gauged a book's promise by its cover—how else are you going to if you haven't yet read it?—and that fierce-looking, brown-skinned teenage boy lunging toward me with his bayoneted rifle instantly took me hostage. I flipped through the pages almost as an afterthought: *John reached out and pulled the towel away looking at Audrey's half-erection... "You ever been goosed Audrey?"... Audrey shook his head blushing... "Lean over and brace your hands on your knees" ... He heard John unscrew a jar then felt the greased finger slide up him. He gasped and threw his head back... "You ever been rosed Audrey?"... Thumbs prying his buttocks apart as John squirmed forward. Pinks eggs popped in his crotch.*

How was it possible I could be reading sentences like this in the Raleigh Springs Mall? How could such a dangerous artifact have slithered its way past the suffocating surveillance of this Southern Baptist-run concentration camp that was Memphis, Tennessee? Already half hard in anticipation of insanely forbidden pleasure, I ambled nonchalantly up to the cash register. The cashier, a girl my own age, glanced at the cover and announced, "Cool! What's it about?" The pretentious absurdity that was my younger self probably mumbled something mitigating like "Oh, it's a famous study of the political dynamics of revolutionary youth movements in Mexico." She bemuses me now, that long-ago girl, how her innocent or at least unjudgmental "cool!" rang in my ears as I slunk away with my pervy contraband.

To claim I read Burroughs's novel from cover to cover for its literary merits would be a lie. I only read the sex parts and skipped everything else—the weird satirical vignettes and Control Machine rants and Vietnam War allegory and Boschian phantasmagoria—but since there were so many sex parts I actually did end up getting through quite a lot of it.

I'd never before read any kind of gay sex scene anywhere, except for that meltingly restrained passage in Nabokov's *Pale Fire*:

> *The two lads were told to wash up. The recent thrill of adventure was superceded by another sort of excitement. They locked themselves up. The tap ran unheeded. Both were in a manly state and moaning like doves.*

That's the thing about the closet: it takes very little gunpowder to set off an explosion.

The Wild Boys, on the other hand, afforded nearly nonstop fireworks, a kaleidoscopic mènage of boys coupling in various eras and locales, from 1929 St. Louis on the brink of the stock market crash to Marrakesh and Casablanca in a calamitous eighties future. Even in my breathless space/time leaps from one blue boy fuck to the next, I soon registered, a little uneasily, that I was essentially reading the same (compulsively exciting, even addictive) scene over and over. "Turn around and bend over" ("Vuelvete y aganchete"[sic—I think Burroughs means *agachate*]) is the narrative's persistent refrain. Never congress in any other position than what the Romans called coitus more ferarum, "sexual intercourse in the manner of wild beasts." The scenes were brief, mechanical, satisfyingly to the point. Except... The repetition soon became uncanny, a kind of erotic déjà vu—sex as ghostly memory obsessively pored over from multiple angles, revisited in multiple dimensions. The compulsive return lent those feral couplings a strange poetry. The crudely efficient peep show vignettes that composed my initial *Wild Boys* may have triggered a gratifying physiological response, but something in the interstices, fugitive whispers I inadvertently picked up on, lingered disquietingly.

> *I remember London stairs worn red carpeting and I could see his pants were sticking up between his legs colored photo had something written on it... "Vuelvete y aganchete" ... I let myself go limp inside blank factual he slid it in out through the dusty little window afternoon hills the old broken point of origin St. Louis Missouri*

Some years passed. I had long been furtively composing my own Burroughs-esque bacchanalias, all pretty mechanical as well, which I stashed in a manila envelope I'd misleadingly labeled MATH ASSIGNMENTS—though I guess those vignettes *were*, in a sense, math assignments: derive from an idiosyncratic but carefully calculated combination of Xs and Ys my own incalculable orgasms. But as time went by, I branched out; I grew more interested in less efficient, more distracting equations including plot and character. I started writing short stories. Perhaps unconsciously I had taken to heart the reforms enunciated by Burroughs's "great Slastobitch": *The blue movies as a separate genre have ceased to exist. We show sex as it occurs in the story as a part of life not a mutilated fragment.*

One of my first more or less fully achieved stories, "Long Days and Warm Nights: How the Revolution Almost Started," told a tale of two ersatz wild boys, angel and tomaso (I thought it revolutionary to leave proper nouns lower case) and their magical-realist exploits in a vaguely Mexicanized village. They didn't wear rainbow-colored jockstraps and Mercury sandals, but they did make vaguely provocative use of their bodies and in the process discover how to "fly," the whole story the kind of flying dream Burroughs's Green Nun punishes Audrey for, and which the novel's wild boys on their hang gliders turn into a species of delirious reality in the Desert of Blue Silence. I composed it under the spell of David Bowie's "Golden Years" at a time when I often wrote while relying on music as an aid to this more sustained variety of orgasm. I didn't yet know how deeply Burroughs's narrative techniques, especially the celebrated cut-up and fold-in techniques, had influenced Bowie's own compositional practices. But clearly, I intuited a connection. What I was trying to recreate in my early twenties was the exciting combination, in both men's work, of estrangement and familiarity that had haunted my adolescent experience of *The Wild Boys*.

Recently I reread "Long Days" for the first time in nearly four decades; it's tame, puerile, embarrassingly derivative, but the story's infatuated prose (*Waiting for angel to come down tomaso skipped smooth stones that left a line of footprints across the surface, until he found himself suddenly swept into angel's arms, carried above the world, and dropped dreamily as sunlight into the mirror of the deep pool, the lava vent that went down and down. Coming upon them one day, the farmer juarez thought he heard the music of doves...*) has maybe not gone completely stale. Crucially, it was the first time I ever dared couple, however demurely, the preoccupations of my private scribbles with a more public-facing prose. I've never looked back.

"Vuelvete"... getting hard in the blue light... "Bend over Johnny"... The boy picked up a tin of Vaseline and slowly with a calm intent expression

rubbed it on his cock... "Bend over Johnny and spread ass"... feeling the eyes
and fingers on his rectum ass hairs spread the slow penetration...

   Another decade went by. At Vassar I would regularly teach a course
called "Gay Male Narratives in America after 1945." I included *The*
Wild Boys on the original syllabus—a no-brainer, I thought. This Vassar *Wild Boys* was necessarily a different beast than either the adolescent masturbation aid or the artist-as-a-young-homo roadmap. The
blue movie sex was still the glue that held the whole together, but there
was so much else worth investigating in this sober academic setting.
The delicious satire of *Le Gran Luxe*, for instance, staged in a 1989
Marrakech overrun by *wild boys in the streets whole packs of them vicious*
as famished dogs. Amid widespread societal breakdown, the fabulously
wealthy A.J., craving *a dinner of fresh hog's liver, fried squirrel, wild aspara-*
grass, turnip greens, hominy grits, corn on the cob and blackberries, goes to
comic lengths to ensure that the hog, *an Ozark razor-back fed on acorns,*
peanuts, mulberries and Missouri apples, arrives in pristine condition. *It*
must be wafted here on a raft slung between two giant zeppelins. My squir-
rels, blackberries and wild asparagrass will of course accompany the hog and
send a farm boy with it a thin boy with freckles. When the hog finally arrives, *there in the sky suspended between two vast blue zeppelins is a piece of*
Missouri trailing the smoke of hardwood forests. Later, to demonstrate his
benevolence toward the locals, A.J. will construct a huge phallus in the
citadel wall that pisses out liquid leftovers (Martinis, soup, Coca-Cola,
hot buttered rum...) into a trough marked DRINKS, and a rubber anus
that spurts solid leftovers (Baked Alaska, salted herring, chili con carne,
peach melba...) into the EATS trough.*Screaming clawing drooling the*
crowd throws itself at the troughs scooping up food and drinks with both
hands. The odor of vomit rises in clouds. A.J presses a button that seals the
balcony over. Ventilators whir and a smell of cool summer pools and mossy

stones envelops the guests. We all stay a month which isn't hard to do considering what is inside and what is outside.

My students in that course were for the most part gay men and their straight women allies. Some found *Le Gran Luxe* moderately amusing; most did not. What did this have to do with being gay? They were confused by the novel's fragmentary plot, frustrated by the fungible characters ("Even less than two-dimensional!"), bored by the fold-ins and cut-ups ("I just started skimming when I hit one of those patches"). Puritanical as only the young can be, they especially rebelled at so much unnecessary sex ("Ugh! Just Ugh!").

"Meaningless promiscuity, misogyny, drug use, nihilism," one student complained. "This book just confirms everybody's worst fears about what gay men are really all about."

In my best literary/critical mode, I tried to get them to ask themselves what all that gay sex might be doing in the novel. "Even if it's quote-unquote meaningless, can it still *mean* something? What narrative work does it perform?"

No response, till after a long silence a languidly elegant student from Mumbai raised his hand. "Well, maybe, you know, the novel isn't wallowing in gratuitous sex for its own sake. Maybe it's actually doing the opposite."

This was promising.

"Can you point to a specific passage, Sachiv?"

"Well, yes. When the great Slastobitch says, *This is the space age and sex movies must express the longing to escape from flesh through sex. The way out is the way through.*"

"What do you make of that? *The way out is the way through?* Anybody?"

Silence.

"Well, so, here's another quote," Sachiv offered. "It's from the Mexican golf course episode involving the dead boy. *I see myself streaking across the sky so blue it hurts to look. I see myself streaking across the sky like a star to leave the earth forever. What holds me back? It is the bargain by which I am here at all. The bargain is the body that holds me here. I am fourteen years old a thin blond boy with pale blue eyes…. What happens between my legs is like a cold drink to me, it is just a feeling cold round stones against my back sunshine and shadow of Mexico. I know that other people think of it as something special to do with how they feel about someone else and there is a word love that means nothing to me at all.*

"And a little bit later:*I am not a person and I am not an animal. There is something I am here for something that I have to do before I can go.*

"And how about this?"On a roll, Sachiv flipped through his copy. He was singlehandedly saving the hour."*I can see what holds me back. It is not a thread like I thought a thin thread that holds a toy balloon a thread that might break and let me blow away across the sky. It is a net that is sometimes close around me and sometimes in the sky stretched between trees and telephone poles and buildings but always around me and I am always under it.*"

"So, you're suggesting?"

"Well, if you repeatedly engage in something, *ritually* engage in it, then don't you eventually develop some kind of power over it? Which means you can exorcise it, eventually you can erase it.Like certain kinds of Tantric sex. Maybe what Burroughs is really trying to do is break the addiction to being. Escape all the suffering that comes with that attachment. End the trap of existence.“

"I think we're getting somewhere important," I said.

The rest of the class squinted skeptically. Except for Jack, the freckled, red-headed boy from rural Iowa who rarely spoke.

"So that makes me think of my Dante class, okay? The *Inferno*, when they get to the bottom of Hell where Satan's confined, which is a pretty gruesome sight, and Dante turns to Virgil and says, Okay, I've seen enough, can we go back up to the top now? And Virgil says, No, we can't, we can only keep descending. We have to climb down Satan's huge gory body, all hairy and matted with blood, till we come out the other side, which is where the stars will be. I wonder if maybe Burroughs is trying to do his own version of that. Write his way out of hell."

The greatest pleasure of teaching is watching fire suddenly take hold. I see Sachiv and Jack, basking in its light, send each other a smoldering look across the seminar table.

Chemistry is everything, though. The next time I taught the novel, there was no Sachiv, no Jack at the table. Despite my best efforts to reproduce their magic, the discussion failed to ignite. Nor did it the third time around. When I taught the course a fourth time, *The Wild Boys* was no longer on the syllabus. I'm still bemused that I felt I had to let it go, but there were so many other "gay" titles out there—*The Folded Leaf, Finistère, The City and the Pillar, Giovanni's Room, A Single Man, Dancer from the Dance, Angels in America,* all distinguished examples of a respectable canon-in-the-making, all collectively supporting the story the gay community wishes to tell (and believe) about itself, a hard-fought struggle from the pre-Stonewall closet to a fully liberated and integrated citizenship in America. *The Wild Boys* refutes all that. It has no interest in gay community or identity or LGBTQI civil rights. Its closest literary relative might well be Henry Darger's *The Vivian Girls,* that 15,000 page, water-colored chronicle of the war storm in the realms of the unreal caused by the child slave rebellion. Like Darger, Burroughs might as well have fallen to Earth from somewhere else. The issues he addressed were certainly queer, but they didn't seem at all *gay,* and most of my students, understandably enough, just couldn't figure out how to integrate him into a course called "gay male narratives," or why they should even try. And I couldn't begin to get them there on my own without more coercive guidance than this in-house Socrates felt comfortable with.

I take the tin and rub Vaseline on his cock feeling it jump in my hand
he is standing there teeth bared gasping... "Vuelvete y aganchete Johnny"...
I turn around and bend over hands braced on knees and let myself go limp
inside as he slides it in

Which brings me to my fourth *Wild Boys*. More than twenty years have
passed since I last attempted to teach it. With some trepidation, I reread
the novel to prepare for this essay, unsure what I'd find, but knowing
all the previous *Wild Boys* would inevitably form the substrata of this
latest encounter.

The satire still stings. I love *Le Comte's* toast: "*I drink to the glorious*
victory of our brave American allies over little boys armed with slingshots
and scout knives." I love the fire-starting BOY with the enigmatic smile
who becomes the hottest property in advertising. Wonderfully haunting phrases float through: *The dead around like birdcalls rain in my face;*
You make gemini with astronaut? Greek youths clad only in beauty and
sunlight?; The boy was footsteps down the windy street a long time ago.
The recurrent Penny Arcade Peep Show chapters, though, are an exercise in diminishing rewards. Sometimes the cut-up and fold-in sections
work, mimicking the eddies and re-circulations of memory, but more
often they're just tedious, and I find myself skimming a bit whenever
the novel makes what feels like a perfunctory shift into word salad.
The flesh gardens and magic jaguars and asexually propagated Zim-
bus interest me about as much as hearing someone else's fever dreams.
The misogyny is persistent and troubling. And the once-cherished blue
movies seem like forlorn artifacts, more quaint than arousing. And yet...
what genuinely moves me all these years later—what I think of as the
spiritual wound at the carnal heart of the novel—are precisely those sex

scenes which I understand now aren't sex scenes at all but instead the sites where the psyche gets stuck and can spend a whole lifetime trying to get unstuck from.

David Bowie astutely described the cast of a typical Burroughs novel as "ciphers and signifiers which are regurgitated, reformed and re-accumulated." A semi-autobiographical Audrey Carsons is *The Wild Boys*'s most fleshed-out "character," *a thin pale boy his face scarred by festering spiritual wounds.* Doctor Moor thinks he looks like *a homosexual sheep-killing dog.* Moor's wife goes further: *It is a walking corpse.* Audrey is inclined to agree with her, *but he didn't know whose corpse he was.* We first meet him in the Green Nun's facility that *looks like a kindergarten but some of the children are middle-aged* and where, *shivering with junk sickness in the icy ward room* and suffering "wrong" dreams about flying, *he is forced to write out i am a filthy little beast ten thousand times in many places,* a punishing mantra that is the through-text of the whole novel.

Into Audrey's St. Louis adolescence (*the old broken point of origin*) comes John Hamlin, *red hair touched with gold, large green eyes well apart.* He drives a magnificent Dusenberg in contrast to Audrey's battered Moon. One afternoon John picks him up. "*Like to go for a ride? ... We could make St. Joseph for lunch... nice riverside restaurant there serves wine.*" Audrey *is thrilled of course. The autumn countryside flashes by... long straight stretch of road ahead*

"*Now I'll show you what this job can do.*"

Hamlin presses the accelerator slowly to the floor... 60...70...80...85...90... Audrey leans forward lips parted eyes shining.

The scene shifts. Old Sarge welcomes top level executives in the CONTROL GAME to a demonstration of "Operation Little Audrey," a military/ corporate/ police state plan to weaponize the young deviant.

Audrey and Hamlin on screen.... Operation Little Audrey on target... Wind ruffles Audrey's hair as the Dusenberg gathers speed... The Dusenberg zooms over a rise and leaves the ground. Just ahead is a wooden bar-

rier... DETOUR sign points sharp left... End over end a flaming pin wheel of jagged metal... The Dusenberg explodes... Audrey and Old Sarge lean out of a battered Moon in the morning sky and smile. Old Sarge is at the wheel.

The CONTROL GAME's hijack of little Audrey is complete. Or is it? Because as the next chapter begins we see, in one of the narrative's rebellious branchings, *a Dusenberg moving slowly along a 1920 detour... A boy stops in front of the car and holds up his hand. He is naked except for a rainbow colored jock strap and sandals. Under one arm he carries a Mauser pistol clipped onto a rifle stock... Audrey has never seen anyone so cool and disengaged... Some distance ahead and to the left he sees PENNY ARCADE spelled out in light globes. Perhaps John has gone in there... Moving with a precision and ease he sometimes knew in flying dreams Audrey slides into a steel chair... In front of him is a luminous screen. Smell of old pain... Later Audrey wrote these notes... I am in the presence of an unknown language spelling out the same message again and again in cryptic charades where I participate as an actor.*

Thus begins the long blue movie detour played out on the Penny Arcade's immersive screens and jerry-rigged stage sets scattered through space and time. Thus begins the long resistance to the CONTROL GAME. With their rainbow jockstraps and Mercury sandals and 18 inch bowie knives (*You don't do things by halves, do you?* Bowie told Burroughs when they met in 1974), the wild boys are *swept into a whirlwind of riots, burning screams, machine guns and lifted out of time. Migrants of ape in gasoline crack of history.* ... "Just kids," says the General. The CIA man grunts. "*Something wrong here, General. They're not all that young.*" Another operative reports, *They aren't human at all more like vicious little ghosts.* What they are is nothing less than Operation Little Audrey gone very badly awry, now airborne and backfiring spectacularly in the flying dream that is the Desert of Blue Silence.

The defiant psyche—unsuppressed, irrepressible no matter how harshly it's disciplined or punished—refuses *not* to return to the old broken point of origin until it has completed that something it is here for, until it has rubbed out its suffering once and for all. The way out is the way through.

he pulled me down onto the sand I could hear myself whimpering my head bursting and flying away like stars that fall in the sky stretched the magic net when I spurted my insides out on the sand the blue spirit filled me

On each of my returns, in each of its incarnations, I have always found *The Wild Boys* an achingly beautiful novel.

TWO LATE WORKS: THE CAT INSIDE AND THE SEVEN DEADLY SINS

JERRY ROSCO

Approach William Burroughs's *The Cat Inside* carefully, just as he would his cat Fletch when it was in a bad mood—"Watch out!" One of his late works, it may be a slim volume but it's very powerful—rich with Burroughs's searing visions, his routines, dream passages, and harsh moral voice.

Cats had always been around during his lifelong travels, but he was indifferent, or even cruel. He remembered cats in Tangier, Marrakech, Algiers, New Orleans. He painfully remembered in Mexico City hitting a cat across the face with a book and seeing it run under a chair. "I was literally hurting myself and I didn't know it."

Things changed when he moved to Lawrence, Kansas in late 1981. Lawrence was the college town of Burroughs's devoted young lover and later great friend, James Grauerholz. On previous stays there, he found it a good place to write. He didn't need the demands of being a cult figure, and he was tired of New York. He rented a fieldstone house five miles outside of town. In the barn and surrounding woods, he could enjoy his target shooting. He had a circle of fond friends. While Burroughs earlier in life had misgivings about his sexuality, in old age he was beyond that. Showing gay wisdom about multiple relationships, now he accepted that James lived nearby with a lover his own age, Ira Silverberg. Bill's assistant Stewart Meyer said, "Ira is the first of James's sidekicks that Bill has accepted to the point of inclusion in his extended household." It would be laughable to ever say Burroughs was at peace but, maybe, it was nearly so. And that's when a new love came into his life. *The Cat Inside* tells the story.

Ruski, at first called Smokey, was a very young cat with green eyes and the blue-gray coat of a Russian Blue. Burroughs put out food for it and other cats, but it was Ruski that first crossed over into the house. Bill found it deeply moving when a barn or outdoor cat wanted to be a house cat. After months Ruski brought along a big white cat that crossed the threshold. Others followed, including a noble gray and white male named Horatio, and a small black and white female with three kittens. A turning point came when Burroughs had to be away for ten days. When he returned, Ruski was tentative, unsure, but when Bill picked him up Ruski recognized him and started purring and nuzzling. That's the moment it was clear he was Bill's cat.

Burroughs noticed that stray dogs didn't come around. Dogs, he believed, hated cats because they charmed humans but offered no services and, the dog thinks, "Worst thing is they got no sense of right or wrong." These amoral cat qualities gradually reminded Bill of Arab boys. Bill wrote, "The cat does not offer services. The cat offers itself."

One day he was target shooting in the barn when he realized the black and white mother cat and her kittens were near his target. He holstered his revolver and the mother cat walked over to him and put her head in his hand. He imagines the cat saying, "I can see you're a good man, Sheriff. Take care of me and my babies." And he thinks: "Thousands of years of female cats in that gesture, and the babies behind her."

At the end of 1983 the lease was up on what he called the Stone House. He decided to buy a house in the area, but he also had to decide about keeping or finding homes for the cats. And he realized that what he considered a journal of the Stone House was really a cat diary—and that it should remain so.

"I have become in the last few years a dedicated cat lover and now the creature is clearly recognized as a cat spirit, a Familiar." By Familiar, he means the cat as a psychic companion and guide. Now he realized he had made contact "…and when any other being is contacted it is sad: because you see the limitations, the pain and fear and the final death. That is what contact means. That is what I see when I touch a cat and find that tears are flowing down my face."

A small bungalow at 1927 Learnard Avenue, surrounded by an acre of woods, became Burroughs's final home. He brought with him Ruski and would have taken Ruski's come and go white cat friend but he had disappeared under ominous circumstances. About its probable demise he thinks, "And why shouldn't the loss of a cat be as poignant and heartfelt as any loss?" Regretfully he left behind Horatio who didn't like Ruski and would remain a protector for the mother cat and her kittens. The new tenant, artist Robert Sudlow, promised to take care of them. And the Learnard Avenue home would soon be loaded with new cats.

Even cat lovers might assume that Burroughs was slowing down, an old guy in his dotage surrounded by cats. No. Through the Eighties the cat diary was just one of his many interests and projects. He signed a seven-book deal with Viking and no longer needed to do readings in rock clubs, but he still did some travel and appearances, there were awards and accolades, he got serious about his art (more about that later), and there were manuscripts to prepare for publication. He wasn't crazy about releasing his nakedly autobiographical novel *Queer*—long buried in his papers—but he owed titles to Viking. In the years he was writing *The Cat Inside*, he was also writing *The Western Lands*, the final volume of The Red Night Trilogy, and mysterious cats appear in the novel. Likewise, the hair-raising language of his fiction often appears in his cat diary: "A cat's rage is beautiful, burning with pure cat flame, all its hair standing up and crackling blue sparks, eyes blazing and sputtering." Or, even more Burroughs-esque: "Easy to imagine a Bat Cat, its leathery black wings all glistening, sharp little teeth, glowing green eyes."

He also devoted time and energy to his visitors with whom he collaborated, including poets such as John Giorno and Allen Ginsberg, and punk rockers such as Patti Smith, Chris Stein from Blondie, Sonic Youth, Michael Stipe of REM, and Kurt Cobain from Nirvana. (Burroughs had a strong premonition of Cobain's suicide.)

Still, with all the demands of his life and work, it is safe to say that in his late years it was cats that most captured his interest and pleasure. They also brought sadness. When Ruski is at the vet's in a close call with pneumonia, Bill feels grief and desolation. He realizes that since adopting Ruski, his cat dreams are vivid and frequent. For example: "I can't find Ruski. I am calling his name. 'Ruski! Ruski! Ruski!' A deep feeling of sadness and foreboding. 'I shouldn't have brought him out here!' I wake with tears streaming down my face."

Cats took on the roles of people in his life. Ruski made him think of Kiki, the beautiful Spanish teen who was his companion and lover in Tangier in the Fifties. He remains the beautiful boy in Burroughs's fiction. But in real life he tired of Bill's being stoned all the time, most of the money going to drugs. "Like a cat," he left and joined a band in Madrid. But one day in 1957, his bandleader boyfriend caught him in bed with a girl and killed him with a knife. Almost three decades later…

I remember the one time I ever slapped Ruski for attacking one of the kittens. The way he looked at me, the shock and hurt, was identical to the look I got from my amigo Kiki. I was sleepy and petulant. He came in and started pushing at me, and finally I slapped him. In both cases I had to make amends. Ruski disappeared but I knew where he was. I went out to the barn and found him and

brought him back. Kiki sat there with a tear in the corner of his eye.
I apologized and finally he came around.

Other cats play their roles well. Calico Jane is like a refined and delicate Jane Bowles. Ginger reminded him of Pantapon Rose, a wise old
madame at a bawdy whorehouse in St. Louis. Ed, an Albino cat, liked
to play the "catch me" game that Bill used to play when his son Billy
was a child—Billy who died of alcoholism and cirrhosis. Orange and
white Wimpy cries at the closed door when Bill is working until he is
let in—just as Billy used to do. Sometimes Wimpy is Bill's father—"the
pathetic appeal and the hurt in his eyes."

Sometimes Kiki is there in face and cat-body when Ruski squeaks
and puts its paws up to Bill's face: "IT'S ME, BILL…IT'S ME."

Another dream: "I am in the house at 4664 Pershing Avenue where
I was born. On the second floor, at the entrance to my old bedroom, I
encounter a little blond child waiting there. 'Are you Billy?' I ask.

'I am anybody to anybody who loves me,' he answers."

Through his cats Burroughs reconciled with people and worked
through grief of the past. "My connection with Ruski is a basic factor in
my life," he wrote. In 1984, a small privately printed piece called *Ruski*
suggested the book to come. But first there was another major character
that would appear in *The Cat Inside*.

James Grauerholz was in town in August 1984 when he heard a cat
crying at full volume. It was a little black male with white markings on
its chest and stomach, about six months old. When James approached
it, it jumped into his arms. Of course, he brought it to Burroughs who
saw Fletch as "an exquisite, delicate animal with glistening black fur, a
sleek black head like an otter's, slender and sinuous, with green eyes."
He quickly came to love Fletch but once again that feeling of *contact*
brought on a psychic vision: "There is also an aura of doom and sadness
about this trusting little creature. He has been abandoned many times

over the centuries, left to die in cold city alleys, in hot noon vacant lots, pottery shards, nettles, crumbled mud walls. Many times he has cried for help in vain." The first week Fletch joined the household, he climbed forty feet up a tree and could not get down. Ruski, though jealous of other cats, climbed up and led Fletch down. Amazingly, a year later, a kitten Bill believed was Ruski's climbed up the same tree and got stuck. This time Fletch climbed up and brought the kitten down.

On April 2, 1985, Ruski squeaked and nuzzled Burroughs who felt a sense of foreboding. Sure enough, exactly a month later, Ruski disappeared. Distressed, Bill sensed the cat's cry for help and suddenly knew where he was. He called the Humane Society which at first denied having Ruski but looked again when Bill insisted. They had him; he'd been caught in a trap.

The closing pages of *The Cat Inside* call out for the fate of endangered species, with a particular message for his readers: "All you cat lovers, remember all the millions of cats mewling through the world's rooms lay their hopes and trust in you, as the little mother cat at the Stone House laid her head in my hand, as Calico Jane put her babies in my suitcase, as Fletch jumped into James's arms and Ruski rushed towards me, chittering with joy."

Burroughs insisted that his longtime friend artist Brion Gysin in Paris create illustrations, and Gysin at first said no. This mattered to Bill because Gysin was one of his closest gay friends and his health was poor. Then it was clear that Gysin's health was failing, and Burroughs used the excuse of joining John Giorno's European readings to visit. He had last days with Gysin and came home with eight abstract brush and ink illustrations for the book.

No entry in *The Cat Inside* is over a page, and most are half that, so they are positioned more like poems, and on quality stock. In 1986, only a limited edition of 133 copies was printed by Grenfell Press, but in 1992, a handsome hardcover was released by Viking, and then a paperback in 2002. Sometimes it's mistakenly called a novella but it is clearly a cat diary mixed with WSB memoir. According to the *Los Angeles Times*, "These are haunting images, from dreams, memory and present day, running from unabashed affection to outrage and indignation." And from *The Guardian*: "Burroughs' laconic prophet's voice was always his strongest suit and, though this is only a small book, he's going, as ever, at full tilt."

In the early Nineties, when I was an editor at *Mandate* magazine, I exchanged several letters with Burroughs, and he put a picture of my black cat into several of his paintings. Here is when he first mentioned the cat book...

October 25, 1992

"I seem to find myself rather grotesquely miscast as the Great Beast. Old school queens half out of the closet cross themselves at mention of my name. And the stories told and believed about my exploits in cities I have never visited...oh well. I have a cat book called *The Cat Inside* ... published by Viking ... should be out now. Should confuse the critics who would foist a tired old tabloid black magic image onto an old man who is fond of his cats.

Blest be

William S. Burroughs"

THE SEVEN DEADLY SINS

Many William S. Burroughs readers know that he was a gun enthusiast and that late in life he began creating "shotgun art," paintings created on wood with containers of paint and a spray of shotgun pellets, often adding drawings or collages. Few, however, know that Burroughs, with the help of a gallery, created a limited edition art book called *The*

Seven Deadly Sins. The book has nothing to do with a famous series of paintings with the same name and subject, created by Paul Cadmus and now in the Metropolitan Museum of Art collection. Cadmus's paintings strikingly show scenes depicting humans committing the deadly sins. Whereas in Burroughs's book, the seven reproduced paintings are abstract, but each one is accompanied by a page of prose in Gothic-style typeface which gives the artist's verbal description of each vice.

Created in 1991, the oversized art book is 9 x 12 and the cover is solid black. But on the center of the front cover is attached a thin 4 x 6 piece of wood, painted red and riddled with dozens of holes left by shotgun pellets. This is an authentic Burroughs shot-gunned artifact and no two can be alike. Below the painted strip of wood are the words The Seven Deadly Sins in red and William S. Burroughs in gold. The inside front and back covers are crimson colored with a brush stroke design. In the front matter is a 1981 Robert Mapplethorpe photograph of Burroughs, full-bodied against a white background, aiming a long gun. Published by Lococo-Mulder of New York, St. Louis, MO, and Amsterdam, the book was printed in Germany but the text is in English. The seven multi-color screenprint images are composed from woodblocks shot by Burroughs with a twelve-gauge shotgun in March and June of 1991, and the seven accompanying text pages were written by him from February to July of 1991.

Burroughs's descriptions of the seven deadly sins are characteristically otherworldly. To give an example of his spooky tone, just one sentence from each of his views of the sins follow on these pages—along with the colors of his art.

SLOTH. *Blue, gold, black and white.* "Sloth says don't stick your neck out, go by the book, never go too far in any direction, stay in the mainstream, don't get involved, don't get mixed up in it."

*AVARICE.Purple, black, green, red and white. "The old miser fin-
gering his gold coins with idiot delight has given way to the deadly,
the disembodied Avarice of vast multinational conglomerates…"*

Burroughs's legitimacy as a visual artist was established late in life
with the shotgun paintings. Some may say that the financial success of
this work was due partly to his counterculture celebrity, and that's fair
enough. But his creative eye and his instinct for art were always there.
Like his lifelong friend Allen Ginsberg, he had an early interest in and
talent for photography. In October 1958, while he was staying in Paris,
Burroughs ran into writer and artist Bryon Gysin who would become
the great influence on Bill's visual art. He had known Gysin only pass-
ingly in Tangier, but it mattered to Bill that Bryon was the very masculine type of gay man that he admired. Now they became close friends,
and Burroughs spent a lot of time watching Gysin work on oil paintings. Through 1959, Bill worked on watercolors and photo collages and
montages, showing his art to Gysin. Then, through the early Sixties he
devoted himself to Gysin's experimental "cut-ups," cutting and rearrang-
ing text in scrapbooks and all through the novels *The Soft Machine* and
Nova Express. Afterwards, he collaborated with Anthony Balch, splicing small strips of film together, to make the short film *The Cut-ups.*

*ANGER. Purple, white and black. "I'd have dropped our national
anthem on the surface of the moon miss head pop singer from escaped alien fan mail making me what the hell kind of an astronaut
who just dropped our national anthem about all the bleeding heart
junk of the free and the home of space alien baloney…"*

*GLUTTONY. Gold, red, black, and four ghostly faces in white.
"Gluttony of the sweets, the sugars, the deadly apples, melting in
the mouth, transmuting teeth and gristle and bone into a toothsome*

sweetmeat. One taste and the deadly process is activated..."

The shotgun art began by accident in February 1982 when Burroughs was trying out a new twelve-gauge double-barrel shotgun, using number six birdshot. The plywood target was left with interesting layers and patterns that sparked his attention. Soon he was creating shotgun paintings using blasted paint containers and adding calligraphy and collage, including photos. When a visiting friend, Dr. Timothy Leary, the LSD guru, insisted on paying $10,000 for a painting, Bill knew he was on to something.

His first exhibit was in 1986 in Lawrence at the University of Kansas. But, as Burroughs biographer Barry Miles pointed out, Bill hesitated to plan a high-profile exhibit tour out of respect for his great gay friendship with Bryon Gysin, a major artist who had never gotten his due. After Gysin passed, however, James Grauerholz, acting as manager, set up 1988 exhibits in New York, Amsterdam, London, Vancouver, Seattle, Santa Fe, and Chicago. Then 1989 exhibits in Cologne, Montreal, Toronto, Basil, Lisbon, and St. Louis. Gallery shows continued through the early Nineties, but what assured his place in the art world was a 1995 museum show at the Whitney. Even better was a 150-piece 1996 show at the Los Angeles County Museum. After Burroughs passed in 1997, museum exhibitions continued in Germany, Austria, Slovenia, and London. Other shows would follow in coming decades.

As for *The Seven Deadly Sins*, it can still be found at this time for about $150 unsigned and at least $400 signed.

LUST. Red, white, purple, black, with figures in the background and a large snake in foreground. "Look at this switchboard, plugged into millions of cocks and assholes, lips and tits, it blares out a blowtorch crescendo."

ENVY. Green, black, white faces, gun and skeleton. "Envy, inordinate by its nature, a need that can never be satisfied…like Virus that feeds on itself for all eternity."

PRIDE. Gold, white figures, purple, black. "Sin is a stuck record, round and round, over and over, always the same, and by being always the same, always deader, the smell of decay always heavier."

While I was corresponding with Bill in the Nineties, I sent him a photo of my favorite cat, Bianca, who had recently died. He told me that he made copies of the photo and incorporated them in his paintings. To be sure I understood, he sent this follow-up note, June 28, 1993: "Did you say 'late' about the little black cat? Is she dead? If so how did this happen? I think it is the most sweet and innocent cat picture I have ever seen. As I told you I have used it in a number of paintings."

My black cat, Bianca, was very mysterious, seemingly appearing and disappearing, and playing tricks on guests. To this day you can hear the thump when she—invisible—jumps down from her favorite window. So, I am not surprised that she was rendered near-immortal in several paintings by William S. Burroughs.

THE BEATS: PICTURES OF A LEGEND

EDMUND WHITE

July 22, 2010

Both Allen Ginsberg and William Burroughs discovered late in life that making works of art is the way to get money. Literature just doesn't do it. Speaking engagements pay, but eventually they become tiring—or one exhausts the market. Neither of the two had ever been money-mad, but old age requires a bit of a cushion. Burroughs turned to painting. He would set up paint cans in front of blank canvases and then shoot at them; *the splatter was the art*. Although these paintings are his best-known artworks, they make up only a small part of his output: he did twenty-four shotgun paintings in 1982 and a few more before he died in 1997. According to his friend James Grauerholz, Burroughs turned out more than 1,500 artworks between 1982 and 1996—including stencils and targets, which were almost all brightly colored abstractions—and had his work exhibited in several museums and more than eighty galleries worldwide.

As Ginsberg said:

If you're famous, you can get away with anything! William Bur-

roughs spent the last ten years painting and makes a lot more money out of his painting than he does out of his previous writing. If you establish yourself in one field, it's possible that people then take you seriously in another. Maybe too seriously. I know lots of great photographers who are a lot better than me, who don't have a big, pretty coffee table book like I have. I'm lucky.

Ginsberg had been taking snapshots of friends with a borrowed camera since the mid-Forties. In 1953 he bought a small Kodak Retina camera for thirteen dollars secondhand at a Bowery pawnshop, and for the next ten years he photographed all his friends and activities in a casual, spontaneous way. It wasn't until 1983 that Ginsberg rediscovered these pictures among his papers.

As Sarah Greenough writes of Ginsberg in the catalog of *Beat Memories: The Photographs of Allen Ginsberg:*

Long a foe of American materialism and convinced that it was better to give to friends, colleagues, and worthy causes than to pay taxes, he found himself in the mid-1980s sixty years old and without much money in the bank. Until his death in 1997, he presented numerous lectures and workshops around the world on "Snapshot Poetics" and attentively worked with dealers and agents to sell his photographs and reproduction rights.

It was also in the Eighties that he added chatty, affectionate, handwritten captions to his photographs, which explained what was going on in them—and which also added to their value by making them into unique objects.

In 1994 Ginsberg sold his archives to Stanford University for a million dollars, but after all the deductions for the auction house, his agent, and taxes, he only had enough money left to buy his New York loft and was back to square one. His photos brought him some income in his last years, though he insisted that most of the profits were plowed back into his work, for hiring an assistant and maintaining a lab.

The pictures are fascinating since few of them are well known and they often show their subjects in their youth—a fresh-faced, toothy, nerdy Ginsberg, for instance, long before he became the bearded guru, and a melancholy, poetic William Burroughs before he became the saurian undertaker seen in his familiar portraits. There's even a shadowy nude of Burroughs in bed during the period when he and Ginsberg were lovers.

Almost all of the Beats were bisexual and one another's lovers. Neal Cassady, the heartthrob of the bunch, slept with everyone, male or female, though he preferred women and was never faithful to anyone. He let Ginsberg sleep with him but mainly as a favor and partly as an experiment; soon after their first New York idyll Cassady left a lovesick Ginsberg behind and ran off to Denver and to adventures with numerous women. Ginsberg joined him there but was ignored most of the time.

Burroughs had as his female companion a woman named Joan Vollmer Adams; the apartment they shared in New York with Kerouac and his first wife, Edie Parker, was a central gathering spot for the Beats in the Forties. In 1951, when they were living in Mexico City, Burroughs shot and killed her during a game of William Tell gone awry. He fled back to the US to avoid jail time. About the incident, he later wrote: "I am forced to the appalling conclusion that I would have never become a writer if not for Joan's death.... [It] brought me into contact with the invader, the Ugly Spirit, and maneuvered me into a lifelong struggle, in which I have had no choice except to write my way out."

Kerouac was mostly straight but he did drink epic quantities and put out for Ginsberg occasionally. Peter Orlovsky, who was very striking when Ginsberg met him, was straight but slightly mad; he let the inexperienced Ginsberg screw him on their first date and then wept, bewildered by what had happened. They stayed together for the rest of their lives though Orlovsky was often so paranoid and out of control that he had to be hospitalized—and occasionally he was hostile to Ginsberg. Not so many years ago I remember asking a straight friend why he had had sex with Ginsberg, and he said, opening his hands palm-up as if it were self-evident, "Dude, he was *Allen Ginsberg.*"

[In their] National Gallery show, [one can see] what a handsome group they are, especially the young Kerouac and Cassady and Orlovsky. Perhaps the most memorable photo is of Kerouac wandering down East 7th Street in Manhattan in the fall of 1953 "making a Dostoevsky mad-face or Russian basso be-bop Om," though I like to think his mouth is shaped in a giant O because he's reciting "O harp and altar, of the fury fused," Hart Crane's ode to the nearby Brooklyn Bridge. Cassady is also a natural Marlon Brando stand-in and a 1955 picture shows him and one of his fugitive loves, Natalie Jackson, posing under a San Francisco movie marquee advertising *The Wild One.*

In another image, the eternally elegant Paul Bowles is shown in a seersucker suit and a rep tie between the grubby Gregory Corso and the frankly weird Burroughs in Tangier in 1961. Burroughs is dressed like a court stenographer in a long-sleeve black shirt buttoned all the way up, pleated trousers cinched high around his waist, and a trilby hat shading his drug-wasted face. The long sleeves were necessary even in the semitropics to hide the needle tracks.

One earlier, campy photo from 1953 shows an unexpectedly suave and theatrical Burroughs giving sophisticated advice in the "André Gide" manner to a browbeaten but adorable Jack Kerouac, an All-American boy right out of a Thomas Wolfe novel (Ginsberg's interpretation). According to Ginsberg's caption, written forty years later, Burroughs is saying, "Now Jack, as I warned you far back as 1945, if you keep going home to live with your 'Memère' you'll find yourself wound tighter and

tighter in her apron strings till you're an old man and can't escape...."
By the time Ginsberg wrote those words he knew that in the interval
Kerouac had in fact become a day-in day-out drunk, moved back to his
mother in Lowell, Massachusetts, and died in 1969 with her in Florida
from complications due to cirrhosis of the liver. He was just forty-seven
years old.

A late photo of 1964 shows, in Ginsberg's words, Kerouac as a "red-
faced corpulent W.C. Fields shuddering with mortal horror..." and re-
sembling his own father. There are equally devastating late photos of
Gregory Corso ("Maestro Poet," Ginsberg notes beneath the image of
his bloated friend, "ancient herald's wand pin, messenger-god Hermes
Caduceus, near his pen, a quiet afternoon in 'The Kettle of Fish,' an old
bar in Greenwich Village under whose sign Kerouac used to drink")
and Herbert Huncke ("Old-timer & survivor Herbert E. Huncke,"
Ginsberg calls him, "Beat literary pioneer who introduced Burroughs,
Kerouac & myself to floating population hustling & drug scene Times
Square 1945"); only Ginsberg himself retains his warmth and humanity to the end. In fact, one of the most touching pictures is a self-portrait
as an old man in the nude, an image that has the dignity and depth and
vulnerability of a late Rembrandt self-portrait.

Early on, when they were just inventing themselves and their original brand of writing, Ginsberg and Kerouac decided to turn all their
friends into myths. They did so by writing about each other and their
holy or zany or heroic or comic exploits, but they also compared each
other to famous people of the distant or recent past. In his late captions to his early photos, written by hand at the bottom of new, "muse-
um-quality" prints of them, Ginsberg quite naturally vaunted the epic
qualities of his friends. In one picture he has posed Burroughs in the
Egyptian Wing beside "a brother Sphinx" in the Metropolitan Museum
to emphasize his sepulchral personality. Ginsberg's description of Kerouac's "Dostoyevsky mad-face," is designed to ally his pal with the great

Russian.

Their letters and journal entries from that period all reveal that they were convinced they represented something new and monumental in literary history. To be sure, Ginsberg was at Columbia studying literature with Lionel Trilling and art history with Meyer Shapiro and, outside school, hobnobbing with the much older poet William Carlos Williams—this heady intellectual company only reinforced his sense of artistic destiny.

Although Ginsberg was usually enthusiastic, especially about his friends' work, sometimes his faith was shaken. During a spell in a mental hospital Ginsberg had met Carl Solomon, whose uncle, A.A. Wyn, was the publisher of Ace Books. Carl convinced his uncle to publish Burroughs's early novel *Junky*, but Wyn was reluctant to publish Kerouac's *On the Road*—and this reluctance gave Ginsberg a temporary doubt. He wrote in his journal: "Carl shook my own self-esteem, threw me into depression. Is there no way we can tell what's good on our own except by personal heart sympathies, going against almost all rational *and* commercial possibility?"

In this early period Ginsberg was working out—as a photographer but primarily as a poet—his doctrine of spontaneity, "First Thought, Best Thought." This principle, which Kerouac probably invented, made *On the Road* a classic work of American literature and "*Howl,*" a daring piece of confessional poetry, so that even established masters such as Robert Lowell took account of it (his next book was *Life Studies*). But the Beats's refusal to edit themselves also led to poems and novels that were repetitious and full of dreary longueurs. Ginsberg was always at his best in visionary poems such as the genuinely inspired free-verse "Wales Visitation":

> *All the Valley quivered, one*
> *extended motion, wind*

undulating on mossy hills
a giant wash that sank white fog delicately down red runnels
on the mountainside
whose leaf-branch tendrils moved asway
in granitic undertow down—
and lifted the floating Nebulous upward, and lifted the arms of the
     trees
and lifted the grasses an instant in balance
and lifted the lambs to hold still
and lifted the green of the hill, in one solemn wave
A solid mass of Heaven, mist-infused, ebbs thru the vale....

In 1949 Ginsberg wrote about his down-and-out pal Herbert Huncke. They lived together briefly, and Huncke was constantly arranging the furniture and burning bits of wood to smell their scent.

Perhaps he had nothing better to do. But I appreciated these activities as touches peculiar to Huncke alone, and therefore valuable, lovely and honorable. They were part of his whole being and "life force." I also enjoyed mythologizing his character. It is a literary trick which Kerouac, the novelist—who has written much about Herbert Huncke—and I exploited in the past.

Not only in the past but throughout their careers. It's really a very simple strategy. You have a small group of friends and you declare them all to be geniuses and you laud all their work and ascribe to them sweet and stormy qualities worthy of the Greek gods. What you're selling is not just your writing but your personal legends.

—Allen Ginsberg

"HE INVENTED SOMETHING": AN INTERVIEW WITH FRAN LEBOWITZ

BRIAN ALESSANDRO

Fran Lebowitz shares her lunch in the Seventies with Burroughs during which he was excoriated by another esteemed writer, discussed the pragmatics of orgies, and complained about footwear. A trailblazer with a singular voice and unconventional career, Lebowitz discusses the influence Burroughs had on literature and the culture.

BRIAN ALESSANDRO: Fran, when I interviewed you for *Interview Magazine* in January 2021, you spoke about the very productive cultural period in New York in the Seventies and Eighties, a period during which Burroughs spent a good deal of time in New York. You knew Burroughs. Can you discuss what your exchanges were like?

FRAN LEBOWITZ: I remember [one time when we had] lunch because it was the longest time I had spent with him. It's very hard to explain to people who are younger than me, which is now all people, how small these worlds were. So, you kept running into people, whether you wanted to or not. I'm pretty sure, and I could be wrong, when I remember absolutely when I saw him, was at this lunch. And the only person who I know for a fact is still alive who was at that lunch was

Vince Aletti, who wrote for *The Village Voice* for a million years, he writes for *The New Yorker* now, he used to write about music, and he's written about photography for many years. He'd probably remember this lunch. The other people who were there were Peter Hujar [the photographer] and Janet Flanner [journalist and author of *The Cubical City*], which was the main reason I wanted to go to the lunch, and her girlfriend, but you didn't say that at the time, and I know you're not supposed to say that now—I'm not up on what you're supposed to say—but she was quite well known, too. Her name was Natalia Ginsberg [author of *Family Sayings*], and she was Italian, and Bill Burroughs was there. Felicity Mason [English memoirist] gave the lunch. She lived half the time here [in New York City] and half the time in Rome. She had this apartment—I can't remember which apartment even though I walk past it all the time. It's on 10th or 11th or 12th Street between 5th and 6th [Avenues]. It was this white building. That apartment was owned by Gian Carlo Menotti [Italian-American composer, librettist, and playwright]. I was very young at the time, maybe twenty-three or twenty-four. At this lunch, I hardly spoke, I know this is hard for people to imagine now, mainly because I was very ... 'afraid' is maybe too strong of a word, but I was subdued in the presence of Janet Flanner, who was a very aggressive conversationalist. Very assertive. She had this very growly voice. And she was yelling at Bill Burroughs through the whole lunch. She didn't like him. They knew each other, of course. I'm thinking if she's yelling at Burroughs, she's going to yell at me. So, I hardly said a word and I remember that Bill Burroughs gave this big recitation about going to orgies.

ALESSANDRO: Intriguing.

LEBOWITZ: That the problem with going to orgies is that people steal your money. So, he showed us he was wearing like a little bag around his neck. Like a little leather thong that had a little pouch. So, he had devised this thing so you could put your money in there. And it would be around your neck. And even if you didn't have any clothes on you would have your money. This is a subject that didn't even interest me then.

(*I laugh.*)

LEBOWITZ: So, let alone now. And then he also started to complain about how he could not find shoes that fit because one of his feet is bigger than the other. This is, by the way, true of everyone.

ALESSANDRO: Was it dramatically different with him?

LEBOWITZ: I guess. I don't really remember looking at his feet.

(*I laugh.*)

LEBOWITZ: But this really incensed Janet Flanner, who screamed at him, "Why don't you just go to a good bootmaker, Bill, and shut up?" So, I was sitting across from her, and after the constant yelling at Burroughs, I really doubt I said anything at all, and she leans across the table, this is more about me than about Burroughs, and said, "What is it you do, anyway?" And I was like really a kid, I was probably younger than twenty-four, and I was thinking to myself, "How can I tell Janet Flanner that I'm a writer?" So, I said in a really soft voice, "I'm a writer." "Speak up I can't hear you." So, I said it again, and she said, "A writer? How very unfortunate."

ALESSANDRO: That's funny.

LEBOWITZ: This is why the lunch was so memorable. Burroughs was a very revered figure Downtown. I don't remember people yelling at him. I have to tell you that this is kind of against the law, but that kind of work has never been, like, my cup of tea, so I didn't love his work, but I understood what he did, I understood that whole, I don't know if you would call it a school, but at this point you probably would. It just never particularly interested me, and I also thought those people were old. That age group. There weren't that many around still. You live like that you don't usually live to be very old.

ALESSANDRO: Yeah, it's amazing he lived to be eighty-three, and passed in 1997. So, he was probably in his sixties during that lunch, a good forty years older than you at that point.

LEBOWITZ: Yes, now no one is forty years older than me. If they are they're on the front page of *The Times*, so Janet Flanner might have been older, so that's the longest time I ever spent with him. These lunches were like the whole day, practically. He seemed to be somewhat intimidated by Janet Flanner. Because he didn't, like, yell back at her. Maybe he just wasn't a yeller, but she barked at people. He didn't do that. He was small and that meant that he was small as a kid and men who are small their whole lives tend not to yell, unless they become billionaires and then they yell at everyone.

(I laugh.)

LEBOWITZ: He didn't have a very dominant social presence. I can't even remember where I saw him around. Parties, probably. I can't really tell you where I saw him. I don't remember him being around at Max's [Kansas City at 213 Park Avenue in Manhattan]. Those people didn't go to Max's. If you could tell me where he went, I could tell you if I saw him.

ALESSANDRO: You're such a trenchant cultural critic. How has Burroughs's literature influenced contemporary writers and artists?

LEBOWITZ: He influenced a lot of people. You'd have to name the people who are noted, but one of the reasons that that thing becomes very influential is because it's illogical. You know, people don't have to even pretend to understand it. I think that people who wouldn't have the ability he had, which is he invented something, so if someone else invents something that no one understands, that was not just accepted, it was lauded, admittedly by a small group of people, and if you can do nothing at all, including inventing this thing, you could easily copy it. So, you know, that's the kind of artist that has really undue influence. That's true of music, it's true of a lot of things, so it attracts a lot of phonies—I know that's not a word you're supposed to say anymore, and there are only six words you're allowed to say anymore, an ever-diminishing list—but he wasn't that, so I never thought that, even though I didn't like him. He wasn't a phony. He invented this thing that had its own internal logic. He didn't wholly invent this. This comes out of Dada and Surrealism.

ALESSANDRO: He even credited Brion Gysin with creating the Cut-Up technique and he kind of co-opted it into literature, into writing.

LEBOWITZ: Even before Brion Gysin. This is over a hundred years old. It's interesting to me that even young kids still do this in all kinds of ways. And they are so far from inventing anything. When the profound essence of the thing is illogic then obviously anyone can copy it. They can say, you just don't understand this. Well, there are many things I don't understand, okay, physics. I don't even know what it is. But I know that there are people who do know. So, if someone is a physicist, I am not going to get into an argument with them.

(*I laugh.*)

ALESSANDRO: Right, it can be known. It's knowable.

LEBOWITZ:It's knowable. But art is very different, so anyone can say anything, and depending on the era, and this particular era that we're living in now is an era not only of—I wouldn't even say lax criticism from a point of view of art—it's intense never-ending criticism of society and zero criticism of art in any real way, and all the criticism of art is basically political, because basically you're not allowed to have these standards anymore because they're politically incorrect. I think this is really in a certain way a good time if you're a young, untalented artist.

(*I laugh.*)

ALESSANDRO: Great quote. Why do you think Burroughs was ambivalent about being labeled a "queer writer"?

LEBOWITZ: Everyone was. This is a particular thing that interests me because all the time I am hearing and reading that people who are young criticize people for having been in the closet. This was everyone. I am seventy, so when I was young in my twenties in the Seventies, we talked about people being in the closet, but we meant to us, to other gay people, not to straight people. Because it was illegal to be gay. People have forgotten this. It was against the law. There were a few people who totally flouted that, but only a few, and they were in danger doing that. You couldn't rent an apartment. You couldn't have any kind of job. Luckily, I have never had a job, a real job where you had to go to the office or something like that. You couldn't be a salesclerk in a store. That was everybody, it doesn't matter who you are, you could be rich, you could be poor. You could be white. You could be black. Some of these environments were much more oppressive than others. Basically, people are inextricable from their era, I don't care who you are, and I would guess, not knowing Burroughs in that way at all, I didn't have to know him, I could guess, that's why.

ALESSANDRO: What did Burroughs get most correct about America? Human behavior?

LEBOWITZ: You know, you never could go wrong criticizing human behavior.

(I laugh.)

LEBOWITZ: You just can't. Human nature is a thing that never changes, no matter what, and it's always bad. You can always look like a genius if you criticize this. Criticizing America is also a thing you can always do, sometimes with more reason than others, you know. It's always fashionable among artists to criticize the United States even when the United States is not being at its worst. Even when the United States was being at its best, which was not exactly in my lifetime. There have been wonderful things done by this country, not recently, I have to say. There are times when even in my lifetime, I was born in 1950, so the United States was more than powerful after the Second World War and it also depends on who you are, you know, how much you would criticize the United States. I am only a second generation American, and I never heard a bad thing about the United States until I was a teenager, but certainly not from my family because everyone was so thrilled to be alive. You know, but I have friends my age who were from more patrician backgrounds, which would be almost anyone, and they might have had several generations of family criticizing the United States, and it also depends how the rest of the world is acting. If you happen to be living in a country where the regime is not the actual Nazis, you're already doing very well, okay? If you happen to be living in a country where the president is Donald Trump, you are mortified. Burroughs was from a rich family, so that makes a completely different kind of person. And even though he was gay, he was a man, and he was white, and he was rich. These things are incredibly important to forming people's characters. More than their character, their personality. He grew up among the ruling class. One way I guess the country has improved, by the way, is that the country isn't controlled by sixteen Protestant bankers, anymore. It's more diverse horrible people who run the world now.

(I laugh.)

ALESSANDRO: We've diversified the horrible people.

LEBOWITZ: Right.

ALESSANDRO: Do you think the current political climate would allow for another writer like Burroughs?

LEBOWITZ: Yes, but I think the danger would be to ... what I said before is just true of artists in general. I mean, the criticism you're most likely to get is going to be political or personal, in these awful ways that are to me so childish. Most people know a huge amount about people now. This is largely the fault of the people themselves, you know, who are constantly talking about themselves, but I mean for instance, when I was young and I wanted to know what a writer was like, here's what you had, you could look at the picture on the book jacket.

ALESSANDRO: That would tell you all you needed to know, huh?

LEBOWITZ: That would tell you all that was available. Other than what was in the press, which used to be called just The Press, so you didn't have that much access to personal knowledge about people. I don't own a computer, but I'm all over the internet because people tell me I am. Many people [promote] themselves. So, if you do [promote] yourself, to me, what this seems like, is a never-ending prison sentence in the 8th grade, social media. It sounds horrible to me. I don't think Burroughs would fare well under this system, but he also wouldn't be the same person.

ALESSANDRO: Interesting. You just said you can't really extricate a person or an artist from their era.

LEBOWITZ: You can't. You just can't. You know, it's what makes you. The era in which you grew up, your generation, that is the thing people have most in common.

ALESSANDRO: You're an icon. Burroughs is an icon. What makes him an icon and is the era of icons over?

LEBOWITZ: It's not a word I adore, but I think it depends on what you mean by it. Now, first of all, people proclaim themselves this.

ALESSANDRO (*laughing*): Self-proclaimed icons!

LEBOWITZ: Yes. Anything you say about yourself is incredibly suspect, I don't care what it is. Also, there used to be fewer categories of artist, you know. There were artists, writers, musicians. Now there are like eighty billion. Because everyone these days call themselves artists.

Bakers say they're artists. Chefs are artists. I'm not saying I don't like to eat. I like to eat but come on. I think that part of it may be that because of the age of Burroughs or anyone of that generation, there is a lot of mystery attached to these people. Even if it wasn't deliberate, in the case of someone gay not saying they're gay, that's a certain kind of mystery, that was deliberate, even though opposed by other people. There just wasn't that much available information. It was considered impolite to talk about yourself.

ALESSANDRO: That's all people do these days, right? I think about the "Me Decade," the Eighties, can you imagine how much worse it's gotten in the past thirty years?

LEBOWITZ: In the past thirty minutes. By the time I hang up this phone it will have gotten worse.

(I laugh.)

LEBOWITZ: I don't have the internet, and yet I know so much personal information about people that I hardly know who they are. More than I know about people I actually know. There are lots of questions I would never ask people. People I know, who I'm friends with. People will say to me, "How can he afford that house?" And I would say, "I don't know." "But you're one of his best friends." And I would say, "I know, but I would never ask him about his money."

ALESSANDRO: It's about manners.

LEBOWITZ: It would never even occur to me to ask anyone about money and that's one of the worst things people talk about all the time. And I always say, if I know how much money people made or what they paid for their apartment, let me assure you, it's because they told me.

ALESSANDRO: You didn't solicit it.

LEBOWITZ: I didn't ask. And people tell all kinds of sexual things about themselves and things about their families. That's just a different era.

ALESSANDRO: Over-sharing, yeah. Several writers have objected to contribute to this project due to their misgivings with Burroughs's "immoral behavior," as they put it, in his life and in his work. What are your thoughts about that?

LEBOWITZ: But killing your wife is, to me, a big thing. This is not the kind of thing that you can say, "It was a different time," "This was the norm of the time," "This was conventional behavior." Killing your wife should never be allowed, okay? Killing anyone—I don't want to confine this to people's wives—I mean, Norman Mailer got away with almost killing his wife.

ALESSANDRO: I know, he stabbed her.

LEBOWITZ: And he is younger than Burroughs, a little younger, and Norman Mailer wouldn't get away with writing those books now, forget, you know, stabbing his wife. So, "writing those books"—that is the era. But killing your wife, that should be an eternal thing you're not allowed to do. So, if people objected to discussing or writing about Burroughs because he killed his wife that to me is separate from "he didn't proclaim his sexuality". And there are people who think that's immoral.

ALESSANDRO: I guess, this is something you touched on with Scorsese in *Pretend it's a City*, you said you wouldn't go to a dinner someone was giving in the Seventies because Leni Riefenstahl was going to be there. It's that perennial question of, "how do you separate the artist from the person?"

LEBOWITZ: It depends on what they do, that's what I think. Leni Riefenstahl was the central propaganda arm of the Nazi party, okay? I don't care how great a filmmaker she was. I don't care, yes, she was a great filmmaker, I think. I'm not alone in this. She was a great filmmaker, which makes it worse. Not better. So there luckily weren't too many people who were like that. At least not invited to dinner parties in New York, at least that I'm aware of or at least that I was invited to, so to me I didn't even think of it for one second. There was a tremendous cult of Leni Riefenstahl around The Factory but there was never a tremendous cult of her around this apartment, which I didn't live in at the time, but to me. To me some things are iffy, that's not iffy. Killing your wife is not iffy. Hiding your sexuality, I think it's a lack of knowledge to criticize someone of Burroughs's age for that.

ALESSANDRO: That's fair. You have to contextualize it. It's the era. Why do you think Burroughs's work has endured and even seen something of a resurgence, lately?

LEBOWITZ: Because it appeals to people who are young. It's what Oscar Wilde said, "Being fashionable means being fashionable among the young." That's not an exact quote. If Burroughs was the toast of retirement homes, no one would care.

THE GARGOYLE ON MY SHOULDER

TREBOR HEALEY

Since I've spent the last five years in Mexico, and having never gotten around to reading *Queer*, I thought I'd give it a go and see how much William Burroughs and I found in common and appreciated in Mexico—but it came up snake eyes. He was primarily a man of the mind in a country that is primarily of the earth and the body, a 1950s expat who thought contemporary Mexico somewhat ridiculous, Mexicans more so—and of course he was after drugs and often straight boys. We were thus at odds on all counts about Mexico or so it appeared at first. Because we agreed about at least one thing. And that was, for want of a better term, the spirit realm, which clearly haunts all three of us—Burroughs, Mexico, and me.

And that is something timeless, much like Mexico itself, and I dare say Burroughs too, who was obsessed with time and its gaping maw, death, which is of course yet another ever-present subject in Mexico. So, even if the glaring reality of our living in two very different times or epochs, not to mention different head/heart spaces, makes our experiences of Mexico almost incomparable, Mexico's very essence inevitably brings us ever closer together, erasing all differences, flummoxing my assumptions about Burroughs.

The fact is, I was nonplussed with *Queer*. The Beat book about

Mexico City I always liked was Kerouac's *Tristessa*, titled eponymously for the main character and meaning sadness in Spanish. I know, so Ti Jean. Anyway, *Tristessa* takes place in Colonia Roma just like *Queer*, but Kerouac dispenses with the expat scene as he's in love with a young Mexican junky woman living with her old man, and describes the Mexicanness of that life—the birds, the dog, the food and the musty overcrowded room, the taco stands on the midnight streets, the beat life of being down and out, impoverished yet beautiful and connected to the sensuality of life while he wallows in his own dissipation. But he's socially immersed! Kerouac breaks your heart, both in his lack of taking care of himself and in his empathy for the similarly broken around him, all of which allows him to enter their world in a way that Burroughs seems unable or uninterested in doing. Granted, there's always something indulgent in Kerouac, but I always had a Burroughs/Kerouac conflict when it came to the Beats, and it was affirmed in arguments with my long-ago junky boyfriend, Z, who loved Burroughs. "But what about the heart?!" I'd shout, shaking a copy of *Visions of Gerard* at him.

"What about it?" he'd deadpan in high Burroughs style, his pupils the size of dimes.

Ginsberg I found too earnest, and Burroughs too cynical, but Jack was the sweet spot in between who saw the hopelessness and vanity of the whole thing and felt it, holding his bleeding heart in his palm as if he'd just removed it himself with a dull knife atop the Templo Mayor of ancient Tenochtitlan. Maybe it was the Roman Catholic in me. Like Jack, I'd been cornered and indoctrinated by priests and had had a rough ride accepting my queerness before dabbling, as did Kerouac, in Buddhism. How could a practical Protestant like Burroughs ever understand, any more than a Jew like Ginsberg, a genuine Buddhist practitioner, who was boldly queer and undefeated by the world? But I'm not writing this essay about Kerouac and Ginsberg. Besides, I matriculated into a world of punk, which in time drew me closer to

Burroughs and his independent and politically provocative way of being gay, a term I always felt was confining and conforming by the Eighties. I certainly fit into the gay world more than Burroughs ever did, but hearing his "Thanksgiving Prayer" for the first time, I felt I'd found a kind of queer soulmate. And though I'm hardly as radical as Burroughs, he's stuck around ever since like a little gargoyle on my shoulder, keeping me in line—even as I attempt to write this essay—in that distinctive voice, "Don't you think you're a tad full of it?" *Just a tad, Bill, forgive me.* "All right then," he mutters, "get on with it."

In *Queer*, Burroughs's autobiographical character Lee goes to Mexico and throws himself into the expat milieu of the early Fifties, encountering the numerous young men wandering around on the GI Bill, most taking a few classes to justify an adventure in a foreign land. Few spoke Spanish. They stuck together, frequenting the same bars and keeping what they seemed to feel or prefer was a necessary distance between themselves and the locals. Burroughs was interested in the locals for sex and to score, but little else, save taxis in which to get around, of course, and the bureaucracy so as to procure visas and the like.

I could relate to the sex part, but with no monkey on my back I related not at all to that other chore, which always makes Burroughs's travels hectic, somewhat miserable, always risky and rather unpleasant, focused as they are on getting that fix. Taxis and bureaucrats can be frustrating as they are in any country where an American is seen as a mark, but speaking the language helps enormously.

There is an insightful exchange in *Queer* where Lee's love interest, Eugene Allerton, referring to a cabbie, says, "Sometimes I think they don't like us," and Lee answers, "I don't mind people disliking me…The question is, what are they in a position to do about it? Apparently nothing, at present…This driver, for example, hates gringoes. But if he kills someone—and very possibly he will—it will not be an American. It will be another Mexican. Maybe his good friend. Friends are less frightening than strangers." And less apt to draw the attention of the authorities, in a country where something like ninety-eight percent of crimes go uninvestigated *unless* it's one perpetrated on a foreigner.

All that aside, I was there for different reasons, essentially to lose my American self as completely as possible—I was as repulsed by twenty-first century America as Burroughs was by its earlier prosperous Fifties—and become as native as my Irish visage and my American-forged psyche would allow. I didn't have to hunt for a room through the near-slums of Fifties Colonia Roma, now utterly gentrified so as to be almost unrecognizable from that earlier time. It was totally uncompelling to me with my desire for immersion, so rife as it is with tourists, Spanish being almost completely unnecessary save the basics. I could simply troll the numerous rental apps instead and find my own neighborhood far off the gringo trail.

And no need for gay bars, or a gay district like the Zona Rosa, which abuts Colonia Roma, and as I recall from my first visits in the Nineties, even then had something of an edge. No longer, as it's now succumbed to gay world culture and is filled with loud dance bars and outdoor cafes catering to middle class locals and gringo tourists. Finding boys isn't complicated at all. There's Manhunt, Grindr, Scruff, ad infinitum, so no need to troll the bathrooms of Sanborn's or the long pedestrian avenues of the Parque Alameda, which were the necessary and more interesting hunting grounds of the Nineties and before. The internet is now as ubiquitous there as here. Why if I were a junky, I'll bet I could even safely score online.

And there's a subway now that didn't exist in the Fifties (built in the Seventies, and one of the most extensive in the world, rivaling only New York City for daily ridership), so I can find a place pretty far away from the tourist locales and still get into the city center, or meet a boy in far off Linda Vista, in twenty minutes or less. So from a queer and an expat angle, I've got it easy, not to mention benefitting from the social changes and attitudes that have washed over both the US and Mexico, especially Mexico City where one can find and make love to some of the most beautiful men on earth—*"One of the boys was so beautiful that the image cut Lee's senses like a wire whip"*—without ever having to play games or get robbed in the process, though all that is still possible. They may not all be "out," as they usually have to live at home with their families, but even that's changing, and once out on the street, they live as gay a life as anyone in the US or Europe, with a robust gay literature documenting it all the way back to the Thirties with pioneering gay poets Salvador Novo and Xavier Villaurrutia, and then into the boom in gay literature after the Sixties, ushered in by Luis Zapata and Carlos Monsiváis, followed by the explosion of queer voices from the likes of Pablo Soler Frost, Jorge Ojeda, Fernando Zamora, Tryno Maldonado and Sergio Loo, few, unfortunately, in translation.

But Burroughs's protagonist Lee is not in *that* Mexico City, and furthermore, he's about the most awkward queer boy to ever grace the pages of American queer lit. Which becomes somewhat endearing as you witness his clumsy attempts to seduce Allerton, who seems uncannily like the junky I once loved, Z., who also looked like a *"sullen child unable to locate the source of his ill temper...tall and very thin, with high cheekbones, a small, bright red mouth that took on a faint violet flush when he was drunk... straight, black eyebrows and black eyelashes...delicate and exotic...never completely neat or clean, but you did not think of him as being dirty."*

Allerton is dismissive of Lee's advances at first, and Burroughs/Lee, having no game, must rely on sheer determination, his heroin cool, and of course the Routine. He has a wicked sense of humor, which protects him and disarms others, even if it consistently goes over Allerton's and most others' heads, so Lee comes off as nonthreatening. In time, I found Lee's lack of game somewhat charming, and even admirable. It's authentic as Burroughs always is, and gay culture is often anything but, especially when it comes to the hunt. We all know what game we got when we cross paths with the gay boys—a well-preserved gringo Daddy type in my case, which Mexicans actually find exotic. And the boys Burroughs encountered likely found him the same, if they weren't just poor straight boys who saw him as a rich mark.

But Burroughs, via Lee, clearly didn't play a gay role among Mexicans or among the expats he pursued like Allerton, for whom his physical characteristics would be anything but exotic, so the point is somewhat moot. Lee's first seduction of Allerton is comically absurd in keeping with Burroughs's world-weary approach. *There was a long silence. Allerton was sitting with his head leaning back against the couch. His eyes were half closed. "Can I show you over the house?" said Lee, standing up. "In here we have the bedroom."* He's a fumbling queer boy who can't fake it, so he surrenders to burlesque, which makes the scene all the more poignant as they innocently get it over with.

But what's all this got to do with Mexico? I wanted to bond with Burroughs over Mexico, not seducing the drab and passionless Allerton. Thus was my hang up—my challenge. About to give up, I got an email from one the editors of this very book. Only weeks from the deadline, and I'd yet to write a word, despairing that I had nothing to say after my feelings of profound disconnect. He recommended I take a look at the *Yage Letters*, and not wanting to disappoint, I did just that.

Bingo. For, while I didn't really find in it much about Mexico, I did find the queerboy Burroughs I'd been looking for as shared in his letters to Allen Ginsberg. His stories about Billy Bradshinkel back in St. Louis, the car sex and trips out to Creve Coeur Lake in the Ozarks, echoing my own horniest years in Berkeley and in L.A. Lots of car sex

with Mexicans who lived at home (one hand on the steering wheel—
"dude, I'm nutting"), and in place of the Ozarks, the redwood forests
above Oakland, and later the idyllic San Gabriel Mountains (even better thanks to the endless summers) where we'd lose our shirts and drop
our pants and unload among the sage and creosote. "Notice I am spar-
ing you the falling leaves," Burroughs quips to Allen, giving away what a
romantic he really is, yet another thing we share. A queer romanticism,
sans dates or domesticity, something more faunlike and friendly, Whit-
man's "two boys together clinging," or a couple of boys at play in the wild
like something out of a poem by Antler. "And I got a silo of queer corn
where that came from," Burroughs guffaws.

But again, what about Mexico? Well, maybe this isn't going to be
about Mexico after all. I picked up *Queer* again, and turned right to the
page where's he's disappointed that Allerton likes to sleep alone. "*Too
bad. If I had my way we'd sleep every night all wrapped around each other
like hibernating rattlesnakes.*" I thought of Quetzalcoatl and feathered
serpents, and realized through those *Yage Letters*, I was beginning to
discover the route to Burroughs's elusive heart, and maybe even the effect that Mexico had had on him. He was certainly more of a romantic
than I'd thought, but he was just so awkward and so clearly interested
in socially-isolating things like drugs, time travel, and Mayan mysticism,
that there were few if any opportunities. So he did what he had to do,
couching it all in the Routine of course, to get what he liked, which was
young men: "(*I thought I was getting that innocent backwoods ass, but the
kid had been to bed with six American oilmen, a Swedish botanist, a Dutch
ethnographer, a Capuchin father known locally as the Mother Superior, a
Bolivian Troskyite on the lam, and jointly fucked by the Cocoa Commission
and Point Four).*" And then he tells Allen that the "*Trouble is I share with
the late Father Flanagan—he of Boy's Town—the deep conviction that there
is no such thing as a bad boy.*"

Maybe that's the real junk we share. Otherwise, I've certainly got my own junk in the form of exercise (certainly much easier on the nerves and the constitution) to fend off my crippling suicidal dark moods that are impervious to SSRIs. Bourgeois as it would likely sound to Burroughs, with his penchant for firearms, drug experimentation and rent boys, if I didn't get my daily fix, I too *would become a sloppy lush or go crazy taking cocaine.* Well a sloppy lush sure thing; cocaine not so much since college. I'm trying to find common ground here, cut me some slack. "All right then, get on with it," the gargoyle on my shoulder grimly mutters.

And was Burroughs's Mexican immersion really only of the mind when all is said and done? Perhaps I was just misreading that or functioning on a grosser level of experience than our drug-addled yage-taker who I soon discovered in the "Mayan Caper" of *The Soft Machine* going for total immersion—and it doesn't get any more physical than a "transfer operation" where one's mind ends up in the body of a young Mayan man via injection...

"*The injection caused simultaneous vomiting and orgasm and several times he finds himself vomiting and ejaculating into the Mayan vessel* ...—*A spermy, compost heap smell filled the room—The boy began to twitch and mutter and fell to the floor in a fit—I could see that he had an erection under his thin trousers—The broker opened the boy's shirt and pulled off his pants—The penis flipped out spurting in orgasm after orgasm—A green light filled the room and burned through the boy's flesh—Suddenly he sat up talking in Mayan—The words curled out his mouth and hung visible in the air like vine tendrils—I felt a strange vertigo which I recognized as the motion sickness of time travel. The boy touched my shoulder and disappeared up the path in jungle dawn mist—*"

Well, I haven't had quite that experience, but I do remember disappearing up a similarly misty jungle path several years previous in search of a small pyramid, El Tepozteco, where I discovered Xochipilli—god of art, games, dance, flowers, song, homosexuals and hallucinogenic plants. Well then. I thought of my late Mexican friend, Javier, an aficionado of peyote and all things hallucinogenic, who died suddenly and shockingly and to whom I was never able to bid farewell. That got me thinking again about Z. and the Introduction to *Queer* where Burroughs talks about the "ugly spirit" haunting him, which leads to his accidently killing his wife, Joan.

Perhaps I'd missed the point completely on the first read through. I'm haunted too—by Z.'s end, who I loved and who loved me, and who I did not visit when I heard he was dying of cancer a decade after we'd parted, after he'd burglarized my apartment and fled for good. It wasn't that I was sore per se. I owned so little and almost nothing of value. In fact, I was able to buy back my books across the street at the used bookseller's *at cost,* and I never used the camera anyway, which the police found at a pawnshop. I was probably more upset that he'd fled for Iowa City where he'd hooked up with a writer in the Iowa Writers' Workshop, which looked to me like an upgrade and was thus a blow to my struggling and dubious writerly self-esteem.

So, I didn't go to him, but mostly because I'd learned he was dying from a person we'd known in common who was potentially dangerous, and in my paranoia, I sensed a potential trap. Yeah, the "ugly spirit" was in the house. I struggled with what to do. I'd loved him and he'd loved me, but he was proud and had a mean superego, and ultimately, I felt he'd resent me visiting him in such a vulnerable state—a reminder of his heartless betrayal. How could I do such a thing to him on his deathbed? Wouldn't that be cruel? A selfless Catholic to the end or a fumbling Jack Kerouac. And the little gargoyle on my shoulder, saying in that flat voice, "Don't you think you're just a tad full of shit?"

Quite a bit, Bill, and I hope Z. will forgive me.

"I'm sure he's seen worse," my gargoyle mutters.

Most natural painkiller what there is. LOVE, was Burroughs's final journal entry. There's the heart I was looking for when I argued with Z. so
long ago, and I hear Z.'s voice again, "What about it?" because my failure
in his final hour proved him right and me wrong.

Burroughs talked about something else in that introduction to
Queer—an observation about Lee as a recovering addict and about why
he doesn't really develop Allerton as a character: "*Allerton was definitely
some sort of character. And what was the contact that Lee was looking for?
Seen from here, a very confused concept that had nothing to do with Allerton
as a character. While the addict is indifferent to the impression he creates in
others, during withdrawal he may feel the compulsive need for an audience,
and this is clearly what Lee seeks in Allerton: an audience, the acknowledgment of his performance, which of course is a mask, to cover a shocking
disintegration. So he invents a frantic attention-getting format which he calls
the Routine: shocking, funny, riveting"*...made up of stories about *Chess
Players, the Texas Oilman, Corn Hole Gus' Used Slave Lot,* all dedicated
to Allerton, *who is forced into the role of approving muse. But Later, as he
develops as a writer, the audience becomes internalized.* This is a profound
observation about both sex and writing as performance and about what
they are for the writer. Maybe Z. and I in our youth, and arguably disintegration, were only seeking an audience in each other. Maybe that was
the message I needed to get from *Queer.* Or perhaps, on a higher level,
that's the wisdom only Mexico could provide us both.

Because Burroughs also said that instead of writing, he *was being
written in Queer,* a characteristically mystical Mexican experience that I
feel I've had myself. Often while in Mexico I've thought that instead of

living, "Mexico lives me." And when people ask me why I've chosen to live in Mexico, I don't give reasons anymore because I really believe that "Mexico chose me."

And so I guess in the end I didn't read *Queer* after all. It read me.

NO HOLES FOR PIGEONS

CHRISTOPHER STODDARD

"There are people who look like junkies and aren't, just as some people look queer and aren't. It's a type that causes trouble."
—*Junky* by William Burroughs

Like a porn star attempting to distract viewers from his soulless eyes via a sexy smile, strong legs and a thick cock standing at attention to the camera, a first novel reveals more about the author than they may have intended. There's something beautiful in the purity of a loosely fictionalized account of an author's fascinating life, however it can be lacking in metaphor and other literary magic tricks that often come with more writing experience. While the author risks alienating readers with all the raw and gory personal details that can border on solipsistic, their voice is at its purest: brutally honest and unnervingly palpable. An author's pseudo-autobiography offers readers a naked perspective on a world starkly different from their own. And when the author's voice and background is as clear and provocative as William S. Burroughs's in his first novel, *Junky*, its reception by readers can be groundbreaking, its celebration infinite.

To better understand Burroughs's later experimental books, his first novel, *Junky*, as well as *Queer* and *The Yage Letters* composed earlier but published later, unveils the man behind the curtain, providing some explanation of the abstract metaphors in *Naked Lunch* and *The Soft Machine*, among several other titles to which he applied his signature cut-up technique. In the more approachable book, *Junky*—from a clear plot and bare language perspective, at least—originally released in 1953 by genre fiction publisher Ace Books, under Burroughs's pen name William Lee, he explores, via his alter-ego-protagonist Bill, his own contradictory sexuality and debilitating drug addiction, and the criminalization of both.

However, to pigeonhole Burroughs as a "gay writer" or some sort of activist who fought the addict-averse bureaucracy just because he wrote about gay sex and heroin in defiance of the pre-Nixon war on drugs would be inaccurate. His anti-establishment position was mainly self-serving. Sure, he was an addict who desired and slept with men—he even cut off his finger joint to impress a guy—and yes, he was a writer. But the interpretation of *Junky* and all fiction should be left to each individual reader, and not be used as a tool to uncover its author's good, bad, and ugly truths.

Ironically, anyone speaking openly about their same sex experiences at the time Burroughs was writing wouldn't be considered a gay writer by today's standards, which implicitly demand support of the homosexual lifestyle. Moreover, a writer is simply a writer, no matter whom they're fucking. Who cares whether Burroughs was gay? Did anyone classify Denis Johnson as a straight writer when he wrote the sex-and-drugs-charged short story collection, *Jesus' Son?* Did we label presumed-heterosexual author Hanya Yanagihara a gay writer when we celebrated her lengthy novel about queer life and issues, *A Little Life?*

No, these authors and their books were recognized for their cultural relevance and literary excellence. When it comes to authors whose sexual preferences lean toward the same gender, we have a responsibility to leave off the descriptor of "gay," as it has the opposite effect of inclusivity. It merely perpetuates the marginalization and isolation of writers and other artists who happen to be homosexual.

If anything, the sexual escapades of Bill in *Junky* read as homophobic. He abhors gay men, especially those who are "obvious"—in other words, effeminate:

> "A room full of fags gives me the horrors. They jerk around like puppets on invisible strings, galvanized into hideous activity that is the negation of everything living and spontaneous. The live human being has moved out of these bodies long ago. But something moved in when the original tenant moved out. Fags are ventriloquists' dummies who have moved in and taken over the ventriloquist."

Burroughs's harsh observations of gay men in the gritty New Orleans bar scene, as seen through the eyes of his protagonist Bill, certainly sound like those of the clichéd self-hating gay guy in the closet, especially during the mid-1900s when sodomy was illegal and homosexuality was considered an abomination. But ultimately, Burroughs and his Bill were just drug addicts looking for their next fix in whatever form they could get it. In the book, when Bill is fresh out of heroin, he buys coke; when he can't score coke, he gets plastered with booze; and after the bars in the French Quarter close in the wee hours of a muggy New Orleans morning, he finds the nearest living thing to take back to his hotel. After Bill is released on bail from a drug-related arrest, he flees to Mexico where he resumes his lifestyle of barhopping, in search of the next high and/or hookup, while further detailing his loathing of homosexuals:

> "Three Mexican fags were posturing in front of the jukebox. One of them slithered over to where I was standing, with the stylized gestures of a temple dancer, and asked for a cigarette. There was

something archaic in the stylized movements, a depraved animal grace... Sodomy is as old as the human species. One of the fags was sitting in a booth by the jukebox, perfectly immobile with stupid animal serenity."

If Burroughs possessed even a modicum of the same sentiment as his Bill (by essentially categorizing gay men as dumb animals), it's difficult to find similarities between his offensive sensibilities and other authors of the "gay writer" variety who wax poetic about man-love. In *Junky*, it's clear Bill thinks of his desire for gay men as a reluctant alternative to drugs when he's out of them, just as the isolated herder is rumored to be inclined to his sheep when he's horny, but that doesn't mean he identifies as an animal.

All of this isn't to say that *Junky* and Burroughs's other earlier works weren't socially progressive in their own right. After all, he slept with men and told the world about it at a time when homosexuals in America were labeled mentally ill perverts. As contradictory and unkind to himself and the gay community as he may have been, he should be applauded for writing about his homosexual experiences.

Burroughs didn't overtly identify as gay, but he certainly was a junky whose lifestyle suffered from counterproductive laws targeted at drug addicts. And his anti-establishment position doesn't necessarily mean he was an activist, either. He could've just been venting about the inconvenience of the police trying to hinder his druggy lifestyle. The plot of *Junky* centers around Bill's relentless pursuit of his next fix, his run-ins with corrupt cops along the way, and his subjection to arrest for abusing drugs rather than being treated for heroin addiction. In the introduction to *Junky*, Allen Ginsberg writes:

"20,000 doctors [were] arraigned for trying to treat junkies, thousands fined & jailed 1935-1953, in what N.Y. County Medical Association called 'a war on doctors.'"

This mid-century "war on doctors" is synonymous with President Nixon's war on drugs that began in the early Seventies, during which he labeled the drug addict as public enemy number one, the sentiment of which lingers to this day. For decades upon decades, society has gotten it wrong. We criminalize the sick rather than help them. We ostracize minorities. Burroughs was brave enough to draw attention to these age-old social issues with his novel *Junky*, however self-serving his inspiration may have been for writing it.

"The chief of police said, 'This drive is going to continue as long as there is a single violator left in this city.' The State legislators drew up a law making it a crime to be a drug addict. They did not specify where or when or what they meant by drug addict. The cops began stopping addicts on the street and examining their arms for needle marks. If they found marks, they pressured the addict to sign a statement admitting his condition so he could be charged under the 'drug addicts law.'"

In this passage, Burroughs-as-Bill recounts the origins of the systemic discriminations of the police state that are still pervasive today. Nearly half of people currently incarcerated in American prisons are nonviolent drug offenders. While the laws have evolved and residents of some left-leaning states are reaping the benefits of the decriminalization of drugs, there are many innocent others decaying in prison and largely forgotten. Regardless of his reasons for complaining about the cops locking up drug addicts like himself, Burroughs shone a much-needed light on the darker side of the law.

"Since no place or time is specified and the term 'addict' is not clearly defined, no proof is necessary or even relevant under a law so formulated. No proof, and consequently, no trial. This is police-state legislation penalizing a state of being... So I decided to jump bail and live permanently outside the United States."

Burroughs is showing readers the tragic result of the puritanical need to keep America great, to sweep the sick and the different under the rug or push them out altogether. Why else does Bill feel compelled to escape the country in which he was born, if not for feeling helpless and rejected by society? In the novel, Burroughs positions Bill's motivation to escape to Mexico as a desire to live in a country where he can get high and fuck whomever he wishes with significantly less worry of arrest: *"In Mexico your wishes have a dream power..."* He's explaining—perhaps without realizing it—why Bill had such a strong desire to maintain his drug habit: his oppressive, intolerant perfectionist of a country was both his trigger and his enabler.

Maybe William S. Burroughs wrote *Junky* simply to provoke readers with his shockingly personal stories of America's underbelly. Maybe he wrote it for the money, or at Allen Ginsberg's urging. Maybe he was just sharing what life was like for him and his queer junky friends via his daringly direct, beautifully bare words. Maybe he was struggling with his sexuality... or maybe he was just trying to get off. We'll never really know, and maybe it doesn't matter.

"WE'RE MIRED IN IT": AN INTERVIEW WITH CHRIS KELSO

TOM CARDAMONE

In 1962, the same year Naked Lunch *was banned in Boston, William S. Burroughs trudged his way across the United Kingdom to the International Writers Conference in Edinburgh. None other than James Grauerholz, in his introduction to Burroughs's collection of essays,* The Adding Machine, *identifies the conference as integral to "the author's first critical apotheosis." In* Burroughs and Scotland *(2021, Beatdom Books) Scottish writer and British Fantasy Award nominee Chris Kelso, with quicksilver insight, delves into how this event and Burroughs's writing marked a seismic shift in the Scottish literary scene, one that still resonates.*

Having read this book while miles above the earth, freshly inoculated against a virus still surging across the globe, waving away the stewardesses' offer of much needed cocktails to better retain my focus on the printed page, I closed this exciting blend of biography-partial-memoir-and-manifesto with several questions swirling in my N95 mask-compressed brain. So, I pinged Chris on social media, and he agreed to the following interview:

TOM CARDAMONE: Chris, tell me about that exact moment you decided that Burroughs and Scotland needed to be put to paper.

CHRIS KELSO: Growing up, I can remember the first time I ever crossed paths with Burroughs, and it was catching a few moments of the David Cronenberg film of *Naked Lunch*. It was the scene where William Lee was feeding the exterminator powder to the Clark Nova, and it was profoundly disturbing at the time. But that image stayed with me for a long time, and then you become a teenager and you start to get into counterculture books and that kind of media and *Naked Lunch* was always sort of mentioned. So, I had this kind of disturbing image from my childhood. And then I went to university, and I had just been dumped by my girlfriend. And rather than studying and trying to power through and channel my energy in a more positive way, I decided to just sort of skip classes and go to the university library. And that's where I decided to confront my inner darkness a bit. Because obviously, you know, getting dumped is devastating, you know, heartbreak. I mean everyone has experienced it—I'm sure you've experienced it at some point, or you've dished it out at some point. But by taking that time in isolation I felt like I was able to meet the darkness head on. But the thing about growing up in Scotland, I don't know if you've ever been in Scotland before.

CARDAMONE: I have.

KELSO: Oh, have you been to Ayshire before?

CARDAMONE: No.

KELSO: Ayshire, it's kind of Burns territory. It can be a pretty bleak place. People are faced with darkness in their everyday reality, they don't want to reflect or cogitate. It's brutalist architecture everywhere. I mean, it's got a beautiful countryside, but the people who are there have a bleak existence, generally. Burroughs work was the best way I could articulate my inner darkness, something I had been taught to repress and hide—because life was fucking hard enough without becoming introspective. So you're kind of well-acquainted with Burroughs's themes, I think, people identify with his kind of hopelessness that he had, because, I mean, Burroughs is the ultimate kind of individualist. He's a heroin addict, which is such an individualist pursuit. And I mean, he was a total alien, as well. And there is something intrinsic to the Scottish experience that is very similar—we're sort of a rogue nation. And we've got a history of oppression from other countries and we're striving for independence from the United Kingdom. And there's just a lot of darkness in the rest of the country as well. We're mired in it. And so, that's the long-winded and clumsy connection; I suppose that that was the kernel of the association. I'm very proud to be Scottish, as well. And I love William Burroughs, so really, I was looking for any excuse to bring the two together. And then when I found that Burroughs had been to Scotland and he had a relationship with Trocchi, and all of these kinds of people, it became just a bee in my bonnet. I wanted to see if I could stitch it all altogether.

CARDAMONE: As a fiction writer, composing your first long-form nonfiction piece must have been an adventure. Were there nonfiction books that inspired you?

KELSO: I'm a big fan of David Shields. I don't know if you're familiar with his work, *Reality Hunger*. He's a great American writer, and somebody who started off writing fiction, but then really moved away from it, like he sort of fell out of love with fiction. And his argument is that the novel is dead. And I had a very similar experience, to be honest. I mean, I've written about twenty-five fiction books and none of them have sold particularly well. I mean, I'm covering a lot of ground with the genre as well, the science fiction was harder to sell, then there was kind of literary fiction, and they all get decent critical reviews, but never anything that, you know, we'd always have to have a job—I could never make a living at it at all. And so, I also found that I really wasn't reading an awful lot of fiction anymore. Maybe it's just the older you get, I've heard of how that happens, you become more sort of conservative the older you get as well. Although that hasn't really happened, but I have moved away from fiction; I'm looking for something to relate to more directly. In saying that, I've always read nonfiction, but really grew up with science fiction and genre fiction. But similar to David Shields, the relationship ended. I can still read fiction, but I'm not compelled to write it anymore at all. Maybe my imagination is used up. My suspension of disbelief has snapped. I'm expecting my first child and have recently got my first teaching job, we're moving house, I'm gonna have a mortgage—all this kind of stuff, I'm unwilling to grant myself that type of escapism. It's good to be rooted in reality now. Yeah, if that makes any sense.

CARDAMONE: That makes perfect sense. I used to read seventy-five percent fiction, twenty-five percent nonfiction. Over the years it's flipped. And I feel like as a storyteller, the reality that wraps us is so unreal. Maybe we should live there and do the work there. I definitely vibe with you on that front. I enjoyed *Burroughs & Scotland* because, while you recorded Burroughs's time and interest in Scotland, you also examined his influence on science fiction, in-depth, I might add. And his influence on the genre gets name-checked a lot, but not often explored.

KELSO: Yeah, I think you're right. And it's funny as well because I always had that association with him. Like when you read things like *Wild Boys* and *The Soft Machine* and some of the cut-up books: the science fiction influence is evidently there for all to see. He was reading science fiction as well. He was an avid reader. And if you have ever read his letters, he talks about reading Samuel Delaney's *Dahlgren*, and all these really interesting sorts of new wave science fiction writers. It was pretty clear that that the things he was talking about—agents and alien beings and otherworldly situations and characters—that's something so very inherently science fiction. But in Scotland as well, we were very influenced by Burroughs's own brand of science fiction. *Interzone Magazine*, which was started in Scotland, obviously takes its name from the Moroccan international zone from *Naked Lunch*.

I personally think of Burroughs as a science fiction writer. I don't know if that seems strange because he was such an omnipresent figure in the counterculture and culture in general. He's been very influential. But I still see him as a science fiction writer—all the tropes are there.

CARDAMONE: It's funny that you mention Delaney. I used to live in Bay Ridge, Brooklyn. And whenever I took the bus, I passed a very truncated street, just a few blocks long, named Dahlgren Place, and I always wondered if he took the same bus during his time in New York and if that's where he got the name.

Writers and artists often talk about how Burroughs influenced their work, even their lives, and usually reference the first book of his they read, almost always *Naked Lunch*. What was the second Burroughs book you read and why? What kept you coming back to his oeuvre?

KELSO: Good question! The second book I read is my favorite Burroughs book to this day, *Junky*. I love *Junky*. And I think the reason why is because *Naked Lunch* is such a challenging read, especially the first time you pick it up. You hear a lot of things about it. It's got this kind of semblance of a plot—there's some kind of dream-logic. But I remember feeling a bit hung over with *Naked Lunch*. And there was something really fascinating about Burroughs's life, and I really identified with how he experienced the world—being an outcast, I wanted to latch on to something, a text that he produced, that I could identify with, and I heard that *Junky* was much more a memoir, it was much more linear. It's still my favorite Burroughs book and it's the most accessible as well, it's the book you might suggest to somebody who isn't a big fan of experimental or overly confrontational reading. Having read *Junky*, I was able to return to *Naked Lunch* with fresh eyes and enjoyed that much more the second time—you realize how much a masterpiece it really is.

CARDAMONE:Now in *Burroughs and Scotland*, you talk about an incident in your youth where you gave a male friend a celebratory peck on the cheek, and the homophobic fallout that ensued. Usually the heterosexual response to such nonsense is to double down on one's own heterosexuality, you know, sports, me-fuck-girls and bragging about it, egregious hatred toward gays to prove one's own hetero-ness. Or maybe that's just The States. But instead, you ended up enthralled with a notorious homosexual, William S. Burroughs. That's kind of counter the usual path.

KELSO: Yeah, I think you're right. And when I was with my classmate, given that that incident happened, and it was very, very innocent and innocuous, I didn't envisage the fallout that came from it. The one good thing about that experience was that it put me in the shoes of a gay person, because where I'm from, Ayshire, the last person who openly came out was literally crucified and burned alive at the side of the road. So that's the environment we're talking about—it's heavily religious, very Presbyterian with a very elderly population as well. I think it's much better now than it was. I should say there are also a lot of fantastic people in this area.

But that incident was a celebratory kiss, as you said, the fallout for that, I mean, I could go outside my door, they were spray-painting things on the side that are still there, there were things spray-painted all throughout town. It was graffiti with my name. So, people had made a decision about me. And my mom and dad were relatively progressive, considering where they were from, and the time period we're talking about. But at the same time, I could tell that they were bitterly disappointed that I had kissed a boy. And I think when I became a teenager, I took that being shunned, like, in a big, public way—all throughout my formative years, that feeling of being somebody who is weird and viewed as depraved. And then of course, you leave the town that you grew up in, you go to university, but you realize that most of the people you are influenced by are gay, that it really doesn't fucking matter—none of that stuff really matters at all. Some of my best friends in fact—many of my best friends are gay men. The majority of writers that I admire, filmmakers that I admire, are gay men. That experience gave me a lot of empathy for people who are living in the margins and outside of society. And Burroughs is the ultimate outsider. He was doing all this kind of stuff in the Fifties. Obviously he was married to Joan, had a child—it was a kind of a sham marriage, rather, he was out, Ginsberg was really out, and they were beginning to receive critical acclaim. And that was a tremendous inspiration for me. And I've always had, I've always felt that kinship and unity with any minority population. Just that one experience was tremendously humbling. I'm not even sure if I answered your question.

CARDAMONE: You answered it beautifully.

You were "othered" and you used it, rather than reject it wholeheartedly, which, unfortunately, is what makes some of the worst bigots in the world. They don't know how to process that experience, so they inhabit that hatred themselves. So, thank you for that.

KELSO: Thank you.

CARDAMONE: I'm a huge fan of Alasdair Gray, and know of several writers who not only adore his work but consider him a personal influence, as do I—I've even eaten in the Ubiquitous Chip! (A Glaswegian restaurant featuring his murals.)

KELSO: Really?

CARDAMONE: And it was before cellphones! So I didn't photograph his work or memorialize it. I had to be in the moment.

KELSO: Even better.

CARDAMONE: Wonderful, actually. I can only imagine he looms large over the Scottish literary establishment, and I'm comfortable linking him to Burroughs in terms of how he really broke open narrative structure and established Scottish literature as a force to be reckoned with. What are your thoughts? Am I on track here?

KELSO: I think you're absolutely right. I mean, the thing I love about Gray is that he is a polymath:he's as good a writer as he is an artist, and I had the honor of meeting him a few times. He used to come to the library that I worked in, and off the record he was a functioning alcoholi-

CARDAMONE: This is the record!

KELSO: Okay, that's fine. So at least he's not gonna read this. He passed away a couple of years ago.So I actually had opportunity to talk to him, not any length because you just couldn't—you couldn't have a conversation because he was being pulled in every direction. He was in high demand, he's kind of the grandfather of experimental contemporary Scottish literature. I did ask him about Burroughs, and he seemed to express a kind of passing admiration for what Burroughs had done as most creatives do owe him a debt in some way. They both cracked open the egg in a lot of ways. Burroughs almost transcended literature because he had such an influence on pop culture and music.

Alasdair Gray had a similar effect on the scene in Scotland as well. For Irvin Welsh's *Trainspotting*. The two obvious influences for him were Alasdair Grey and William Burroughs. So, they do have that kind of tenuous link. A wee bit. The thing about Scotland is it's got quite an uninteresting literary scene and it always has—with works like *Trainspotting*, or Gray's *Lanark* and *1982, Janine*, they come along and blow the whole thing apart. But generally, we revert back to memoirs and those kind of things, or books about Scotland that are very dry. Gray is very important. To me, he is the Scottish equivalent of Burroughs. People think maybe Trocchi is, because he was hanging about William Burroughs and writing for the Olympia Press, but I think Alasdair Gray was a much more daring writer. And much more prolific as well . . .

CARDAMONE:Last question: I think people come to Burroughs twice. Once in reading him, and then that second time, when they hear his voice. That voice! It really impacts how you take in his written word forever after. When did you first hear him?

KELSO: I've been brought up with YouTube. I'm a millennial, so I've always had that access to whatever I wanted, I'm totally spoiled when it comes to those things. I've always enjoyed watching him read. My favorite piece that he does is the Doctor Benway routine—when they're on the ship, and he's performing surgery. He goes into the roles of the characters and he's got real comedic timing; he's a talented operator. Have you ever heard the album—let me just quickly double check the name of it—I had this record, because I'm a bit of a hipster, it's called *Spare Ass Annie and Other Tales*.

When I was at university, it was a prominent feature amongst the more bohemian students, as well. And that was an album that was in popular rotation. So, straight away he's got that presence and that color, there's a kind of performative side that I really appreciate. Because, if you just look at the books, like I was saying before, the first time you read *Naked Lunch*, it is like wading through treacle, it gets quite challenging. But then you can listen to him read excerpts, and it just completely comes away. And it's really, really, funny. It's a great companion to his work—the spoken word legacy that he's left as well.

his voice . . .

TIM YOUNG

At the teen age when I was searching library shelves, looking for queer voices, I chose down and rough and dirty and ready types like John Rechy and Jean Genet. I held William S. Burroughs at arm's length. He was ambiently present in the books that I shelved at the public library. I remember the colorful cover of *The Western Lands* and the other volumes in his late trilogy. I learned to listen politely as straight friends of mine went on and on about his writing, his short stories, and the film adaptations that brought his paranoid characters to life. It is never a good thing to tell a twenty-year-old what they *should* be reading; even worse when that young person is a dedicated book recommender himself. Every push toward Burroughs was another reason for me to stand fast in my ignorance of his work.

I saw Burroughs principally as a Beat writer alongside those selfish macho characters Jack Kerouac and Neal Cassady. Buff, swarthy, MEN who flaunted their patriarchal privilege under the oversize flag labeled "finding oneself." When I did encounter their work, I didn't like it, so I refused to approach it. I am not a fan of William S. Burroughs. But you can't grow up as a reader without confronting him.

But in the same way a reluctant child gets tricked into eating something bitter and healthy, there was a mode of entry into his work: his voice. I discovered it by way of Giorno Poetry Systems, specifically the 1981 album *You're the Guy I Want To Share My Money With*—a landmark project that deserves praise for many things: its title, the full-blown introduction to the wider world of the genius of Laurie Anderson, and its innovative format, a four-sided double vinyl LP set, one side each by Anderson, by John Giorno, and by Burroughs, and the fourth a multi-grooved side that played one of the three writers depending on where the needle landed, (a triumph of analog that cannot truly be duplicated digitally). These recordings show Anderson at her most interesting phase of development and allow Burroughs to assert his presence for another generation of listeners and readers while keeping Giorno, an underappreciated national poetry treasure, in the mix. Burroughs shows himself to be a master storyteller and joke-maker. A later Giorno Poetry Systems compilation, *A Diamond Hidden in the Mouth of a Corpse* (1985), with its Keith Haring cover, put Burroughs in the shared company of Hüsker Dü, Sonic Youth, and Cabaret Voltaire, introducing him to an even wider audience. Therefore, my acquaintance with William S. Burroughs didn't happen by my reading him.

Instead, Burroughs read to me. It was an aural acquaintance, and it pretty much remained on that level. His voice was the gateway—an amalgam of mesmerism, threat, calm, and matter-of-factness that aligned with the memory of my own grandfather's animated tale-telling. I grew up listening to family stories. This medium of interaction was a welcome and happy one for me. I was a dedicated reader from the moment I could hold open a book, but eventually I realized that the oral tradition was important in my family: jokes, histories, bizarre accounts of something that happened to the acquaintance of a friend of a relative. I suppose Burroughs came on not like a stranger in a bar but as a weird uncle who communicated a passel of anecdotes relating to our much wider family history.

And Laurie Anderson? What branch of the family did she belong to? I could trace part of her genealogy to Lou Reed, her genius life partner, who was also influenced by Burroughs, was promoted by Andy Warhol, and who studied with Delmore Schwartz ("My Dedalus to your Bloom . . ." from "My House", *The Blue Mask*). But this masculine thread would only be a footnote to any explanation of the very deep queer kinship I feel with her.

Burroughs's voice has a long history. Parallel to—and in a sense equal to—his writing. His first spoken-word record, *Call Me Burroughs*, was recorded in Paris in 1965 and issued by The English Bookshop with a US edition pressed in 1966 by ESP-Disk. The record, although issued in a limited edition, had a major impact on a number of writers and musicians of the era: The Beatles, David Bowie, Bob Dylan, even Steely Dan

The next major audio effort by Burroughs was in the form of a double LP made with John Giorno in 1975. It included passages from fan favorites, such as *The Wild Boys* and *Junky* but also featured a newer work, a long section of *Cities of the Red Night*, which would be published in 1981. The real breakthrough of Burroughs as a stand-up reader happened in December 1978, at the three-day Nova Convention celebrating his work and bringing him together with younger artists he had influenced, including Philip Glass, Patti Smith, and Laurie Anderson. Giorno Poetry Systems issued a pared-down recording culled from the event in 1979.

Burroughs late-life career as a touring showman was launched, and it would hold him in good stead (or at least in rent money) for several years. More records followed in the 1980s and 1990s: *The Doctor Is On The Market, Break Through In Grey Room*, a pair of popular releases from Island Records, *Dead City Radio*, and *Spare Ass Annie And Other Tales*, both produced by Hal Willner (long-time music consultant for

Saturday Night Live and producer of albums by Anderson and Reed and many essential tribute projects), audiobooks, and then, after his death, the inevitable remix project: *William S. Burroughs In Dub* (2014).

Burroughs's voice is now readily available. You can find him on iTunes and Spotify and many other digital locales. So, it is much easier to encounter that monotone that is, in fact, not monotonous, and the drone that is not truly droning, the detached voice that in reality holds you and reassures you that there will eventually be some moral to his story. The danger of this availability is, of course, its decontextualization. Burroughs, like any artist online, is disembodied in a way that makes one element of his art fungible. Thus, some listeners might only encounter Burroughs in samples used by other artists such as Cut Chemist and Meat Beat Manifesto or in the form of the supremely enjoyable distillation of *Naked Lunch* that is Bomb the Bass and Justin Warfield's "Bug Powder Dust" (the Kruder & Dorfmeister Session, natch).

    This entrée via sampling is what reminded me more recently of the power of his voice. About fifteen years ago, I picked up an odd compilation of songs by Malcolm McLaren, *Tranquilize*. This CD features the track "Mexico, Manhattan and Malibu" which begins with an excerpt of Burroughs reading from *Naked Lunch*—specifically the section "Bradley the Buyer" (the first work on the talismanic 1965/66 album, *Call me Burroughs*) laid over Willie Bobo's 1962 instrumental track "Trinidad"

> *Drove all night, came at dawn to a warm misty place, barking dogs and the sound of running water.*

> *"Thomas and Charlie," I said.*

> *"What?"*

"That's the name of this town. Sea level. We climb straight up from here ten thousand feet." I took a fix and went to sleep in the back seat. She was a good driver. You can tell as soon as someone touches the wheel.

Mexico City where Lupita sits like an Aztec Earth Goddess doling out her little papers of lousy shit.

"Selling is more of a habit than using," Lupita says. Non-using pushers have a contact habit, and that's one you can't kick. Agents get it too. Take Bradley the Buyer. Best narcotics agent in the industry. Anyone would make him for junk. I mean he can walk up to a pusher and score direct. He is so anonymous, grey and spectral the pusher don't remember him afterwards. So he twists one after the other....

Well the Buyer comes to look more and more like a junky. He can't drink. He can't get it up. His teeth fall out. (Like pregnant women lose their teeth feeding the stranger, junkies lose their yellow fangs feeding the monkey.) He is all the time sucking on a candy bar. Babe Ruths he digs special. "It really disgusts you to see the Buyer sucking on them candy bars so nasty," a cop says.

McLaren segues from Burroughs to an interview with Jayne Mansfield from the early Sixties in which she expounds on her love of Californian modernism. Like so many things McLaren created, he took opposite cultural aesthetics and paired them just by the fact of their shared temporal existence, allowing the listener to discover linkages. This work made me find Burroughs again even though it still didn't make me a true reader of his works. I suppose long before then I had reached an equilibrium regarding how close and how deep I wanted to be to him and his world. I'm just not that into him. I listen and observe from a remove, a bit like stopping to peer through a murky window at a boxing gym versus jumping into the ring while still wearing your flat leather shoes and street clothes. I'll leave that be. I want to maintain my distance.

I had a friend—my best teenage friend—who, shortly after I found he was not gay, became enamored of—no, nearly obsessed with—Burroughs. So much so that he moved to Lawrence, Kansas to be near the man and his aura and reputation. So, in allegiance to this friend, I did pick up Burroughs's books again, intending to encounter the man on paper. But it didn't stick. I gave up on his printed word. To be honest, I give up on a lot of books, in the same way I allow myself to walk out of movies that don't agree with me. I feel it's no badge of honor to force myself through a work for the sole virtue of adding a title to my list of accomplishments. Life is short.

In library school, I came to respect the view that Burroughs's first paperback pulp editions had risen to the highest ranks of bibliomania. For me, this added another layer of credibility to his life and removed a small increment of my resistance. This is really to say that I looked long and hard in used book shops for a copy of the Ace paperback of *Junky* by William Lee, which, of course, I never found since it was already a well-known quantity in the rare book world I was just then entering. As I write that, I realize that I just confessed to desiring the material reality of his text, not the content.

That realization may be the heart of my contentious contrariness which I have about so many things: desperately wanting to have a reason or definition for my attraction or repulsion to/from things and at the same time not ever wanting to dispel every bit of that mysterious attraction or repulsion. Burroughs and Anderson, like Pedro Almodóvar and Klaus Nomi concurrently in my acculturation, provided a queerness that was satirical, humorous, and also somewhat surreal but very,

very satisfying in all the ways that the best experimental artists of the twentieth century can be. They showed that being *fabulous*, as wonderful as that can be for many people, is not the sole measure of achievement for queer folk. One can be garrulous and contrary and confusing and frustrating and insecure and totally weird without giving away one's soul. Add to the list above Gus Van Sant, Agnes Martin, Leigh Bowery, Lily Tomlin, and John Waters, and call it a pantheon of queer-ish performers, makers, creators, and talkers. Each of them defines their art with their voice, even if it manifests in the decision to withhold their voice; to illuminate their art or let their art speak on its own. While we're at it, let's go ahead and throw in Missy Elliot because all of these Super Friends put it down flipped it and reversed IT. The IT here being themselves and their transformations of their selfhoods into art. In a simple-stupid phrase, they were all so fucking weird. It took me a long while to even start to understand them or to admit that I remained confused, but fascinated. But ain't that the soul of wholesome queerness?

After I reached an impasse in composing this essay, realizing that I am doing a form of bait-and-switch (Wait? So, you don't like Burroughs, but you admit that you've read only small bits of his work? How is that a convincing argument?), another friend gave me the words to better define my stance: "... your respect for those [other queer] artists created a new patience for his voice in you." Yes ... patience, queerness, voice, ... in me. I am at a loss for another metaphor, or I am realizing I don't need one. I can respect Burroughs, I can place him in context and admire his life and work while not immersing myself fully in his work. Maybe this means I am focusing on the *punctum* in his oeuvre while ignoring the *studium*? Maybe.

So now, after all that high-falutin', thesaurus-consulting folderol, I will admit that there is one actual written text by Burroughs that I love, and which inhabits a part of my brain. It is "The Discipline of DE (do easy)", one of the chapters from his short story compilation *Exterminator!* I know it from Van Sant's early short film he created in 1982. It makes sense to me as it likely does to many other OCD folks since it gave me a flipped version of Zen that didn't ask me to calm down but told me how to use my hyper-attention in a way that brought ease and value to my daily life and routine. It was about paying attention and learning from retakes. Burroughs assured me that "Every object you touch is alive with your life and your will." It may well be a parody or a satire, but the truth about fiction is that you never know what you'll end up taking away from something you encounter. And if a work makes a body appreciate its particular context or pushes it to start doing something a bit more easily, then it's out of my/your/our (the writer's) control, and all for the better. Burroughs himself taught me to put my socks on before my pants. He let me know that I simply needed to use "just the amount of force necessary to get the object from here to there." He showed me that there's a queer little system that makes sense in one's queer little life.

TOWARDS A PORNOGRAPHIC FREEDOM: WILLIAM S. BURROUGHS AND HIS WILD BOYS

JASON NAPOLI BROOKS

I arrived to William S. Burroughs's work through accident, not attraction.

When I was twenty-two years old, my parents rented a beach house in Stone Harbor, New Jersey for a Thanksgiving celebration. I was expected to drive there from my grandmother's house in Philadelphia, where I had been living, to join them and extended family for the weekend. Instead, I went to my parents' house, my childhood home, in Northeast Philly, which I knew would be unoccupied at the time, popped some of my mother's Valiums, downed a vodka-rocks, and sunk into the sofa while a VH1 docu-special on Queen played. I remember hearing "Another One Bites the Dust," and then conking out for the duration of the day. This was before cellphones were requisite for everyone on earth, and so there were no missed calls from worried family, and I can only imagine what they were thinking when I didn't show up. I had become increasingly withdrawn from family and friends the months prior and my parents had started keeping tabs on my comings and goings.

The next morning when I regained consciousness, I phoned my therapist and she insisted I check myself into a psychiatric hospital.

I went on to spend eight weeks at Friends Hospital, founded by Quakers in the early nineteenth century as an "Asylum for the Relief of Persons Deprived of the Use of Their Reason." My stay was comprised of countless hours of group therapy and long, supervised walks around koi ponds, as well as one-on-one sessions with a psychiatrist that my Trinidadian nurse described as "not fit to treat a dog."

Upon admission, I had been asked if I felt like I was being watched. Eying the four closed-circuit cameras mounted at each corner of the room, I forthrightly answered, "Yes. I do, right now." This led to a diagnosis of "acute paranoia" and I was administered hefty doses of an antipsychotic that kept me out of sorts for most of my stay. While hospitalized I was a bona fide paranoid, but solely because I thought there was something gravely wrong with me that no one was telling me about. I think most young queer people feel this way, drugged or not.

The psychiatrist treating me reinforced this, reminding me that homosexuality had been listed in the *Diagnostic and Statistical Manual of Mental Disorders* and that if I had "urges," they could be medically treated. This was in 1998.

My father visited me at the hospital every day. I had requested my mother stay away, at least until I had grounded myself. I asked him to retrieve some of my clothes and books from my grandmother's house, where I had been living before the Thanksgiving incident. One book was the *Empire of the Senseless* by Kathy Acker; the other was Rimbaud's *A Season in Hell*. He left the latter behind, prudently surmising, "I don't think you need that one in rotation right now."

At each visit my father would ask, pointedly, what was it that had *really* brought me here? The vague answers I gave him about postgraduation stress and a breakup with a long-term girlfriend didn't land. Maybe as a parent he wanted to gauge his culpability, or maybe he already knew that coming to grips with my homosexuality was causing me to disassociate from reality. What I was not yet prepared to tell was what had transpired a few months before: that one of my college classmates, a gorgeous Filipino guy named Alex, had become my best friend there, that we were both straight and had girlfriends at the time but ended up having an ongoing, white-hot affair. That where we studied, Shippensburg University of Pennsylvania, consistently listed in all of those vapid real estate magazines as one of the nation's "top ten small towns," was undergirded by an illicit drug trade and brutal, random acts of violence. That Alex and I made it through our time there by working out together, listening to industrial music, watching World War II docs, and then fucking like animals. It was all very *Sun and Steel*, and if I hadn't already been an ardent communist without knowing it, probably could have been construed as a bit fascist. That I had graduated a year earlier and had to leave Alex behind, as he completed his senior year at college. That one afternoon while I was trying to get my life together in Philadelphia during the low-key fascist, corporate hellscape that was the Bill Clinton Nineties, I got a call from a mutual friend who told me that Alex had been raped by a townie named Earl. That Earl had broken into Alex's house, had his way with him, and then hacked up Alex almost to death with a kitchen knife. That Alex was clinging to life, having been airlifted to a hospital in York. Alex requested I drive out and retrieve some of his belongings from his house. That I did so, and arrived at a Victorian single-home with a lattice-work porch slathered in Alex's blood. Alex and I had exchanged all manner of fluids, but I had never seen his blood and now it was everywhere—the air was fragrant with iron. I was horrified that such violence had been exacted on a body so beautiful. That the puddles of blood betrayed a hitherto unseen and fragile architecture that sustained his beauty. That the perpetrator had, incredibly, been granted bail so I grabbed handfuls of his t-shirts, underwear, and socks in a mad scramble to get in and out of that blood-

bath. That it was daylight when this all happened which made everything more terrifying. That when I arrived at the hospital, Alex's mother
met me in the lobby, collected his things, and told me to keep away from
her son forever or else she would kill me herself. Alex, tripped out on
morphine, had let slip that he and I had been lovers. She blamed me, an
obvious homosexual, for her son's rape and near murder. That, maybe,
in some ways, I agreed with her. That when you're young and queer and
not out, you intrinsically understand something is "wrong" with you,
and horrors that unfold around you are, more or less, your fault, if not
directly, then through some spectral malevolence you project.

I was discharged from Friends Hospital that following January, or
at least I remember it being January. Back then it was always, always January. I was still not prepared to come out as gay and the feelings of guilt
and paranoia were far from subsiding, but I was able to move more flu-
idly through the day and get myself out of bed, bathe, and eat, that sort
of thing. I also appeared stable enough for my friend Beth, a poet and
former college classmate, to trust me to sublet her studio apartment off
Rittenhouse Square in a building that perpetually smelled of Old Spice.
It had a creaking gated elevator and was packed with loony neighbors,
like the schizophrenic woman next door, who seemingly wore the same
soiled nightgown every day, and blasted the Turtles' "Happy Together"
twenty-four-seven.

Beth had left behind exactly two books: Derrida's *The Post Card*,
and Burroughs's *The Wild Boys*. I had already read *The Post Card* and
consumed an inordinate amount of Derrida for a person my age, having been mentored by the poet John Taggart while I was studying at
Shippensburg. John was a father figure to me those years, and he was
a deconstructionist freak. His poetry descended from the Objectivist
school and had me reading loads of George Oppen, Louis Zukofsky,
and H.D., for which I was grateful.

John was also a wonderful snob who, if he liked you, would let you in on his snobbery. And so, if John pronounced another writer as a hack, that word became law. Case in point: I once brought up wanting to read *Naked Lunch*, but John scoffed at this, dismissing Burroughs's oeuvre as "smoke and mirrors." In the end, I was left with the impression that Burroughs, both the man and his writing, were the embodiment of a quasi-intellectual rock star author that budding, serious writers should steer clear of.

In Beth's empty apartment, I had a lot of time to fill and no money to buy other books, so, I read *The Wild Boys*, and quickly realized I had, at last, stumbled upon a voice of reason.

Confidants seem incredulous when I confess that nothing in *The Wild Boys*, or any of Burroughs's other work, makes me hard. When I read passages such as "He spreads his legs and I slide it in slow feeling the ring squeeze me and I can tell when he spurts," I cannot get the oft-recorded sound of Burroughs's nasal grumble out my head. It's a *major* turn off. Herein lies the peril of the writer's cult of personality surpassing artistic intent. Though I would argue that titillation is not the ultimate intent of Burroughs's erotic writing.

The Wild Boys is much more than a work of queer erotica, it is one of America's enduring texts on freedom, in good company with *The Adventures of Huckleberry Finn*, *Walden*, and *Their Eyes Were Watching God*. The lurid scenes of orgies and onanism that Burroughs meticulously renders in the novel are all in service to self-determination, and the sex portrayed in the novel is meant to be transformative, both for the characters and the world they seek to disrupt.

Burroughs's Wild Boys are adolescents of an indeterminate age who assemble from all corners of the globe to form a dissident group that barrel through the Middle East enlisting further recruits with a siren call to overthrow the heterosexual, capitalist power structure. The boys act as roving incarnation of what Hakim Bey calls a "temporary autonomous zone," a transient utopia that eludes control from the state. Integral to the Burroughs vision of such a revolution is fucking—and lots it. To that end, the novel is tumescent with depictions of oral, anal, breeding, and party and play, with the drug of choice ayuashuasca.

The use of ayuashuasca reveals Burroughs's intent and his greater world view of how the sexual act can effect societal disruption, and thereby change for the better. As described in *The Yage Letters*, he was particularly interested in the telepathic aspect of the drug, which was reputed to connect the minds of users when employed through proper set and setting. For Burroughs, the use of the hallucinogen and group sex were not meant to be solipsistic—the goal was to generate collective sexual energy that could be harnessed and directed toward the dominant power structure.

Along with the supposed telepathic properties conferred by ayuashuasca, Burroughs had been drawn to the research of Willem Reich and his theory of orgone energy, that libido was bioenergetics and could be accumulated in the form of a battery and then directed into the atmosphere as a dynamic entity, a change agent. And this is what the Wild Boys' sex accomplishes throughout the novel: making change atmospheric by animalistic fucking.

As a writer, I learned from Burroughs that the sex your characters experience has to be transcendent. Sex is revelatory, enabling the death of the ego, causing them to emerge post-orgasm as a new person. Georges Bataille taught a similar lesson in "Madame Edwarda" and the "The Dead Man."

The timing of the publication of *The Wild Boys*, in 1969, coincided with the Stonewall riots and a mass, nationwide coming-out. Queers were now moving from the closet—a place Burroughs viewed as another temporary autonomous zone—into a more visible position in mainstream life. At the time, Burroughs was skeptical of such a move, fearing that the radical nature of queerness, which mostly emanated from the queer ability to stay hidden and do as one pleased, would be lost. It's a sentiment that's resonant of Martin Luther King's fear that, at the conclusion of the Civil Rights Movement, that Black people were being "integrated into a burning house," the house being capitalist, warmongering America.

I am now at the age of forty-five and revisiting *The Wild Boys* after almost two decades. Upon re-reading, I can admit that Burroughs's vision of societal evolution is imperfect. For one, women are not part of it, and I think for any revolution to be successful women have to be a driving force, if not almost entirely at the helm—you're going to want a Rosa Luxemburg or a Nora Astorga. Another stark reality is that the novel depicts sex among adolescent boys. I've rationalized that it's not pedophiliac because the sex is between boys and not boys and grown men. And in real life, boys have sex with boys. The pornography in the novel is so relentless that it does not titillate, but gets the reader to let his guard down so that he can be recruited for the revolution.

OUT OF CONTROL: WILLIAM S. BURROUGHS, QUEERNESS, AND THE CUT-UP METHOD

PETER DUBÉ

THE MEETING

The work of William S. Burroughs put a crack in the shell of reality, and, because as I've written elsewhere "[w]hen something opens up things move through it in both directions" (Dubé 59), it offered me a way out of the ordinary world. I am indescribably grateful for it.

I came to the work at exactly the right time, just after high school, somewhere in my first or second year of college. The discovery was the fitting culmination of an important arc in my early intellectual and creative development. I was at the time a card-carrying member of the post-punk/industrial music youth subculture and had already plunged deeply into the writing, art, and theory of surrealism. Moreover, an unusually cool English teacher had introduced me to the Beat poets a couple of years earlier. Thus, I had the good fortune to enjoy some appropriate context when I came to Burroughs. I recognized his work's importance at once. Over the next few years, I read through the corpus, if not quite systematically, then at least with dedicated passion.

As many do, I began with *Junky* and *Queer*; as an already-out gay boy who'd paid the price for coming out so young, and at that particular time, the latter title resonated deeply. However, as I continued my exploration, the vibing became more general and more intense, shaking both my picture of the world and my sense of self—a wine glass in the presence of a particularly powerful soprano. Still, I had no idea what weirdness was lurking on the road ahead. Soon enough, I came to the cut-up novels and was set back on my heels. They read to me like some of the surrealism with which I was familiar; they too were filled with what seemed likedeep images conjured from the unconscious, and they echoed the rebellious zeal that was so much a part of the surrealist movement, but there was something else going on here, and with *Queer* still in my mind—and this is my topic here today—it felt really, really gay and more than a little dangerous.

When I opened *Nova Express* and saw this on its first pages my consciousness leapt into a new space:

> "*LISTEN TO MY LAST WORDS anywhere. Listen to my last words any world. Listen all you boards syndicates and governments of the earth. And you powers behind what filth deals consummated in what lavatory to take what is not yours. To sell the ground from unborn feet forever—*
>> '*Don't let them see us. Don't tell them what we are doing—*
>> '*Are these the words of the all-powerful boards and syndicates of the earth?*
>> '*For God's sake don't let that Coca-Cola thing out—*
>> '*Not the Cancer Deal with The Venusians—*
>> '*Not the Green Deal—Don't show them that—*
>> '*Not The Orgasm Death—*
>> '*Not the ovens-*'"

(Burroughs, *Nova*, 3)

Power - Filth
Seeing-Telling-Doing
Orgasm - Death
Cancer - Venus

What links was Burroughs making? What connections? Some of
the pairs were startling and some were archetypal images with deep
roots in the cultural imagination. In those pages I began to see strange
relationships being made, lines of force and information shaping a web
of language, image, and power, a web I recognized without understanding how. Struggle and secrecy, desire and extinction, language and silence, the mechanisms of power. I made out a mobile, elusive pattern,
one that framed everything, including my own life. I was beginning to
see what, I would later learn, Burroughs called CONTROL. A simple
word, and a terrible truth. And I sensed that understanding more about
this thing, this pattern-making frame, could be *useful*. Still, on first reading, I didn't understand *how* Burroughs made those connections, it was
after all my first encounter with "the cut-up method," and at that point I
had no idea what that was. Still, even at first, uninformed contact I was
floored and curious, so I kept reading: *The Soft Machine, The Ticket that
Exploded,* and, crucially, *The Third Mind.*

THE MANEUVER

Burroughs's essay "The Cut-Up Method of Brion Gysin" appears in that
last named collection and it proved most useful in my manic research.
Tzara's famous remarks about how to compose a poem by randomly
"pulling words out of a hat" was already familiar due to my deep dive
into dada and surrealism, so I was thrilled when I saw that a reference

to him opened the essay. "There's a tradition of this sort of thing," I remember thinking. The enthusiasm grew when I discovered the systematic experimental use Burroughs and Gysin (a fascinating artist/writer/ thinker in his own right) made of the technique in creating "Minutes to Go" and other texts. "The Cut Up Method" read:

> *"The method is simple. Here is one way to do it. Take a page. Like this page. Now cut down the middle and across the middle. You have four sections: 1234..... one two three four. Now rearrange the sections placing section four with section one and section two with section three. And you have a new page. Sometimes it says much the same thing. Sometimes something quite different—cutting up political speeches is an interesting exercise—or in any case you will find that it says something and something quite definite. [....] Cut-ups are for everyone. Anybody can make cut-ups. It is experimental in the sense of being something to do. Right here. Write now."*
>
> (Burroughs and Gysin 29-31)

This lucid explanation of the mechanics of the method, the examples provided, and the outline for its extension into related techniques such as the "fold-ins," and even into other media, fueled a long period of exploration on my part, in which I confirmed Burroughs's findings; sometimes the cut-ups produced rather unremarkable results and sometimes astounding ones. I also learned the importance of the source material, starting one's research in the right place as it were: cutting up history, scientific texts, and other prescriptive kinds of writings led to some of the most startling findings, as did, sometimes, using porn, while naturalistic prose worked best when sliced up with some other writing, in my experience. But no cut-up came up completely empty.

This work on my own also led to a much richer understanding of Burroughs's work. It pointed me toward a source of deep, psychologically complex, and sometimes troubling imagery and it gave me broad kinds of permission! I was ecstatic, needless to say. This was exactly what the gay outsider and aspiring writer I then was needed most at that time. The cut-up told me that language *was stuff* and could be handled as such; it could be shaped, moved around, torn apart, and put back together in new and interesting combinations, and that such processes revealed enormous things about both language and the world in which it operated. Language was, in short, *material*, and that insight has stayed with me forever. Then, given that so much of the world we live in, and our experience of it, is the product of language, of discourses, it meant that the world itself is transformable. Moreover, the method, like surrealist automatism, made subtle shifts in consciousness happen almost naturally, andwas able to put truly startling, thought-provoking verbal tableaux like these before the mind's eye: *"The cold heavy fluid settled in amountain village of slate houses where time stops—Blue twilight—Place Of The Silence Addicts—They move in and corner SOS and take it away in lead bottles"* (Nova Express, 124) or *"ANGLE BOYS of the cosmos solicit from lavatories and broom closets of the Biologic Court Buildings charge out high on ammonia peddling fixes on any case..."* (Nova Express, 133). Such tantalizing juxtapositions, and there are many more, sketched out a parallel world behind the ordinary one and gave me the sense of a shadowy, ontological queerness that meant everything.

Silence - Addiction
Angles - Solicitation
Biology - Courts
State House - Time

More evocative connections, More links made. And running beneath, something that hinted at how queerness wasn't merely a thing in the universe, something that just existed, but was, rather, a *way of existing.* The whole thing felt overwhelming and, somehow, at the same time, completely affirming.

The Wild Boys, which came to my hands next, brought that implied queerness out into the light. In that novel, gangs of feral young guys, ferocious partisans of freedom, wage war on the armies of repression and normalcy, while having loads of horny good times together. Good times that were, in themselves, part of their struggle for freedom. Every other page seemed to contain unforgettable lines and hallucinatory, erotic visions. I was swept up in it; it was for a time, my bedside book, and though far from what one might call a "how to" manual, it was, in many ways, a plan, a map of psychic and affective possibilities, or so I imagined and that was enough. Burroughs subtitled the work *A Book of the Dead,* a highly suggestive reference to the *Egyptian Book of the Dead,* which is a guide filled with spells and rituals for helping the newly deceased successfully navigate their way into the next world, and travelling between—or creating—new worlds was, and continues to be, a profound mental/spiritual and political drive within me. It is one of the things that drove me to become a writer.Thus, the conjunction of such a title and the incendiary contents was pure evocation, and I read the book looking for signs. And, if not part of the so-called "Cut-up Trilogy" itself, the text is marked by many signs of the technique and the experience of it is marked by similar juxtapositions and disruptions operating at the sentence and diegetic levels at once, as in this passage:

> "*Fifty boys with portable tape recorders record riots from TV. They are dressed in identical grey flannel suits. They strap on the recorders under gabardine topcoats and dust their clothes lightly with tear gas. They hit the rush hour in a flying wedge riot recordings on full blast police whistles screams, breaking glass crunch of nightstick tear gas flapping from their clothes. They scatter put on press cards and come back to cover the action.*" (Burroughs, *The Wild Boys,* 139)

The "meta" dimension of such descriptions, in which the mechanics of the cut-up method meet and are embodied in the very depictions, the weapons and combat strategies of the Wild Boys themselves, pointed towards the still more radical potential of cutting things up as a creative and psychic strategy. Even as the Boys used cut- up recordings as a weapon in the narrative of the novels,[1] Burroughs had suggested the cut-ups' expanded possibilities in his nonfiction.

"The cut-ups can be applied to other fields than writing. Dr Neumann in his Theory of Games and Economic Behaviour introduces the cut-up method of random action into game and military strategy [...]the cut-up method could be used to advantage in processing scientific data. How many discoveries have been made by accident [....] The cut-ups could add new dimensions to films..."

(Burroughs and Gysin 32)

Burroughs would shortly demonstrate this extensibility of the method with the release of his own film collaboration with Gysin and Anthony Balch, *Towers Open Fire* (1963) in which the construction of the film takes up the methodology he developed in his novels. I was also, given that I was then at the high point of my fanboy immersion in popular music and its subcultures, aware that David Bowie had appropriated the cut-up for his own compositional practice, slicing and

---

1   Burroughs did experiments with cut-up recordings himself. They would be released in 1981 by Industrial Records as the LP *William S. Burroughs - Nothing Here Now But The Recordings* . See:https://www.discogs.com/label/9095-Industrial-Records. Moreover, Burroughs famously used cut-up tape recordings, not unlike those deployed by *The Wild Boys*, as one of the components of a curse he cast on a restaurant where he felt he'd been treated poorly. I've read the account in several places, most recently in Genesis P-Orridge'smemoir *Nonbinary*.

splicing lyrics and bits of tape into the new forms and strange images that became fundamental components of his now world-renowned oeuvre, while saying "[w]hat I've used this for more than anything else is igniting anything that might be in my imagination." (Cited in Curcio 103). However, no artist with whom I am familiar made a more systematic and rigorous use of the cut-up method than Genesis P-Orridge (later Breyer-P-Orridge). Beginning with their work with performance art group Coum Transmissions, in which they explored various forms of arbitrary gestures and behavior in art contexts and daily life, and through the musical project Throbbing Gristle with its wild collages of sound, tape loops, and patches of noise, the cutting up and reassembling of reality is a hallmark of the artist's production. In the later stages of their career, P-Orridge and his partner Lady Jaye would go still further "applying the cut-up method not only to word, sound and image but to the very real of their own bodies and selves, in a *Third Mind*-esque project of their own that they coined 'Pandrogeny'" (Sinclair 203). As the project's title "Pandrogeny" suggests, this was an attempt to cut up gender, but it was also an effort to cut up identity itself as P-Orridge and Lady Jaye endeavored to become one person in two forms, using the surgeries they undertook in an attempt to make them look more alike.

THE MESSAGE

This extensibility, this secret integration of the cut-up into all forms of human creative activity in order to rearrange perception, to turn our understandings of what things mean or are, upside down was gold. And as both *The Wild Boys* and Breyer-P-Orridge's work suggest, it was queer, or *participated in* the queer. I'd established that to my satisfaction, beyond simple satisfaction in fact. I *knew* it down to my bones. The cut-up negates or undoes the naturalized surface of language, sound, images, to reveal not only their component parts, but their logics, limitations, and normative and disciplinary foundations. They show us what such things do to us and the world, even as they suggest ways of reorganizing things.Queerness operates similarly to reveal—not simply all of the above—which are component parts of queer life too, but also how such norms and limitations operate in the order of relationships, both intimate and broader social connections as well. It is likely Burroughs's queerness put him in a position to see the arbitrariness of dominant social structures, their *constructedness*..,, and allowed him to see the value of the cut-ups and their wide applicability, creating, it often seems, a feedback loop between method and man; a reading of the textual world from an eccentric position leading immediately to a sense of its malleability, its transformative potential, and the restructuring/cutting up of which gave rise to new textualities, new discourses that opened up new possibilities again.

Wide swaths of queer life, certainly large parts of gay life as I've experienced it, are marked by more open and diverse approaches to sex and sexuality, family structures, gender presentations, language and more, and the new formulations are often undertaken by dismantling, or cutting up, normative ideas. Partners, throuples, fuck buddies, chosen families, and leather families…. show us the rigidity, even the coercive power, of the traditional family and its superstructure, the capitalist state, even as they undo it in some ways. Further examples spring to mind readily. Certainly, I have heard the word "daddy" for example used to denote at least four or five different kinds of relationship, and have used it myself in at least three different contexts. And, in acknowledging such basic coinages, we have scarcely begun to look at a vast range of manifestations of "cutting things up" as a practice we hinted at earlier. Consider the way in which the collective homes that were a prominent part of the early gay liberation movement, or current gay leather and biker clubs, or voguing houses, reconfigure absolutely foundational notions of "kinship" in ways central to countless queer lives whether lived in the dominant social mode or within the more subcultural LGBTQ+ world. And what of practices like street or park cruising and the manner in which they cut up public space, transforming its normative uses and creating new affective forms?

And if the cut-up is about change, transformation, and that focus is why it strikes back at the hegemonic understanding of reality, which we may just as well, joining with Burroughs, call CONTROL, by taking the raw material of subjectivity and the social, and transforming it, queerness does much the same. Like the cut-ups, it creates zones of freedom and creativity within the social space of discourse. It opens up, to reprise the image with which I began, a crack in the world, one that has proven to be more capacious than I might have imagined starting out. It is big enough to escape through.

WORKS CITED

William S. Burroughs. *Nova Express*, New York, Grove Press, 1992 (1964)

———-*The Wild Boys*, New York. Grove Press. 1992 (1971)

William S Burroughs and Brion Gysin. *The Third Mind.*New York. Seaver Books/ Viking Press. 1982 (1978). pp 29 - 31

James Curcio,*Masks: Bowie & Artists of Artifice*. Bristol and Chicago. Intellect. 2020

Peter Dubé. "Furrow," in *Beginning With the Mirror*, Maple Shade, Lethe Press, 2017

Genesis P-Orridge. *Nonbinary*. New York. Abrams Press. 2021

Vanessa Sinclair, *Scansion in Psychoanalysis and Art: The Cut in Creation*. New York. Routleddge. 2021.

JUNKIES

CHARLIE VÁZQUEZ

For Miguel Algarín (1941—2020)

"Well?" Diva said, awaiting an answer.

A thousand thoughts stormed through my mind as she held out the needle alleged to be clean, the heavenly reprieve from a hard life it could deliver, the anguishes of addiction I knew too well. The bearded guy who'd shot up when I arrived nodded off on the sofa at the back of the apartment, by the windows facing the bustle of West Burnside Street.

Diva seemed much older than twenty-five, her cobalt blue extensions frayed into messy yarn reaching halfway down her back. She'd applied eyeliner thick and Egyptian-like, the black lines contrasting the pancake foundation slathered over pockmarked vestiges of bad acne. A haze tinted her gaze, equal parts ecstasy and agony, wisdom imploded into itself.

I took the needle.

Diva had held out another object prior to this offering, the curiosity resting on my lap. "He's real," she said while lighting a cigarette.

She leaned back in her recliner to enjoy the smoke as gray afternoon slinked in through the window blinds, the seven foot bookshelves behind her crammed with paperbacks, photographs, coffee mugs, and secondhand debris. Cigarette butts spilled out of a seashell ashtray on the coffee table between us. Bowie's *Heroes* whispered in the background.

I took my glasses off to examine the odd artifact, the hue browner than expected, smoke stains dulling its earthly patina. Chunks had gone missing, the gaping orifices staring back at me.

I set the curiosity aside to fire up my metal pipe, filling my lungs with mossy smoke. Diva belted out a blast of sinister laughter when I choked, leaning forward to blow a silver blue Marlboro ring in my face. Our fumes fused into a fog that hung suspended like a galaxy, before expanding and settling to imbue the piles of trash with its steely hue.

She cracked a fiendish grin of missing teeth and said, "Give him back."

"Where'd you get it?" I said, returning it.

"None of your fuckin' business, faggot."

Diva set the human skull onto a shelf behind her, where it sat level with her head like a witness from another dimension. Where it stared into my eyes. She dragged her cigarette and whipped her extensions aside, the metal beads strung onto them clinking and clanking. The light in her eyes hardened into a reptilian panic I didn't understand, an ecstasy I'd avoided.

The bearded guy at the back of the apartment (what was his name again?) mumbled something and threw his legs up on the sofa and passed out, striped by daylight breaching the window blinds, which sliced him into a hundred pieces.

Diva's boyfriend Danny rolled over on the futon tucked into the corner; a shirtless dark-haired country boy with a barrel chest, so unlike the men I'd grown up around. He'd caught me checking him out and winked while shifting the lump in his jeans the week prior, a flash of tongue. A ten-year stint in San Francisco had taught him how to use what he had to get what he wanted, and I'd entertained countless fantasies about him while alone.

"Check these out," Diva said, passing the stack.

The covers were wrinkled and creased, the pages fading like news-print brought to light after centuries. Pulp fiction cover art, white middle-aged men and women burdened by the ravages of crime. Volumes titled *Junky*, *Queer*, and *The Wild Boys*, the author's name familiar even though I hadn't read his work yet. He'd scrawled his name onto the title pages of *Queer* and *Junky*, smears of blue ink a decade old in 1989. They had to be worth something.

I held on to *Queer* and returned the others.

"I promise I'll bring it back," I said.

"Fuck no, you're not."

"Fine."

"You can borrow it if..."

"If what?"

Diva twisted around to rummage through the shelves, moving jars filled with coins aside before offering the needle, which I clenched in my sweating hand. She unfolded a wad of aluminum foil and pulled out a lumpy substance, pinching a bit away and placing it into a bent-over tea-spoon. She sprinkled droplets into it from her water glass on the table.

"I can tell it's your first time," she said.

"Hold up."

"I'll show you how," Diva said, heating the spoon with a lighter.

"Look—"

"You get hooked," she said, staring into the flame as the solution bubbled, "and it's your fuckin' problem, queen. I'll hook you up seven days a week. Only until midnight."

"I'm not doing it," I said, setting the needle down.

A devilish grin spread across Diva's lips. "You can lay down with him if you get sick," she said, raising her eyebrows as if to tempt me. She pointed her lips at the futon, where Danny tossed and turned shirtless. His Roman jawline stubbled black with desire, his chest and forearms covered in dark hair. I'd lie next to him whether I got sick or not.

"He fucks around with guys when he's high," Diva added.

I shouldn't I thought, getting hard in my jeans.

Better yet: *What if I do?*

Days later, I scanned the shelves of the Central Library downtown, the sky smoldering charcoal beyond the tall windows. *Queer* wasn't there as I'd hoped, but *Junky* and *The Wild Boys* were, as well as other titles I hadn't heard of yet. I took the hardcover edition of *Junky* to the reading room, a ritual I'd brought from home, where I'd studied for high school exams at the New York Public Library on 42nd Street and 5th Avenue in the Eighties.

Two hours or so later, I reached the middle of the novel, chilled by the dry and cold delivery. The dialogue rang as deadpanned and desperate, the deprivations all too familiar. Sentences clean and sharp as razor edges. My stomach grumbled in protest, so I wrote the page number in my notebook and zipped across the street for ten dollar, all-you-can-eat buffet at India House, where handsome waiters served cucumber-infused water from glass pitchers, quite an extravagance for a busboy.

Junky was there when I returned, ready to wrap up business like an eager hustler. I became familiar with a world kept secret from me while in plain sight, the brush strokes of a life as anguished as the one lived by the man I was named after. His expression crossed and distorted by a burden he never discussed, a stranger I never knew in many ways, yet who I'd come to resemble as I grew out of adolescence and into manhood.

Protagonist William Lee confesses that he "formed a romantic attachment with another boy" early in the prologue, while exploring the landscapes of their Midwest suburbs in high school. By the next page, he advances to his college experience while expressing disappointment with "rich homosexuals," which he refers to as "jerks"—the queer élite.

Once in New York, Lee hangs out at 42nd Street hustler bars and sells morphine, even though a trust fund provides him with $150.00 monthly (about $1,600.00 in 2021). He befriends Roy, a stylish "junk hog" with an East Texas accent, an old lady, and an "asymmetrical skull." They team up and scheme on scoring prescriptions (scripts) written by shady doctors in Brooklyn, the Upper West Side, and The Bronx, wherever they can get them.

In my favorite sequences, Lee gets desperate for drug money and decides to "work the hole" (subway) with Roy for cash. They spot a "flop" on a platform bench at 149th Street and Grand Concourse and exit the train car to "lush roll" or pickpocket him while he's passed out. Lee sits next to the drunk and opens a newspaper for cover while Roy goes through his pockets. The victim stirs and mumbles something, shifting his posture. Roy manages to work eight bucks out of him, which he splits with Lee.

On another night, they enter the Times Square subway station and spot a "flashily dressed" mooch. They follow him to Brooklyn while spying on him from between subway cars. Once he passes out, they move in. Lee spreads out *The New York Times* (to look like a businessman!) and Roy gets to work. When the victim stirs groggily after feeling something and awakening, Burroughs writes: "A Negro sitting opposite us smiled."

They work the drunk for cash but not before he wakes and confronts Roy. The victim recognizes them and even knows their swindle, disclosing the newspaper trick and teamwork for everyone around to hear. He demands his money back. Lee and Roy beat him up and make a run for it, splitting the six dollars they've stolen while trying to avoid arrest on the street.

Their fiercest competitor, "The Fag," has earned his name by feeling up his victim's legs to spook them while working them for as much as

$1,000.00 (about $10,000.00 in 2021). While discussing the origins of his street name, despite his being the most successful pickpocket they know, Roy declares: "He's no more a fag than I am... not as much, in fact."

While the majority of *Junky*'s primary characters are substance abusers, queers come in at a close second, from the jet set élite Lee dismisses in the prologue to the redheaded hustler he hunts down with his gun after getting robbed in New Orleans. The line between the two is just as blurry at times, yet what struck me most upon rereading it thirty year later was Lee's absolute contempt for queer men. The reason is never addressed, self-hatred one could suggest.

William Lee seems to prowl the pages of *Junky* while in search of something beyond a fix, beyond sex, that which will provide healing for a wound never identified. The post-war New York landscape of soot and heartbreak lingered well into the Seventies when I was born, the decade when my father started taking me into Manhattan on the subway. While much will never be known about his torments, clues have endured to reveal the truth behind his silence.

"The Nixon campaign in 1968, and the Nixon White House after that, had two enemies: the antiwar left and black people. You understand what I'm saying? We knew we couldn't make it illegal to be either against the war or black, but by getting the public to associate the hippies with marijuana and blacks with heroin, and then criminalizing both heavily, we could disrupt those communities. We could arrest their leaders, raid their homes, break up their meetings, and vilify them night after night on the evening news. Did we know we were lying about the drugs? Of course, we did," John Ehrlichman, aide to President Richard Nixon

1978: the subway doors jolted apart. My father and I stepped onto the platform on 149th Street and Grand Concourse, where William Lee and Roy lush rolled a drunk over twenty years prior. The crowd dispersed around us, wheels screeching on rails. Once on the 5 Lexington Avenue Express, my dad buried his face in the *New York Daily News*. I was left to study the residents of my native city, such as those I'd be introduced to years later in *Junky*, a novel my dad would've enjoyed reading.

He'd left his native Puerto Rico while in his teens, after contending with bad luck most of his life. His mother, Dolores Vázquez-Ginorio, suffered a chronic asthma attack at home when he was a boy. The town doctor arrived and administered the wrong medication by accident, killing her in front of her husband and three sons. The youngest was too small to understand, yet my father, seven, and his oldest brother, nine, never recovered from the shock.

He led me into a storefront once we surfaced in Manhattan, a low-lit place like a number's joint. A tall, Black gentleman in a flashy suit and tie approached and pulled my dad aside for a word in private. A feather stuck out of the side of his rimmed jazz hat. He and my father chatted "in code" to conceal the nature of their discussion, though it was apparent to me at seven years old that there were things I wasn't supposed to know about.

The dark-skinned dandy kneeled before me once they finished. "You need to love your daddy," he said with a soft hand on my shoulder. "He's trying. He's a strong—"

My dad yanked me away before the man could finish, saying goodbye while zipping off. In a cruel and fast world such as that of *Junky*, where the desperate grabbed on to whatever dignity they could find while projecting façades of normality and cool, despite the temptations to succumb to demons hidden behind dirty jokes and small talk.

Heroin was popular by the time my father arrived uptown in the late Sixties. Salsa singers such as Héctor Lavoe were known to shoot up as did many of their fans. The Fania All Stars lorded over the Latin music world of Seventies New York, fronted by vocalists such as Lavoe, Cheo Feliciano, and Ismael Miranda, successful bandleaders as well as heroin addicts.

My dad hadn't developed a habit to be trendy.

He'd incurred a knee injury in a car accident shortly after arriving, according to my maternal grandmother. Morphine was administered at the hospital. Whatever was prescribed after his discharge didn't work, so a friend turned him on to heroin. My father battled addiction for the rest of his life, wandering the streets of a cold city.

One can still witness this tragedy at the 125th Street subway stop at Lexington Avenue, which was immortalized by Lou Reed in the Velvet Underground's "I'm Waiting for The Man." The scourge that exploded during the Vietnam War persists along 149th Street in the South Bronx, close to where my father hid out of shame until dying at age sixty-one in 2008. Near where William Lee and Roy exited a subway car to "lush roll" a drunk passed out on a bench.

Not far from where I live.

In Portland at age seventeen, I started frequenting The City, a self-described "gay underage nightclub." It was a popular target for the police department as well as an obsession for born-again Christians who conspired to save whoever they could by the entrance on weekends. The upper level featured the post-punk, Goth rock, and industrial music I'd discovered on New York radio, where you could dance, get high, and listen to hard music.

The City stood in a rundown warehouse quarter known as the Pearl District, up the block and around the corner from Powell's City of Books, my healthier refuge. The Henry Weinhard Brewery churned away night and day across the street, the ales it produced served in the gay bars along Stark Street. I'd crash with punks from California I'd met through work, mostly straight, working-class white guys who'd put me up whenever I missed the last bus.

The industrial band I cofounded, Factor Red, rehearsed in the basement of the house where our singer lived with his dad, Michael. A native Los Angeleno, he had hustled on the streets of Seventies Hollywood. "The fags worked Santa Monica [Boulevard]," he'd explain, "the girls, Sunset, and the trannies, Hollywood. I'd meet her on Sunset after making money," he'd add, referring to his wife, who was also bisexual and worked the streets.

An out gay man by the Eighties, he'd lost nearly all his friends and lovers by the time he turned forty, though Robert Mapplethorpe, who he'd met in California, was living his final days. It was Michael who I came out to, once I confessed my attraction to a painter he was mentoring. That artist, Jeffrey, would become my first boyfriend of nearly three years.

Michael had studied art history and English literature; we'd talk for hours. As a rebel of the Sixties, he'd also read the major works of the Beats. "Burroughs was always my favorite," he'd say on our epic drives through the Mojave and Sonoran deserts, "since he was an Aquarius like Mozart and Oprah." He'd pause before adding, "And me, of course."

In autumn 1988, word started getting around that William S. Burroughs was shooting a movie in town with Matt Dillon, of all people. Friends spotted him on the Southwest Park blocks and at the St. Francis Hotel, a Twenties single room occupancy holdout which has since been demolished. Burroughs vanished by the time we heard about a crew filming in Northwest Portland, though he reappeared a year or so later when *Drugstore Cowboy* started screening across the street at Cinema 21.

I'd learn of his teaching alongside Allen Ginsberg at Naropa Institute years later, as hired by founder and meditation master Chög-yam Trungpa Rinpoche, whose lineage I've since joined. Trungpa also coined the term "crazy wisdom," which captured the spirit of the post-war rebels who inspired me, those intent on building a future centered on creativity and equality. Many, such as Michael's contemporaries, wouldn't live long enough to make it happen.

The medications and therapies for HIV/AIDS that many take for granted in the twenty-first century didn't exist back then, and a positive diagnosis often meant early death. Few people I knew beat the odds in the Eighties. It was common to chat someone up at a club over the weekend only to learn of their passing soon after. The City Nightclub was no exception and acquaintances and nightlife stars started dying just as I began exploring the queer underground.

Am I ready to die for this? I wondered often.

Michael became the mentor, the father, I needed. He didn't waste time in explaining how his sexual behavior had changed since the arrival of HIV/AIDS, how he'd managed to remain HIV- when his friends hadn't. I didn't take his wisdom for granted and reserved it for the future since I'd only been with Jeffrey. Needles and bareback sex would never be an option.

"Assume you're positive, and do what you can to keep your lovers safe," he'd tell me. "Assume the same about them and protect yourself."

It didn't take long before I started messing around with a musician and photographer I was collaborating with, an alleged criminal, which didn't intimidate me. Vince and I tried to avoid a crisis once we fucked around, but we were too immature to do the right thing. We snuck around when we could, though once I caught him shooting up, I broke things off with Jeffrey. We'd grown apart, and I couldn't risk infecting him since Vince was an HIV+ top.

I allowed myself to fall in love against my better judgement. The times spent driving through the mountains and watching sunsets on the coast were worth the heartbreak. It was easy to ignore the drugs and infidelities, though Vince's HIV status became cause for concern since I was intent on remaining HIVnegative. Most of my friends were seropositive back then and I understood the complications this invited.

Then he was gone, off to Hawaii to clean up.

Heartbroken and inspired by *Junky*, I started drafting stories based on the relationship. Depression followed. I took whatever drugs I could find, losing count of sex partners after twenty or so, the tally increasing with each outing into the dark Oregon night. Vince had introduced me to sex in the woods, which I resisted while with him, but I soon sought the adrenaline rush in his absence.

I worked on stories all the while, however unschooled for the trade I was. They piled up, though they never quite captured what I wanted. I'd also read a few of Burroughs's books by then; *Junky*, *Queer*, *The Wild Boys*, *Interzone*, *Exterminator*, *Cities of the Red Night*, and *The Ticket That Exploded*. Why I never finished *Naked Lunch* I'll never know.

The Portland Eagle became a portal for exploring the boundaries of orgasmic possibility, for mining story material, where in corners one could fumble for cocks and lips to suck and lick in the rock and roll darkness before the lights came on whenever the cops arrived to harass us. Ceiling-mounted TVs flashed XXX porn as men cruised one another in the hard shadows.

Bar sex proved to be quite the allure for a Gen X punk raised on the hairy chests and bulges of Seventies television, the hedonism of the gay, punk, and hip-hop subcultures of Eighties New York City. Life had done a demolition job on my generation's formation. The Nineties had arrived to offer catharsis, adrenaline. We partied and got naked and messed around to make up for all the drugs, drinking, divorce, and domestic violence we'd put up with as kids.

In 1998, I befriended a tattooed bartender, Mark, who worked at a local gay bar. He confessed to being a fan of *Cities of the Red Night* and *Naked Lunch*, which he'd read in jail. We bonded over lounge music and horror films and illicit substances, and even though I knew it was wrong, I developed a crush and sought him after work and on weekends.

We took ecstasy after he finished working one night and wound up in a porno video booth. The next thing I knew, I was between his legs, his underwear wrapped around his ankles, a scenario I'd fantasized about many times. And then we switched places, much to my surprise. Another night on the town. Everything under control.

Someone knocked on the door quite suddenly. I got up to answer, figuring we'd be arrested. A man who looked like he'd wiped makeup from his face with a single swipe of a wet rag stood there, ranting on about something he was selling. He took one look at Mark's erection and tried to enter. I pushed the ghoul out with all my weight, but my date stopped me. Mark wanted to know what the freak was selling and bought two *I-sill-don't-know-whats*.

"Swallow," he said, shoving one in my mouth.

I wrote a story about the experience called "Angelic Snot," which Alyson Books published in 2003 in the anthology *Straight? Volume 2: More True Stories of Unlikely Sexual Encounters Between Men*, my first publishing credit.

The same year, I reunited with Michael in Palm Springs after he'd moved. We drove through the desert until reaching Tijuana one evening, where I fell in love with the coast, the people. He suggested I live there a while to photograph his art collection for an insurance policy. It was in Playas Rosarito that I revised the stories I'd been compiling for years, far from where I'd written them. They'd grow into my first book, inspired by *Junky*.

Mark was still working at the bar when I returned to Portland in fall of 2004. The bar-back stopped to introduce himself as I was having a beer one evening, a tall and handsome fellow with blonde hair and farm boy looks, which was never my thing. His grin inspired me to consider otherwise. Intelligence shone intensely in his gaze, the ultimate turn-on.

He rested the lip of his bus tub on the leather belt holding his Levi's up before wiping his hand on his towel and holding it out. "You're the writer he's always talking about," he said, the stink of bleach thrilling me. "I'm Bill. It's great to meet you."

A darker truth awaited discovery beneath his wholesome veneer, though his confessing to admiring experimental literature and film should've sounded the alarm. Perhaps I was too distracted. Maybe I was wondering why blond guys had yet to turn me on.

We talked about writers we liked, and The Beats came up. Bill preferred Ginsberg to Burroughs and Kerouac, but I wasn't ready to shoo him away quite yet. He mentioned a poetry manuscript he'd been working on. An infatuation was born.

And as I'd hoped, it happened one day. "We should hang out," Bill said with a smirk while lighting a cigarette at the bar. "My treat. My place."

"Cool."

"In case you're wondering," he said. "I'm not gay."

Bill picked me up when the day arrived. He kept his eyes fixed on the road as we drove into the twilight of Oregon dusk in autumn. I tried not to stare at him, though it became impossible to not to see his legs in the periphery, which looked strong beneath denim. Veins bulged along his forearms whenever he gripped the steering wheel to take on a turn.

"We can't go to my place," he said, averting his gaze.

"Mine is fine," I said, "as long as you're not afraid of spiders."

"Can I ask you something?"

"Sure."

"Will you do something with me?"

"What did you have in mind?"

"Just some heroin."

Here we go again, I thought. *What if you get high and come on to him like those other guys? What if you get pulled over while in possession? Don't do it, Charlie...*

"Fuck yeah, I'll do it with you," I told him.

Bill parked on a dead-end street. "Wait here," he said.

I lit a cigarette as he scaled a ten foot fence separating the end of the road from a grassy hill dropping to the highway. He landed on the other side like a ninja, vanishing into the evening. The scent of fallen leaves and burning fireplaces electrified the air.

Bill plopped down next to me ten minutes later and locked the driver's seat door, securing his seatbelt. "I've been waiting to do this for a long time," he said.

"Heroin?"

"Can I read you something after we do it?"

"Whatever you want."

We entered the basement I was crashing in after I'd arrived broke from Mexico, sneaking in as to not be heard. Hens in the backyard shrieked in terror as soon as we sat down, my roommate scrambling outside from his bedroom upstairs. The surprise made it hard to relax, and I got up to investigate. A family of racoons had attacked them as I'd learn later.

"Come here," Bill said.

He set his poetry journal aside and spread his legs, the light in his eyes glinting with the prospect of pleasure. I sat next to him as he fumbled through his pockets, my heart pounding when I caught a whiff of his sweaty hair. The thought of his letting his guard down once we got high filled me with hope, but also with dread. Yet another adrenaline rush.

The skull seemed to judge me from the shelf.

"Needles freak me out," I told Diva.

The thought of lying next to Danny had tempted me, but not enough to make me change my mind. Why I should've cared what an addict dealer had to say seems strange looking back, but it doesn't mean it wasn't true. It was as if the spirit of my father, who was battling addiction more than 2,400 miles away in the South Bronx, forbade me through the gaping eyeholes.

"You're one of those," she said.

She raised her eyebrows to express disappointment. "Fine," Diva said. The junk dealer reached for a coffee mug next to the skull, whose gaze continued to penetrate my conscience. *What the fuck are you doing here?* it seemed to ask.

Ten years later, I sat with Bill the barback in my spider-infested basement. My roommate had calmed the chickens in back. I stuck Bowie's *Station to Station* into the CD player, wondering what would happen. The night hummed peacefully. In the hours to come, I'd awaken to another day of selling vibrators and leather harnesses and poppers at Spartacus Leathers.

"Well," Bill said, "I don't want to let you down."

"What do you mean?"

He parted his poetry journal as if preparing to read. Then he removed the ballpoint pen, pulling the ink tube out. Bill snapped the cylinder in half and gave me a piece.

"That's how I do it, too," I told him.

"Cool," he said, preparing it. "You know what I love when I'm high?"

"What?"

"A slow wet blowjob."

"Okay."

He spread his legs in anticipation while firing up the sauce in the spoon. Once it cooled, he snorted half through each nostril, throwing his head back when it burned. I took the works and cooked up my bit as *Station to Station* pulsed on in the squalor. My nasal passages caught fire when I snorted my share, my limbs going heavy when the warm feeling spread.

Bill got up and stumbled to my bed after a while, where he collapsed faceup to stare at the spiderwebs dotting the ceiling beams in decay. "Come here," he said, unzipping.

I fell next to him, the smell of sweaty hair closer.

"You can suck it now."

"All right."

"Well?" he said, after some moments passed.

"I can't move."

"Damn," he said, "but doesn't this feel great?"

"You never read me a poem," I said, as *Station to Station* started over. I melted into the mattress as he lay like a corpse beside me, his hands folded over by his zipper, his eyes closed. The thought of pleasing him was more entertaining than the effort required to do it. He lay still for hours, as if contemplating a cease-fire with his demons. Neither smiling nor scowling, just heavy under the weight of an ocean.

And then he left.

I wondered about his silence as the CD looped over from the beginning, what drove him to seek the mirages of intoxicating substances since I knew why I did. My father's heartbreak became clearer with time. Burroughs's torments still jump off the pages whenever I revisit his earliest work, the clues to the murder camouflaged in the crime scene, the motive never found. If the primary cause of addiction can be traced to trauma, then we're all junkies.

CALLING DR. BENWAY! CALLING DR. BENWAY! EMERGENCY! COME RIGHT AWAY!

JERRY L. WHEELER

I was introduced to the work of William S. Burroughs on September 23, 1970. It was my birthday, and, coincidentally, the day the first report cards from eighth grade came out. Of course, I was on the honor roll—the all "A" honor roll, in fact. This entitled me to a fifty-dollar shopping spree—twenty-five for my birthday, twenty-five for the grades—at my favorite establishment, the Little Professor Bookstore.

Mom happily doled out the cash, carefully cadged from the grocery money without my dad's knowledge. She was all about bribery for good grades and although I would have studied without the promise of easy money, I wasn't averse to whatever trickled down. My dad was less than enthusiastic about the practice, however. He preferred dealing in negative consequences. "He ought to have his ass beat if he *doesn't* make the honor roll," he'd said. According to him, an ass beating cured a multitude of sins.

My shopping excursion, then, had to be on the down-low. The catch was that the bookstore was too far for me to ride my bike, so we'd have to do it on the way to pick up my dad from work. I could always hide the bag under the seat and sneak out to the garage after supper when he was ensconced in the bathroom, but it also meant I'd only get about ten minutes to spend my money. He'd ask questions if we were late, and my mom couldn't lie to save her ass. Or mine.

By the time we got to the strip mall where Little Professor was, I had my hand on the door handle ready to bolt. I didn't even wait for the car to stop moving before my feet hit the concrete. As usual, Mom sat in the car and lit up a Viceroy. Meanwhile, I hit that place like an amped-up housewife on *Supermarket Sweep*.

I'd pre-shopped in my head. First off, I grabbed a hardcover Ray Bradbury collection, *The October Country*, which I'd had my eye on. Fifteen bucks right there. Then, I hit the science fiction/horror section, snatching up the three James Blish *Star Trek* novels I'd been lusting after and a handful of *Weird Tales* reissues. The latter was an especially good deal because you got three magazines with at least ten stories each shrink-wrapped as one for four bucks. That just about blew the wad, but I still had enough for a couple Tarzan books.

Piling up my booty for the cashier, I checked the clock and saw I had three minutes to spare. Perfect. I handed over the money, got a handful of change back, grabbed the bag, and made it out to the car before Mom finished her cigarette. She asked me if I'd gotten what I wanted, and I assured her I did.

Mom never seemed to care what I was reading, only that I was reading. "He always has his nose in a book," she'd say to friends and family, but she said it like she was proud of the fact, not with the derision my dad found in the same phrase. She never questioned my judgment or forbade me any book, no matter how lurid the cover was. "They're just words," she'd tell anyone who gave her static.

Her philosophy was the same with movies and television. I had an old black and white portable in my room, so I watched whatever I wanted to, but we usually watched horror movies together. She loved them. The bloodier the better. Only the year before, we'd left my dad sitting home and went downtown to the Fox Theatre to see the re-release of Hitchcock's *Psycho* and stop at Farrell's for ice cream. "You weren't scared, were you?" she asked me later. "It's only a story." I never told her I checked behind the shower curtain every time I went to the bathroom until I was well into my twenties.

Clutching my books, I climbed in the backseat of the Delta 88, tore open one of the *Weird Tales*, and stashed the rest. It was about an hour to Plymouth and back, so I let Clark Ashton Smith, August Derleth, and Theodore Sturgeon entertain me while we picked up my dad and went home to Mom's hamburgers and chocolate cake for my birthday.

"Remember we're going to the matches on Saturday," Dad said, reminding me of his gift. "The Sheik and Dick the Bruiser. Should be bloody." One of our few common interests was pro wrestling, although we both enjoyed it for entirely different reasons. Maybe. My mom always pretended she wasn't into it, but when the heels came out of the dressing room, she'd be standing up and booing and throwing popcorn along with everyone else in the Olympia.

Familial duties discharged, my dad headed for the bathroom. I waited until I heard the first series of grunts—he was eternally constipated, something I always found ironic due to the amount of shit he used to give me—and then I sneaked out to the garage. When I came back inside, I checked the hall to make sure he hadn't left the session early. Coast was clear.

I fondled the Ray Bradbury hardcover lovingly. That was a real score I'd save until later. I thumbed through the *Star Trek* books and tore the shrink-wrap off the *Weird Tales*, looking at all the tables of contents. Cool. More Lovecraft, three new Robert Bloch stories, two each by Manly Wade Wellman and Robert E. Howard—it'd take me a month to get through these alone. Then I checked out the Tarzan books. But one of them wasn't Tarzan. It wasn't even by Edgar Rice

Burroughs. It was by William S. Burroughs.

I'd never heard of him, but this didn't look like any Tarzan book I'd ever seen. It had a yellow background with lots of black shadows and forms I'd later recognize as junkie paraphernalia, but had no clue at the time. The title was intriguing, though. *Naked Lunch*. I opened it up and read the first paragraph:

I can feel the heat closing in, feel them out there making their moves, setting up their devil doll stool pigeons, crooning over my spoon and dropper I throw away at Washington Square Station, vault a turnstile and two flights down the iron stairs, catch an uptown A train...Young, good looking, crew cut, Ivy League advertising exec type fruit holds the door back for me. I am evidently his idea of a character. You know the type comes on with bartenders and cabdrivers, talking about right hooks and the Dodgers, call the counterman in Nedick's by his first name. A real asshole.

Devil doll stool pigeons? Spoon and dropper? What the hell was Nedick's? And shouldn't some of those sentences have periods? It didn't make any sense to this fourteen-year-old. Well, most of it didn't make sense. I definitely knew what a fruit was. I'd heard my dad refer to a couple of fruits who did business where he worked repairing RVs. Besides, I *was* a fruit.

I feel very fortunate to have accepted who and what I was at a pretty early age. Certainly, long before junior high school. That doesn't mean I didn't have the same trauma and difficulties and reasons for hiding it as the rest of us did, but I felt no shame internally in being gay. Once I figured it out, I was pragmatic about it. I went to the library and looked up "homosexual." Not the school library or even the local library in Belleville where I might run into someone I knew. I hopped a bus downtown to the Detroit Public Library on Woodward Ave. where no one would recognize me. I read everything I could lay my hands on about homosexuals, but I only believed about half of it.

I was a skeptical kid. Lots of what I read seemed to agree my life was going to be pretty miserable based on me being a fruit, but that didn't make any sense. You had choices, right? The guys my dad talked about had each other, they had jobs, and they had enough money to buy an RV despite his revulsion. All I had to do was lay low and not say anything until I left home and was out on my own. Then I could do what I wanted. Sure, it seemed like forever, but I wasn't about to let anyone tell me I couldn't be happy if I wanted to be happy, no matter if I was a fruit or not. I trusted myself. Always have and always will.

So, could this *Naked Lunch* be about me? That would be different from anything else I had on my bookshelf. I was way too young to recognize the gay subtext in some of the science fiction I was reading, especially Delany, though I did get the concept of otherness that runs through the genre. But this wasn't science fiction. Or was it? Other worlds are other worlds even if they're on Earth. I decided to keep reading—no, I was *compelled* to keep reading. It was Edgar Allan Poe all over again.

When I was ten, I fell in love with a book of abridged Poe short stories. I carried it around until the cover fell off. I spent almost two months' worth of allowance to order a hardcover Poe collection—but those stories were *not* abridged. It was like someone had taken the stories I loved and layered all these words on them. Some in French or Latin. But I was determined to get through them with dictionary, thesaurus, and all the help my teachers could give. It took me a while, but I finally found the stories again under those words. The light came on during "The Cask of Amontillado," which is my favorite to this day. I was holding the same kind of challenge, and I joined the battle enthusiastically.

I couldn't, however, carry *Naked Lunch* around. Though my mom had never said anything about what I read, there was always a first time and that title might just do it. I didn't even want to think about what my dad might say. And my skirmishes with *Naked Lunch* were different from Poe. For the most part, I understood the words themselves, but fitting the paragraphs together was more problematic. Just when a string of two or three started to make some sense, he'd change tracks and start again somewhere else. I was used to more chronological narratives; stories that had a beginning, middle, and end. They weren't all middle.

Even so, it was dizzying. And addictive. The drugs, the sex, the language, the bizarre punctuation, the absolute and unabashed *queerness* of the whole seedy epic engulfed me. I didn't have the words for it at the time, but it was transgressive. Moreover, I *knew* that all of it, every single word, phrase, paragraph, and chopped up chapter was forbidden territory for a fourteen-year-old. This was grownup shit. And I loved it.

I read *Naked Lunch* three times in two weeks before I was satiated enough to move on to something else. I had nightmares about the Mugwumps and Dr. Benway. I tried to find Cunt Lick, Texas on the map. I cringed at the racial slurs. I even jerked off to parts of it. And when I was finally able to put it down and start Bradbury's *October Country*, it took a while before I was able to hang with a story that didn't sound as if it needed to be scrubbed with antiseptic soap. But I couldn't stop thinking about it. So, I took the inevitable trek downtown to the library to do some research.

The first item I hit in the card catalog had a red sticker, which meant it was a record. The album was *Call Me Burroughs* and featured excerpts from *Naked Lunch* on one side and *Nova Express* on the other. I found it in the stacks and went to set myself up at a listening station. I had no idea what this queer junkie dude would sound like, but I didn't expect it to be like my uncle Morgan from Cheboygan. Once I heard that flat, twangy Midwestern drawl of his—dry and uninflected, drawing out the last syllable of a word as no one except W.C. Fields could, I knew I'd hear that voice in my head forever. I checked out *Nova Express* and *Soft Machine* that day.

From Burroughs, I went on to other Beats but didn't find any who captivated me the way he did until I hit Jack Kerouac, but that's another anthology. From there through high school, my literary education grew on two separate stalks: Burroughs, Kerouac, Lenny Bruce's *How to Talk Dirty and Influence People* and anything drug or counterculture-related on one, and my first love of sci-fi, fantasy, and horror on the other. But I always returned to *Naked Lunch*.

The summer after I graduated from high school, I hung out downtown a good deal, making lots of friends—mostly junkies, drunks, potheads, and speed freaks, but I also met a lot of my queer brethren. Went to my first gay bar. But the inevitable happened, and I had to try what I'd been reading about all those years.

I knew a guy who knew a guy who knew another guy who dealt almost anything you wanted out of a basement apartment of the Statler Hotel across from Grand Circus Park. All it took was a little courage and forty bucks, and I was looking at two grams of the fine white powder I'd read about for years. I wasn't even sure how much to snort. He measured some out that could have been enough to kill me for all I knew, but I figured he wasn't looking to have a dead junkie in his apartment, so it was probably okay.

It didn't hit right away, but as soon as we said our goodbyes and I got halfway down Bagley, it was like a sunflower opening up in my chest, as Lenny Bruce said. I felt great except for a buzzing in my ears, but I even came to love that after a while. Burroughs said you could pick up a habit in about a week, so after a month and a half of never not being high, I was well on my way to full-blown junkiedom. I never shot up because I hated needles, but it didn't matter. I knew I was flirting with a big problem. I had a time limit, though. I was going to the University of Colorado in Boulder come late August. It was all arranged and mostly paid for.

By the time August came, I'd had enough anyway. I was too lazy to do heroin. You had to *live* that shit day and night. The hunger. The phone calls. The waiting for the dealer because he's never in when he says he's gonna be. The score. The assholes—*always* the assholes. It wasn't quite as romantic as advertised. I checked out and kicked upstate at a friend's cabin near Houghton Lake. It wasn't as bad as I thought it was gonna be, but it wasn't a party either. I had blankets for the chills and a whole lake to ease the sweats, and even though I was junksick for two weeks, I was one with my heroes. I *had* been there, and I *had* done that.

I hit Boulder in the fall of 1974 with a couple grand I'd saved from four years of summer jobs and whatnot, augmented by some money from my folks, but they couldn't really afford much. Paid my tuition and put down a deposit on an apartment on The Hill close to campus. I'd have to get a job, but not right away. I could coast for a semester. I even had enough for a little shopping spree. Winter was coming, and I needed some warmer clothes anyway.

I headed down to this place called Boot Hill a couple blocks from my apartment and bought myself a few pairs of jeans and some t-shirts—a big fist with its middle finger extended, a Che Guevara, and one with the famous Colorado cannibal Alferd Packer—along with a pair of Frye boots, which were all the rage at the time. On my way out of the store, however, a sweater caught my eye.

It was a cream-colored belted cardigan that reeked of suburbia with its contrasting brown pockets and cowl collar. So middle class. So bourgeois. I had to have it. It was the perfect accessory to an Alferd Packer t-shirt and my puka shell choker, never mind that it looked like something straight out of the *International Male* catalog. That was exactly the outfit I wore when classes started on Monday. Not one person I saw on campus was wearing a cream-colored belted cardigan with contrasting brown pockets and a cowl collar, but I didn't care. It was a statement, and I wore it every goddamn day.

Prowling around campus before the fall session started, I became aware of a new school called The Naropa Institute. Founded by a Buddhist monk named Chogyam Trungpa Rinpoche a few months earlier, it was originally supposed to be a meditation center, but Rinpoche had attracted Allen Ginsberg, Gregory Corso, Anne Waldman, and others to teach poetry at its unofficial subsidiary, The Jack Kerouac School of Disembodied Poetics. The second I heard Ginsberg's name, my ears pricked up. Beats. In Boulder.

I called and found out they were finishing up the summer session and weren't offering any more courses until the summer of 1975. However, the person who answered the phone said I might be able to audit a couple of the remaining classes. I showed up a few evenings later, and the place—not large to begin with—was packed. I didn't even get a glimpse of Ginsberg. I went home disappointed, but Naropa was never far from my thoughts.

Second semester, I became friendly with my Comparative Religions professor, who was also involved in Naropa. When they started gearing up for the 1975 summer session, I asked him if they had space. They didn't, but he said he'd see if he could at least get me in to a few classes. It was, needless to say, a hot ticket. I tried not to get my hopes up, reasoning that they didn't even have a degree program yet, but that Beat attraction was strong. I eventually got in to a few of Ginsberg's classes, but he wasn't the draw for me. Wonderful writer, lousy teacher.

The draw was William S. Burroughs, who was also lecturing that semester. His sessions were always full, and I mean lines-out-the-door full—a fact I understand Ginsberg was pretty touchy about. They were expensive, too. Much more than I could afford as a lowly food service worker in the dorms. But I had to meet him, and this was as close as I was ever going to get. I got there early every Wednesday hoping to catch him on the way in, and I stayed late, thinking I might be able to talk to him afterward, but the timing was never right. And when I was able to catch sight of him, he was always surrounded by people.

I'd been working this angle for a couple of months and was feeling pretty dismal about the whole thing, but I was determined. Then, one Wednesday, I was at Herbie's Deli on the Hill, having a 3.2 beer and a corned beef sandwich before I started downtown. Naropa hadn't bought the building on Arapahoe yet, so their classes were all over Boulder at the time. I put down my copy of *The Gulag Archipelago* to take a bite of my sandwich, turned my head, and saw a familiar figure in a rumpled grey suit and a battered fedora facing me, talking to someone leaning up against the window.

Burroughs.

I dropped the sandwich in my lap, smearing yellow mustard and fatty corned beef all over my jeans as I scooted out of the booth and bolted for the door, not even bothering to wipe my hands. The belt from my sweater caught in the door and ripped one of the loops out, the whole affair flapping in my wake as I raced up to the pair and tried to stop, my momentum carrying me far enough to plow into Gregory Corso, who I nearly put through the window. He gave me a look of death, but I didn't care. William S. Fucking Burroughs was standing right in front of me.

I first noticed how blue his eyes were. I don't think I've ever seen a photograph that captures that. They were also pretty impassive, despite the crazy college kid literally slamming into his conversation. But I guess if you're William Burroughs, nothing much surprises you. Or impresses you. He stared at me, his eyes penetrating, his mouth the same grim line as when Corso had been talking to him. I have absolutely no idea what I said. My mouth just opened and words started coming out. They could have been brilliant or moronic, but based on previous experience and his unchanging expression, my money was on the latter. And all while I was rambling, I could feel Corso glaring at me.

I finally stopped. Burroughs silently looked me up and down, from my Chairman Mao cap to my Frye boots. The right corner of his mouth rose slightly, whether in amusement or contempt I wasn't sure until he spoke.

"Nice sweater, kid," he said in that inimitable Midwestern snarl, sarcasm as thick as the stench of mustard filling the air.

"Fuckin' asshole," Corso said, grabbing Burroughs's arm and hustling him away.

William S. Burroughs had just insulted my sweater, and Gregory Corso had just called me an asshole. That was more personal contact with the Beat Generation than eight months of dealing with Naropa had managed to provide. I had to call it good, I thought as I watched them get into a car down the block.

I eventually lied, charmed, and bullied my way into a couple of Burroughs's lectures that semester, though I didn't dare wear the sweater. Wonderful writer, lousy teacher. But I could have listened to his digressions all day long, and I would have been ecstatic. Ginsberg would have just annoyed the fuck out of me.

I think it was Emerson who said, "I cannot remember the books I've read any more than the meals I have eaten; even so, they have made me." And they have, but I'll always remember *Naked Lunch*. Not to mention that meal.

Or the way Gregory Corso rolled down the window and flipped me off as they drove away.

"HIS THOUGHTS WENT TO KNIVES AND GUNS": AN INTERVIEW WITH ROCK JOURNALIST AND PUNK MAGAZINE FOUNDER LEGS MCNEIL

BRIAN ALESSANDRO

Legs McNeil, founder of PUNK Magazine and former editor of SPIN and NERVE, was friendly with Burroughs from 1975 through the Nineties. After numerous interviews with Burroughs, McNeil shares insights into Burroughs's role in popular culture, his importance to American music, his dark world view, and his "unnerving" voice.

BRIAN ALESSANDRO: You first met Burroughs in 1975? How often did you see him?

LEGS MCNEIL: Yes, I believe, yeah. 1975. I'd see him maybe once a month.

ALESSANDRO: So, pretty regularly. You guys were very friendly, then?

MCNEIL: I was more friendly with Victor Bockris [biographer of

Burroughs, Andy Warhol, and Muhammed Ali], who was doing a book called *Reports from the Bunker*. I became friends with James Grauerholz [Burroughs's secretary and bibliographer], and I'm still friends with James. He's a great guy. And through James, I met William. You know, I was a kid. I was nineteen years old.

ALESSANDRO: Quite young.

MCNEIL: When I'd spend my money on alcohol and was too drunk to get home, I'd call James and he would let me into The Bunker. I did that a couple of times. And they were always very, very, very nice to me. I'm sure they wanted to get into my pants and stuff, but no one ever hit on me or anything.

ALESSANDRO: Well, it's cool that they were respectful of your personal space but were still inclusive and inviting.

MCNEIL: And William knew that I was friends with Norman Mailer, and so I would pass messages back and forth to them, and so I was kind of the conduit to the Norman straight world.

ALESSANDRO: We will return to Mailer soon! In your *SPIN* interview with Burroughs, you mentioned that being in his presence was "unnerving." You specified that it was his voice that most unnerved you. [McNeil wrote, "I still found being in his presence unnerving. No, it wasn't that sneer of his that made you feel like you were sharing a laugh with the Grim Reaper himself. No, it wasn't his ghostly looks or his piercing intensity. No, it wasn't any of that stuff, but *The Voice!* It's a deep crackly thing that enunciates every syllable with an evil distinction. And after all this time, I've still never heard anything like it. It's a kind of Midwestern drawl, mixed with equal parts professorial rattle, sarcastic howl, and agonizing moan. It's the type of voice that, even when it's making small talk, is so filled with the gravel of hard roads traveled that I always expect everything that comes out of it to be of monumental importance. Like the voice of God. Or the Devil."] What year was that article published? Do you have anything to add to that now? Was there anything else about Burroughs that unnerved you?

MCNEIL: The article was published in 1989 or 1990. He was such a gentleman. He was like this Midwestern guy who always wore a suit and tie and that was a little unnerving!

(McNeil and I laugh.)

MCNEIL: You know, for me, in my black leather jacket and t-shirts and my dirty jeans and my sneakers, you know. But he was a really wonderful guy.

ALESSANDRO: From a rock journalist and popular culture perspective, why is Burroughs significant to American culture?

MCNEIL: Well, he was cool, you know, in a time when we were trying to figure out what that meant. He had gone to places that not many of us had traveled to, and he wouldn't judge anybody, but he would say, "Well, you might want to watch out for that."

ALESSANDRO: Debbie Harry said that, too. She said he was especially *not* judgmental. You could talk to him about anything.

MCNEIL: Yeah, but he seemed to post … maybe "yield" signs … he never posted "stop" signs. He would post, "You might want to look out for that!" We were a bunch of malcontent angry artists who didn't listen to anything, and so here is this guy in a suit and tie who was drinking and smoking pot with the rest of us and doing whatever and seemed to know a few things, when not many people seemed to know a few things. A few things that were real, you know!

ALESSANDRO: When you said that "he went to places that not many of us had traveled to," do you mean literally or intra-psychically?

MCNEIL: Spiritually. I mean, he shot his wife, you know. He killed her! That's a heavy thing to live with. Besides all the jokes, "You don't want to play William Tell with him," you know. You could see it in his eyes ... that he'd been through enough.

ALESSANDRO: I remember reading that he said he didn't think he'd become a writer if that hadn't happened.

MCNEIL: Yes, absolutely. Had he not shot Joan.

ALESSANDRO: Yes, it put him in touch with his "Ugly Spirit," as he called it.

MCNEIL: That quote stayed with me throughout my life.

ALESSANDRO: It *is* a heavy thing to carry. I can't imagine.

MCNEIL: Yes, yeah.

ALESSANDRO: In the *SPIN* interview, several things stood out to me, including Norman Mailer's quote—"There is a sense in *Naked Lunch* of the destruction of soul, which is more intense than any I have encountered in any other modern novel. It is a vision of how mankind would act if man was totally divorced from eternity." Where do you imagine Burroughs's dark vision came from?

MCNEIL: I think it started with him reading Jack Black and becoming the kind of guru to Ginsberg and Kerouac and those guys. I can see why they were attracted to him. And the other early Beats.

ALESSANDRO: Chris Stein said in his exchanges with Burroughs that "Bill" believed war to be a sort of cleansing action. Can you speak to that?

MCNEIL: I'm sure we spoke about war. I was managing shrapnel at a time when they were dressed like soldiers. And we thought of everything as war, you know.

ALESSANDRO: In the *SPIN* interview, you share photos of Burroughs target practicing and discuss his love of guns. Can you share any insights into the origins of his affinity with firearms?

MCNEIL: I don't know, actually. He just was fascinated by them. He just loved guns, you know. [Imitating Burroughs]: "And here's the little one that shot Bobby Kennedy!" Stuff like that. I was like, "Okay, Bill!" You never called him "Bill." You always called him "William." He wasn't a "Bill" kind of guy. He was a "William," you know.

ALESSANDRO: I want to talk about music for a moment. The band name Steely Dan, the term Heavy Metal, and The Doors album *The Soft Parade* were all directly mined from Burroughs's books. Why do you think he had such an impact on American music?

MCNEIL: He wasn't writing these things with a ... most books in

American culture have a moral center, right? You know, *Moby Dick.* "I'm gonna kill the whale." William didn't seem to have that, which was very, very freeing. There wasn't your common normal "this is good, this is bad." When you opened his books, it seemed like the opposite was true.

ALESSANDRO: No moralizing.

MCNEIL: Yeah, none. It inspired musicians to think more outside the box.

ALESSANDRO: Burroughs told you that he was aware of his homosexuality in the Twenties when he was still a teenager and felt like an outsider. His discovery of *You Can't Win: The Autobiography of Jack Black* provided some consolation, helping him decide that "the life of a criminal was his calling." Do you believe that there was a connection between his desire for criminality and his queerness?

MCNEIL:Probably. It probably forced him ... because it was such a Draconian time. To be gay was ...

ALESSANDRO: Illegal.

MCNEIL: Illegal! It was a crime. You were a criminal. When you woke up in the morning you were a criminal. So, he took it to its ... logical ... or illogical ... conclusion.

ALESSANDRO: Burroughs claimed that the misinformation about his supposed wealth, of having a trust fund, was created by Jack Kerouac because Kerouac wanted to fabricate that myth around him. Did Burroughs ever discuss this with you?

MCNEIL: He spoke about William Lee, his uncle, who worked for the Nazis. That was fascinating! *The Adding Machine* ... the corporate world was, "ah, who cares," you know.

ALESSANDRO: He probably wasn't impressed with all of it. His thoughts and interests went to something deeper than just money.

MCNEIL: His thoughts went to knives and guns.

(We both laugh.)

MCNEIL: That's where he seemed to be happiest and what he wanted to talk about. He didn't want to talk about fucking adding machines, you know. Jesus Christ!

From McNeil's SPIN interview, regarding Burroughs's myth of wealth and his family's connection to Nazis:

> "William S. Burroughs was born on February 5, 1914, into the upper-middle-class home of Mortimer and Laura Lee Burroughs, where he should have had "forty million reasons not to write." His paternal grandfather, William S. Burroughs I, for whom he had been named, was the inventor of the first adding machine, a partner in the Burroughs Adding Machine Company. But William, Sr., proved a better inventor than a businessman, and at the time of his death in 1898 left Mortimer only 485 shares of the company compared to his partners 16,380. By 1920, the company had grown to assets worth $430 million, and the Burroughs family trust convinced Mortimer to sell his shares back to the company until nothing was left.
>
> If the invention of the adding machine weren't enough of a

legacy to ensure that the Burroughs name would live forever in the annals of modern corporate America, William, Jr., had an uncle on his mother's side, a Mr. Ivy Ledbetter Lee, who also made a contribution that revolutionized the way America does business. Only this tool was far more sinister than an adding machine, and one that William, Jr., would spend his entire life, consciously or unconsciously, trying to rectify.

"Ivy Lee started the idea of press releases; he invented modern corporate public relations." Burroughs sat over his customary afternoon vodka and soda, happy and relaxed and ready to remember the past. We had just returned from a morning of target practice at the Stoneyard, a weathered old gray barn outside Lawrence where weekly Burroughs fulfills his need to drill holes in things with big guns. "Ivy Lee said, 'They'll come to us, and we'll control the information.' He turned the tables on the press. He was a real evil genius, there's no doubt about that."

Hired by John D. Rockefeller to improve the family name after the infamous Ludlow massacre, where Rockefeller sent in the troops to quell his striking Colorado coal miners, Ivy Lee came up with the idea of sending Rockefeller into the mines to talk to his miners, hang out with them looking like he cared. It was Ivy's idea that as long as you looked like you were caring, you could get away with murder.

It was also Ivy's idea for John D. Rockefeller, Sr., to hand out dimes to the poor, and the whole concept of the Rockefeller Foundation. But then Ivy Lee fell on the public relations disaster of the century. He was hired by the Nazis just before World War II to make their image "acceptable."

"Ivy Lee was dying of a brain tumor at the time he was working for the Nazis. The last time I saw him, he said to me, 'I just saw Hitler and he told me, "I have nothing against the

Jews!"

    Burroughs sipped on his drink, grimacing at the thought of one of his relatives helping to invent the Big Lie."

ALESSANDRO: I was struck in your interview with Burroughs when he said about psychoanalysis, "I think psychoanalysis is nonsense at this point. At the time, I thought there was something to it. But as time went on, I saw less and less. I think people are only too anxious to talk about their *me*, their individuality. What comes in from the outside is much more interesting. The whole dichotomy of inner and outer reality is a basic error of western thinking. It's not inner reality or out reality, it's one continuum of the whole organism in relationship to its total environment." Can you talk more about his Buddhist orientation? Is it fair to call it Buddhist?

MCNEIL: I'd probably say he was Buddhist, yeah, when you put it like that. You know, that we're a part of the Whole. And I agree with him about therapy-speak and all that ... everyone is always talking about their feelings. You know, who gives a fuck?

(We both laugh.)

ALESSANDRO: Can you say more about your friendship with Mailer and how it connected to William, how you were the intermediary?

MCNEIL: It happened by accident. Completely by accident. I just happened to know him, and I met Mailer at this girl, Martha Thomas's, who'd done some of the transcribing of *The Executioner's Song*, which is a really good book.

ALESSANDRO: There is that incredible quote by Mailer where he said that "Burroughs might be the only American writer possessed by genius." Did you ever speak with Burroughs about that?

MCNEIL: And he would say that genius came through us from somewhere else. That we only put our names on the cover.

ALESSANDRO: This idea that artists and writers are just these conduits, that something larger works through us, and we just have to seize it in that moment and be lucky enough to capture something.

MCNEIL: Exactly! Exactly! Because, you know, it's like where does an idea come from? Which is a really interesting kind of question.

From McNeil's SPIN interview, regarding the possession of genius and Mailer's quote:

> "Norman Mailer said I might be possessed by genius," he started, catching me off guard. "Well, *that's* the point. You don't possess it. You aren't a genius, but you're lucky when you're possessed by it. The more you're thinking about your individuality, or your *me*, the less you're going to be contacting anything of the slightest bit of interest.
>
> "You become the tool. Exactly. Henry Miller said, "Who writes the great books? Not we who have our names on the covers.' The writer is simply someone who has an antenna of which he tunes into certain currents. Of times, when he is lucky. A medium, as it were.
>
> "You see, when I paint my self-will is not involved at all in the process. But in writing, you can't help but see what's in front of you. So you have to know what you're doing, but your sense and characters come from God knows where!"

"How do you get out of your own way?" I asked as we stood looking over the garden, staring at the sunset. Burroughs was leaning on his cane, enjoying the serenity of it all.

"Well," he started slowly, "It's a matter of emptying yourself."

ALESSANDRO: Thank you, Legs.

MCNEIL: Thank you for asking me to be a part of this.

LANGUAGE IS A VIRUS FROM OUTER SPACE: DIVINING BURROUGHS

JESSICA ROWSHANDEL

ABSTRACT

William S. Burroughs is dead. The following is a conversation between Burroughs and a living human being. The divination method used to communicate utilized digital versions of Burroughs's texts, the copy/paste function on a laptop, and an online tool called The Cut-Up Machine. For this study, the diviner asked Burroughs specific questions and the cut-ups were Burroughs's responses. When asked what makes them qualified to do this, the diviner quoted Burroughs, "The cat does not offer services. The cat offers itself." After a brief pause, they added, "Plus, we're both queer, we're both writers, and we're both assholes."

LANGUAGE IS A VIRUS FROM OUTER SPACE: DIVING BURROUGHS

Communicating with the dead as a living person can be challenging. First, there is no universal definition for death. Second, to speak with the dead assumes that death is a transition, not an ending—rather, a changing of forms from human to spirit. Within this realm of belief, humans cannot typically see or hear spirits unless a person is naturally gifted in extrasensory perception or specially trained in such interactions.

For the purpose of this paper, communicating with the *undead* does not qualify as communicating with the dead since the undead are both dead and alive. By definition, death does not bring life along with it. Here, death operationalized is a series of infinite moments that begins when a human individual's essence changes from corporeal to spirit, which may or may not begin at the same moment as medical death. What it means to be medically dead is still debated and of no concern here. Although important, how to define a person's essence will not be tackled nor will the mechanism of its transfer, nor the chemical makeup of a spirit. These are beyond the scope of this paper.

Laurie Anderson borrowed from Burroughs for her song "Language is a Virus (from Outer Space)." Perhaps through song the virus is celebrating itself. Perhaps only a few humans figured out the truth about language because both the song and Burroughs have been relegated to the avant-garde for quite some time. And perhaps death is the moment the virus returns home, last breath by last breath.

This paper documents a conversation with William S. Burroughs, who is dead. He died in 1997. The Dadaist cut-up method that he popularized for both literary and divination work was used to communicate with him since speaking with the dead requires divination, which is a broad category of practices that includes speaking with the dead; foretelling the future; and non-empirical methods to obtain knowledge, like reading palms and tarot cards, astrology, and consulting psychics. Anything can be used for divination, even belly buttons (omphalomancy).

FROM DIVINATION TO DAMNATION AND BACK AGAIN

~~Monotheistic religions warn that divination is evil and will lead to eternal damnation. The patriarchy has infested religion and likewise spreads its tumors throughout the scientific community. Avoiding damnation to a European scientist during the Enlightenment (and to this day, really) meant relegating these practices to the realms of superstition at best and charlatanism at worst. By extension came the belief that divination practices were inferior to science, i.e. other cultures (read: people of color) were inferior. Witch hunts in Europe and the Thirteen Colonies reflected this specific intersection between sexism and racism that eventually spread throughout their own cultures, as all effective oppression eventually does. However, try as they might, such practices refused eradication thanks to the syncretism that hid them in plain sight...~~[Cut this section, out of scope of this paper]

WILLIAM S. BURROUGHS BELIEVED IN MAGICK

Magick is spelled differently than the performance art to differentiate itself as occultism. Burroughs believed in magick. And that is why he believed that the cut-up method was a form of divination. He once said, "I remember a film called *Dead of Night* where the ventriloquist dummy starts talking on its own. Well, a writer must encourage this phenomenon—create a dummy and induce it to talk on its own. Now this is known as 'an ear for dialogue' in the trade. But, you see writing is, in fact, a magical operation. If you know the right spells (and what are spells but words) you can call all the living, all writers living and dead, to write for you, to work for you. The Cut-Up, (the) use of Cut-Up is a key."

METHODS

No Institutional Review Board (IRB) approval was obtained for this paper since the subject is deceased. Currently, IRBs in the United States only concern themselves with human subjects that have physical three-dimensional bodies that are observable by the five senses.

THE CUT-UP METHOD

There is no one way to use cut-ups for writing or divination. Burroughs used a blade to slice through the middle of a page, horizontally and vertically like a cross. Then he rearranged the four resulting squares. Alternatively, an individual can cut out each word of a text and then mix them up in whatever way they choose. Once mixed, they randomly pick out words and form a new text.

Burroughs had a grandfather who became rich from the exciting new information technology of his time—adding machines, which did the manual work of humans just like the internet does for us now. Because information technology has evolved, the Burroughs diviner used modern technology to "cut-up" text. Instead of physically cutting up paper, digital text was copied with the Control+C buttons on a laptop keyboard and then pasted (Control+V buttons) into The Cut-Up Machine (languageisavirus.com), which scrambles pasted-in text.

This paper's author served as the diviner and asked Burroughs their specific questions, using the cut-up method to obtain answers. The texts used were from Burrough's essay, "The Cut-Up Method of Brion Gysin" (Answers 1, 3, and 5 below) and his text from his book *Queer* (Answers 2, 4, and 6 below), both of which were found for free via internet search.

In line with other divination practices, the number of words copied or their location in either text was chosen by the diviner's intuition. The cut-up text is presented unedited. The diviner then interpreted the cut-up text.

When asked what makes the diviner qualified to practice any kind of divination, they responded with, "Bill is the writer, and I am the dummy." Never have they knowingly spoken with the dead. They are not sure if they even believe in magick.

RESULTS

Question 1
William, tell. Did you purposely kill your wife, Joan?

Answer 1
would how the to sense an to two as them write fast how to not talk make they of argue for push ups that fall is another being cut Anybody to assumed fall fall twice Cut and ups object everyone did about see in off It as something philosophers now object and here Greek words can occur and heavy Not Right see logically experimental something are they the do as twice objects the table Cut the It

Question 2
Is there any point to life? Ultimately, it feels very pointless.

Answer 2
the air so first sand there city 1940's and liked sky shade of of was blood end Mexico blue with first that circling the that raw When people it blue sparkling a with visit of one day vultures the from and clear lived in menacing pitiless City million goes at of my well Mexico Mexican special City the I I the

Question 3

Were you a pedophile? Be honest.

Answer 3

to twice occur fall argue that words It about Greek push and how something something an now the assumed they fall off would as another to Right see talk them to the Not philosophers twice how see write two as not object fall fast and the to Cut here objects object logically did they do heavy and table as

Question 4

I read an article by Genelle Chaconas on myumbrella.com that said you had such internalized homophobia that you couldn't stand flamboyant gay men. Can you explain why people say this about you? Tell the truth.

Answer 4

they little is in sadness and from knelt crying He crying his little crying wondered standing someone group hear dream a of arms he precognitive came Ship He doing deserted A what in looked was the were in front shack He Ahoy place against the his The people down closer Here Convict there his Ecuador and child were there He of of saw chest in son sound suits Willy Cotter's The was could and took standing held Lee close wave why a of

Question 5

What are your thoughts and feelings as you watch along from the afterlife while genderqueerness becomes more and more visible and accepted than it was when you were alive?

Answer 5

cut random predict strategy data to accident? order since up The We your be knowing advantage by have by can from opponent gain not discoveries he not your to processing used many the advantage scientific made factor will could no How method move produce accidents been can in

Question 6

Should I read any of your works? I have heard disturbing things about you, so I've been turned off. But maybe I should give you a chance. If so, where should I begin?

Answer 6

time the American Cola the took walked neither his the pushed since dyed It a Lee Lee around was not that The you a door ran long of past as bar at Mexicans waste and Why soda At G He There and with was paid stools during rancid a juke young come waiting A checked made was left leather in Lola's finished beer He of covered girl where and Lola's the a a patronized far the full for the There boy legs opposite kitchen a Bar wall drinks Coca red Ship people students small and into a screeching certain the down cab was in exactly spent caps box There stools sweep the to and had as was fag here? meantime Allerton yellow as tube slovenly daytime Mary time at an makeup in of by night ice when fat Chimu counter where side fried for was cook and room lost he metal the the Ahoy maid bar were a with beer to I again the met and with the two box which soda in room chess the glazed frequented carefully future and back in second there them had came horrible everything lined place in nor he one playing hair When rubber the who in out noises Tables was around bar the thought looked with drink applied counter a was joint The the Lola's the along night

DATA

Question 1

William, tell. Did you purposely kill your wife, Joan?

Interpretation

We were two people unhappy with each other. We argued. But if you assume that I fell from grace, then I fell twice—once when I actually fell, and once when you made that assumption before trying to find out the truth. That being said, everyone did see it happen but twisted their words like philosophers, making you hear Greek. It was a heavy experience because it wasn't right. I thought the game, William Tell, was logically experimental—if I miss she'd live, right? And I thought I'd miss. I meant to miss. But there was something inside me, like I existed twice inside myself, and one of those things lays all my cards on the table. That. It, the one I couldn't cut, that's who did it, and did it on purpose.

Question 2

Is there any point to life? Ultimately, it feels very pointless.

Interpretation

In the Forties, the sky was a shade of blue, Mexico blue. Yet the sky was so raw that it looked red. The air was like first sand. When people visited the blue sky, they sparkled… until vultures from their menacing, pitiless city also visited the sky, circling that raw blood. There were millions of them in the Mexican blue, where I was once special, where I was once well. It's all a circle. Better to be dead.

Question 3

Were you a pedophile? Be honest.

Interpretation

Yes. Twice. And you assume again, so twice I fall again. And a twisted philosophy made words Greek again, like with Joan's death, like with any lie. The boys, they were righteous and honest, and I ruined their lives. They fell too, fast and hard, like I did. It was that heaviness, two objects inside me, having an extra one is exhausting because they're heavy. I tried to reason with the bad one, to object logically, to no avail.

Question 4
I read an article by Genelle Chaconas on myumbrella.co that said you had such internalized homophobia that you couldn't stand flamboyant gay men. Can you explain why people say this about you? Tell the truth.

Interpretation
You convince yourself that it's just a little sadness, but I've fallen to my knees, crying. A boy inside me was crying, wondering and afraid that others could hear his dreams. I could see the future, and I would be a ship, deserted and dilapidated like a shack on a beach for all to see. And I could see a man from Ecuador, a convict of some kind. His name was Willy Cotter, and he was there with his son, Lee. Willy Cotter held Lee close to his chest before the waves could wash the boy away.

Question 5
What are your thoughts and feelings as you watch along from the after-life while genderqueerness becomes more and more visible and accepted than it was when you were alive?

Interpretation
Was it random and accidental or was it part of the strategy all along? It's the order of things. When the direction is up, things go upwards. That's just logic. It would have been an advantage for opponents to have known before queers were more out, to have gained time before queers processed their existence and discovered themselves in each other. Science isn't a factor here, so the opponents can toss that "advantage".

Question 6

Should I read any of your works? I have heard disturbing things about you, so I've been turned off. But maybe I should give you a chance. If so, where should I begin?

Interpretation

I'm as timeless and American as cola. Read the one about Mexico, and Lee, and Lola who went to a bar for the hot kitchen boys. What a waste; they were fags, but she didn't care. Standing around this juke in her rancid leather, all she waited for was a boy's come.

I will tell you about students with their sea legs who disembark from a red ship, tumble out of screeching taxis, visit that same bar, and get drunk in the daytime. One of them, Slovenly Mary Allerton—last night's makeup smeared on her face, checked from a tube of yellow paint and box of ice cream—gorges on fried food at the metal counter with fat Chimu and is so drunk on beer she yells "Ahoy!" over and over to the barmaid, forgetting that she is no longer at sea.

She should instead drink soda and play chess, but at the mere thought of it, her eyes glaze over from the horror of it. Like the other students, she pretends to be from the future visiting the past. A boy sat on a stool next to her and played with her hair before they started fucking right there on the table. Everyone could hear him go in and out of her without a rubber, but Slovenly and the boy were too drunk to care. Lola never did find the come she wanted from the boys at the joint, but she'll get along okay.

DISCUSSION

Close your eyes. Unfold your origami lungs. Take a deep breath. Untie the white string holding the butcher paper that swaddles your guts. Open your eyes. What do your guts tell you, diviner?

CONCLUSIONS

Being queer and being Dadaist are similar in some ways, at least in theory. While Dadaists aren't an oppressed class, antiestablishmentarianism vibrates strongly throughout both. Burroughs was both queer and Dadaist. The corporeal mechanism—belief in divination, essence, dead spirit, omphalomancy—Burroughs lacks perception; however, he believed definitions.

Communicate it, the vice. It's consulting and completely begins by versa—the conversation, no decisions, non-paper cannot. What belly makes paper the defined will of astrology: tarot. Prophecy is form, is interpretation, is mediums, is the Tea. First make up Anything, or perhaps define a bit, same of buttons. And divination can 1997 a future moment for him, or gift it to foretell an individual's changing—both human.

REFERENCES

Don't believe anything you read until you corroborate it with your virus.

HOW BURROUGHS SHOWED US THAT THE WORD IS A VIRUS AND AN EMPIRE WHICH MUST BE CONSTANTLY CRUSHED AND REBUILT (OR: THE INTERZONE VIA KANGALARIA)

DENNIS LEROY KANGALEE

"Every time you say it—the white man laughs.
And so does his little voice in-side.
All the words were the same. Vile and empty with a little hanging inside each one.
Single space. No more clock. Hands rule the empty waves.
The word—
The word—
The word
hurts."

I always had the desire to turn the screenplay format into a personal mode of expression I felt I could break, contort, dismantle, and rekindle. The way William S. Burroughs did with the novel. Unlike B, I was—

am not—a genius. But the temptation to make others "see" in a new way appealed to me; it seduced me from being an entertainer who became an actor who conceded, almost painfully at first, that he was an artist. There is something almost traumatic taking that leap, admitting to yourself that everything you previously believed and pretended to believe were not real, meaning they had no gravity. They were just examples of traumas of the authentic man struggling in an inauthentic world.

I often wonder if that is what a closeted homosexual might experience, if those experiences could be similar in some way.

What I do know with full certainty is that when you approach the work of a major artist you don't learn much—you just feel humbled. You have entered a church of someone else's making and you have no idea how it was formed, how it was actually built. The stories, the tales and legends mean nothing when confronted with something so awkwardly beautiful and recalcitrant. And for the writer who lives words and reimagines them—this is everything. Being enraptured by the possibility, the endless vistas of

The Word.

As a young theater director, Ginsberg's dithyrambic poems meant more to me and were more in sync with the Dionysian fervor of the type of theater I wanted and the art that I could fully metabolize, but years later—because of his mystery—it was Burroughs's writing that I can now claim to be closer to, if only, because of its alienness and clinical surreality. At twenty, full of Artaudian fervor, I wanted art to be like guns, blazing. At thirty, despite my punk inclinations, I preferred a cerebral Brechtian approach, welcoming an editorialized world of creativity. At forty, the two collided, but now crawling into the halfway mark toward being a half century—

    I see it all

    words

    emotions

    actions

    gestures

    visions

    sounds

    as beautiful contents of an arsenal I have no control over.

Unlike guns, they don't need to be cleaned or kept locked away and they don't exist to annihilate.

    Sticks and stones may break my bones

    but words

    can

    kill

    . . .Sometimes they do. In every conceivable way. Sometimes—at its best—art heals. After the aim of trying to liberate oneself, then another...you can only hope to heal.

    How does that happen?

    I haven't the slightest clue. Neither did Burroughs. And he couldn't spend too much time dwelling on this for there were far more enticing rabbit holes he desired to go down. Besides he had cats to tend to. He was a big lover of cats. Any Aquarian who likes cats has *lots* of problems on his plate even before he gets to the dining table. Yoko Ono. Huey P. Newton. Paul Newman. All Aquarians. All interested in dissolving and recreating their passions. And with Burroughs, the passion overwhelmed him, almost possessed him (he had a literal obsession with possession) and, as he admitted, had he not accidentally killed his wife he never would have become a writer.

    Words can impact you like nothing else, even a casual remark. The words you use and choose are moral choices as Godard remarked about certain film techniques: everything is a question of an inner morality. The personal is political, the political personal, the choice is a reflection almost as accurate of the one that stares back at you in your literal bathroom mirror. Unless the light is off or its overcast. Ever notice how freakishly comforting you feel when its overcast and you look in the mirror? Because in that zone you actually look as you feel. Least I do. But the struggle was never reconciling my physical problems or attributes. It was making sense of what I felt and thought and finding a way to write them down.

Burroughs understood the strange power of literature and its command over us. He was suspicious of the Government's use of words and language, and the only way to recover one's soul is to combat it with your own sense of language. Your own sense of writing words.

In the beginning there was The Word.

All religions begin with The Word and all wars start and end with the promise or the period of a poem.

December 1995. I read somewhere "Language is a virus from outer space...a disease communicable by conversing,". These words by B made the hairs on my arm stand up.(Listen to the Laurie Anderson song.)It had never dawned on me until I was nineteen and was a patient in New York's Paine Whitney Mental Health Clinic that language could actually be the basis of a new form of acting or theater or what have you. Isn't that what all young people are supposed to be excited about? It was at this age that the idea of revolting against form in art (and life!) began to take hold. The Dadaist cut-up technique popularized by Burroughs and artist Bryon Gysin inspired my attempts to create drama—or rather, original scripts for that matter—for it re-organizes language (linear sense) and gives it new, personal meaning in an attempt to short circuit the control and oppressive nature of the Establishment.

At the end of the twentieth century, it was time to figure out how we could reinvigorate this into modern art. 1999 was approaching. But what did that bring us? Not chaos and new meanings: just more order and Rudolph Giuliani's Reign of Terror and the end of Times Square, freakdom, weirdness…and essentially art in NYC. Order. Control. These were becoming the shiny talismans of the era; Apple and iPhone were merely a step or two around the corner…Fascism was creeping in via consumerism. We were giving up. "Control needs time to exercise control. Like death," wrote Burroughs, "Control is a parasite living off of the human organism."

Summer 1997. My own drug experimentation had always been to expand my consciousness (or in the case of the old "marching powder"at least to work longer and harder through the night.) And though I later abused it and self-medicated, I was able to relate seemingly unrelatable things to each other. That goes beyond tangential connections. It strips things naked so you can make them join hands easily. It's what jazz musicians do in great unexpected moments. It's what a compelling actor does by breathing from one moment to the next in a unique way. It's what B's writing does in hard steely prose. It's fascinating that a famous heroin user, never known to be aggressive, was so "active" in his experimentation of words. But then again, Charlie Parker, another famous heroin addict, was fast and airy and…well, we know him as "Byrd."

I'd never enjoyed or was attracted to heroin until much later when mania no longer kept my demons at bay. And even then, terrified of needles, I only snorted it on rare occasions. But I understood the value it had for certain artists who saw it as another way to the unmapped territory within us…I read *Junky*, which was interesting but perfunctory. Leafed through *Naked Lunch* and appreciated his imaginative leaps but was left unmoved. His *Interzone* collection of short stories was far better but it was his later essays/poems of the mid-Sixties to the Seventies that really grabbed me (check out "The Burroughs File"). His greatest novel, in my opinion, however, was the underrated *The Wild Boys*, about a band of homosexual radicals bent on destroying Western civilization. Brilliant!B was a big influence on the punks and the grunge movement of the Nineties (Kurt Cobain was a fan).I remember once reading how Ishmael Reed would cite a text as if it had been something Malcom X wrote, then revealing to the audience that it was Burroughs. I have been looking for that text for nearly a decade.

"Grovel symbols" Burroughs called them. These are our pop culture idols (as they relate to our enslavement and obedience). So therefore, kill your idols so at least they remain as the person/ideal you first fell in love with, you first believed in. Baldwin, a contemporary of Burroughs declared: "Fathers, like idols, must be destroyed." The queer artists in my early twenties informing my sensibilities Both Baldwin and Burroughs never publicly made a "big deal" out of their homosexuality, interesting enough. They didn't see it as a crutch or anyone's business. Of course, it had different resonances—Baldwin suffered terribly in certain radical circles because of his homosexuality—but like Genet, the two seemed to be split down the center of equating their gay proclivities as a simple line in the sand against "white straight society" and history of empirical oppression. In a sense, never pugnacious or self-conscious like Genet. They were simpler outlaws. Burroughs specifically could not live any other way and he did not have the social, political, racial, or familial responsibilities that James Baldwin had. Burroughs could be on the outside of anything. He had the money to do what he wanted…and oddly, Burroughs always remained staunchly honest in his commitment to warn us that we were all being held prisoner to something we do not believe in. *The Wild Boys* demonstrates this succinctly and, like Genet believed or even a fascist Mishima—it was the queer radical who could both destroy and save civilization.

I was in awe of such artists. Genet wanted to be feared, Baldwin to be left alone, to stop having to explain to white America their problems, and Burroughs simply wanted to find "a way out of here." His intentions were enough, nestled in his words. The other Beats? Bob Kaufman, perhaps the most original spoken word poet ever and a mercurial visionary ("the Black Rimbaud" as the French referred to him), took a vow of silence when JFK was murdered and did not return to spoken word until the end of the Vietnam War; Kerouac took up relying on Mama Kerouac for his literary expeditions despite his many talents; associated writers like Bukowksi and Baraka had carved their own separate niches and on different coasts, fighting the battles that had been laid out for them. But as Ginsberg followed the hippies and became more communal in his reach for literary nirvana, Burroughs remained staunchly separate from his contemporaries, seeking refuge in the solitude of a few close friends and his imagination. If he could plot and plan out the visionary resolutions to our social problems, he would do so. But he would not be beckoned to join the hippies as Ginsberg had, even following Bob Dylan for a few years.

A poster of William S. Burroughs's face, a bizarre collage stuck to the back wall of the Slaughtered Lamb bar/restaurant off of 4th Street in NYC in 2000, watched over us while we waited to score drugs from 'R,' a waitress who worked two blocks away. She never spoke, but she loved Burroughs and was offended when I told her his later work trumped his earlier work. She was a gay junkie herself but like B, she knew everything about every drug she ever took. Her ex-husband was a pharmacist in Jamaica Estates. She claimed she knew a lot of wealthy people and they all bored her. She first introduced me to James Fogles's

Drugstore Cowboy: A Novel. I told her I saw the film and Burroughs was brilliant in it. She was offended that she had not seen it. She said she didn't "believe in watching movies."

"How to Play William Tell When You Have Writers Block"

Rule 1. Never ever use a real apple

Rule 2. If you can avoid it never ever use a real person

Rule 3. Guns are only as accurate as the finger that writes

In my brief association with R., who was always clean and manicured and well made up (she was pushing seventy), I realized that that generation of "serious drug takers" was passing; meaning these were addicts who knew how to handle themselves even when desperate for a fix. They also knew everything about what they ingested into their bodies. R. noted obsessively all the ingredients and mixtures of drugs along with vegan recipes and ideas for natural remedies to cure bronchitis, respiratory problems, and stress-related issues like low immune systems. I remember her telling me to ingest ghee, a clarified butter, if I was going to continue snorting cocaine. She also would regale us with her own stories of knowing Burroughs. There was always a bizarre patrician attitude to Burroughs's acknowledgment of his lifestyle. R. hated druggies and even more despised heroin users. She said, "only a real stable gentleman could ever hold me off" (help tie a tourniquet and inject her arm).

For that perhaps Burroughs is the ultimate responsible drug taker/addict in all of modern art. Despite their stunning collaboration of Burroughs's short story in 1992, "The Priest They Called Him" (maybe his best solo short story), he was always afraid of Kurt Cobain's pain; in a way that Ravi Shankar could not quite understand the emotional torture of John Coltrane, although Coltrane, like George Harrison, was a devotee of the Indian modes of classical music and culture and food and found the sitar a mesmerizing window into a spiritual grace. But he was full of angst. Angst is something that Burroughs seemed to have no connection to as he grew older especially. There was a practical approach and sensibility he had to virtually everything…had he been a director or conductor he'd have led his ensemble with a scalpel.

I could not see past Burroughs's obsession with guns and shooting. I still find it incredible that even after killing his wife, Joan Vollmer, he was still obsessed with aspects of violent expression; expressions that were purely between him and the weapon: the rat-a-tat Uzi of writing his stream of conscious imaginings that actually made sense and his passionate reverence for the symbols of Americana: guns.

There is no way in hell that in 2020 there could exist a celebrated living author and thinker who gravitated towards guns and had such a casually violent past as William S. Burroughs. Especially an LTBGQ writer (a moniker he would have detested.) He didn't want understanding. He may have sought justice and gave warnings, but Burroughs was not a queer obsessed with acceptance. At all. This was a man dressed in suit—somehow looking like an eternal salesman from the Fifties to a defrocked priest from some hamlet festering behind God's back.

Burroughs may have actually seen God's back and maybe that's where his insistent desire to refrain from the swirl of hippiedom and "movements" and identity politics came from. Always one for the underdog, there was nothing Burroughs had to prove, certainly not to guilt ridden liberals. He had no guilt about being a "white man" as he had no personal involvement in the lynching of Black or Brown people (Yes, all guilt-ridden Liberals feel inside that they themselves tied the noose on some poor coolie's throat or a North American African Man such as myself, with a short stature and a big mouth!).

Burroughs was perfectly at ease with his own political beliefs, even the dodgy conscience he wrestled with his whole life. But it had nothing to do with being "white" or not doing enough for "the oppressed," for he himself was both oppressor and oppressed; victim and victimizer . . .

The universe of art is a dreadful place; not one intended for the weak-hearted or the brittle minded. It is a bastion of contradiction, not hypocrisy. All artists are the sum of their contradictions. The more talented, the more contradictory, often leading to more despair. The creative impulse—the mind—is a raw nerve.

Baraka said, "He who cannot think cannot feel." It is a Western imperialist mythology that emotions are the opposite of thought. And through words and "rational" texts, this argument has been made for the past 400 years alone. Burroughs was aware of this. He had seen it all under/through an eyelid as the terror of the rest of the universe played out in the other. Did you know you could have two separate dreams in either eye under the influence of heroin?

The Horse gallops in one, neighs within the other. That's queer.

Queer? Indeed.

The term "queer" never meant much to me growing up until I became accustomed to "Queer Cinema", introduced to me via VHS at Kim's Underground video store in the West Village. Out of all the video stores, they categorized most progressively: Third/Pan-African Cinema, Women Directors, Queer Filmmakers, and Left Wing Radical Directors.

"Queer" had always been a term I knew to have multiple meanings—strange, odd, gay, homosexual—but Burroughs, like Genet, made queer a political identity in and of itself. He wanted to be a little strange, off-putting to the oppressors and suspect to the establishment.

Burroughs was tormented by many things, but he always respected his readers. Listen to recordings of his later college talks and readings. He really hopes they get it.He always reminded me for some reason of the lost logician trying to simply convince us that people who are corrupt and are rich always treat each other nicely.

Eulogies abound certainly; but fuck the past—leave a fragment of a future. An outline of a map (we both know it's unfinished) and let's bounce.

THE VIRAL REVOLUTION/ RETRO-LUTION

LAURA SCHLEIFER

One could say that we live in the Viral Era. Of course, this is not the first time a virus akin to La Corona has ripped through humanity, sucking the life out of millions along with it, but in our own virus-addled era, those microscopic minions of the living dead are but one part of a much larger viral culture overall. It is eerie to think now that just a few short years ago, the first association that might have come to our minds upon hearing the terms 'virus/viral' might have been a computer infected with a Trojan horse, or a meme or YouTube video that "went viral."

The coronavirus is but one symptom of a globalized, hyper-connected world filled with billions of beings passing around billions of ideas, images, memes, messages, money, body fluids, pathogens, and pathogenic versions of all of the above. Viral videos, viral memes, viral trends, viral mass movements, viral terrorism, viral mass shootings, viral police shootings. Livestream. Dead streams. Free trade. Sex trade. Sexually transmitted viruses. Blow your load. Viral load. Coronavirus. Papilloma virus. Adenovirus. SARS. MERS. Zika. Ebola. AIDS. Viruses spreading like wildfires. Wildfires spreading like wildfires. A planet devolving into a crowded, sweaty, flammable flaming ball, a giant controlled animal feedlot operation whirling through space, all life turned into live stock on the stock market, burgeoning with zoonotic diseases borne of frenetic dis-ease. A planet that, as William S. Burroughs once described it, he would take one look at and, "ask to see the Manager."

In this current moment, Burroughs's fascination with viruses both literal and metaphorical, and specifically with the idea of the word—and by extension all forms of media—as a virus, speaks to our times. This idea of the word as virus appears repeatedly in Burroughs's work, so much so that when a compendium of his lifetime works was curated, it was simply entitled *Word Virus*. In his essay *The Electronic Revolution*, the author provocatively asserts that the written word is a virus that infected our ancestors and set us apart from the other primates. In the beginning was the Word, and the Word was God, and the Word was flesh. And in Burroughs's rendition of the Genesis story, the Word is virus, Burroughed in flesh, Burroughing its way into Adam's brain—and ours, Dear Readers—infecting all subsequent generations. Of course, if the written Word is a virus, then the *Bible* itself might just be the ultimate infection.

Viruses, it should be noted, can infect and control minds, from *Entomophthora muscae*, aka "destroyer of insects," which uses a fungus to control insects' brains before killing them, to the viruses that invade the mammalian brain and leave a path of encephalitis in their wake, to La Corona herself. COVID sufferers with no known prior mental health conditions have been reported to exhibit symptoms akin to paranoid-schizophrenia after having been infected with the virus: trying to commit suicide, trying to kill family members because they think their loved ones are plotting to murder them, wild hallucinations, and in one case, a woman trying to pass her child through a drive-through window because she was certain that she was being followed, and that "they" were after her child. Much like the effects of hallucinogenic drugs on the brain, viruses can make the lines between reality and surreality quite blurry.

It is clear that the target of the Word virus is the mind, though once the mind is infected, it can affect the rest of the body, as well. According to Burroughs, the Word virus is a uniquely human pathogen—indeed, the very foundation of our separation from the rest of animalia. In choosing the written word as the place to draw the invisible boundary line of the human/animal construct, one could say that Burroughs makes a fatal error typical of men who come from his background—i.e. white, wealthy, and patrician—by wiping the vast majority of humanity out, for most human languages never had a written counterpart. Thus, in striving to determine the essential quality that makes one human, Burroughs uses colonizer logic by setting the standard of humanness to that of the colonizer culture's normative. In so doing, he implicitly animalizes all those who come from cultures where the Word was not written, a construct that has been used as a foundation of and rationalization for oppression within human society for centuries.

Yet, unlike other members of the colonizer class, Burroughs does not necessarily think that this difference is a *good* thing. Words spread ideas like a plague. If they are merely spoken, they only infect those they are directly spoken to, or who are close enough to hear them. They remain local in the damage they do. Recorded words, on the other hand, have the potential to become a pandemic, infecting millions or even billions around the globe. They also have the potential to infect generation after generation with the disease, causing Alfred Korzybski, the Polish theorist and founder of General Semantics whom Burroughs references extensively, to describe humans using written language as "time-bending animals."

It is for this reason that Burroughs makes the bold claim that while most people believe the spoken word preceded the written, in reality the written word preceded the spoken, for human spoken languages would never have evolved the way they did if not for the fact that this particular primate's languages were infected with a virus—the written word. The written word was, of course, the original version of the virus, but since then it has mutated into much faster-spreading and more potent variants—first through the printing press, and then far more rapidly through TV, radio, video, film, and in our own era of split-second transmission variants, smart phone cameras, social media, YouTube, the entire world entangled in a hyper-connected wwwweb of influence. One word can infect billions of brains within seconds in a single spray.

It is interesting to note that Burroughs himself did not start writing in earnest until after he accidentally killed his own wife, Joan Vollmer, in an incident in which she mocked his hunting skills, and he attempted to prove them by shooting a glass off her head a la William Tell, but ended up shooting her in the head instead, thus proving her entire point. Or perhaps, more chillingly, unconsciously proving his.Burroughs immediately fled back to the United States, where he was convicted of manslaughter in absentia and received a two-year suspended sentence but never went to prison because the crime had occurred outside US borders. To deal with the trauma of that event, Burroughs began working through his thoughts on paper, but with an extreme ambivalence about and even revulsion toward that process. He often stated that Vollmer's death was the sole reason for him becoming a writer. In the introduction to his autobiographical novel *Queer*, Burroughs wrote:

> *"I am forced to the appalling conclusion that I would have never become a writer but for Joan's death… The death of Joan brought me into contact with the invader, the Ugly Spirit, and maneuvered me into a lifelong struggle, in which I had no choice except to write my way out."*

One can see in this early work, written in 1952 although not released until 1985 because the censors were so scandalized by its content that they prevented it from being published, that the germ of the word virus concept was already present in Burroughs's mind. To him, writing was a vehicle to transport the "invader," the "ugly spirit," out of his own mind and into that of the readers. If the word was a virus to Burroughs, writing was the vector, and publishing the spike protein. Moreover, another incident in Burroughs's formative years may have set the foundation for his antagonistic feelings about the written word, despite ultimately becoming a scrivener, as he put it, himself. Although he had started writing at the age of eight, as a teenager attending an elite boarding school, a seminal incident scarred him for life when his unrequited crush on another boy was discovered and outed. Burroughs immediately dropped out of school, utterly disgraced. Months later, when the school sent home his belongings, he methodically burned every page of his diary that referenced the crush. For many years after that, through the psychiatric conversion therapy his parents subjected him to and beyond, he never wrote a word again, but rather blurred out his feelings with the drugs he conned the psychiatrists into giving him, and the opium he smoked with his family's housekeeper, who allegedly introduced him to the lifelong junk habit his name eventually became virtually synonymous with.

While we can never know whether it was the diary itself that led to him being outed in school, it is clear Burroughs began associating written words with danger and destruction as early as adolescence. The theme comes up repeatedly in his other works as well. In *The Ticket that Exploded*, Burroughs refers to language as "a virus from outer space. ... Language infects us; its power derives not from its straightforward ability to communicate or persuade but rather from this infectious nature, this power of bits of language to graft itself onto other bits of language, spreading and reproducing, using human beings as hosts." In the film version of *Naked Lunch*, which Burroughs collaborated closely on with filmmaker David Cronenberg, typewriters become giant cockroaches who literally talk out of their own asses, commanding him to massage their lips and their keys to write reports from the Interzone—a sort of Moroccan-inspired netherworld where Western sexual deviants can escape into anonymity. Repulsed and horrified, the protagonist shoots the typewriters-as-cockroaches, stomps on them and otherwise destroys them—and therefore, his actual typewriters—multiple times.

The only time he is able to type on them is when he is high, usually on the very substance used to kill the roaches, which thus necessarily kills the awareness of his writing as well. At multiple points, the protagonist says that writing is dangerous and resists doing it, insisting on a vocation as an exterminator until a fellow writer friend convinces him in the end to write, a fictional reflection of the real life incident in which Jack Kerouac convinced Burroughs to go back to writing.

Significantly, the only time the protagonist is able to write without shooting up first is when his typewriter is reshaped in the form of a mugwump, the very creature who knowingly maneuvered him to escape to the queer haven Interzone after he shot his wife, despite the fact that at that stage the protagonist was still in denial of his true sexuality. One gets the sense that only when Burroughs's alter ego is able to face and embrace his queer identity he can make peace with the typewriter enough to write on it without sporadically wanting to kill it. Yet, his ambivalence toward the written word shows up yet again when, in the final scene, he is pressured by guards into "proving he's a writer" by "writing something" on the spot, and his response is to pull out a gun and replicate the killing of his wife on a woman whose visage is her reincarnation, William Tell-style glass on her head and all. The guards respond approvingly and allow him passage into Annexia, the totalitarian state they guard. In order to prove one's legitimacy as a writer, one must expose and exploit one's own trauma over and over again for public consumption.

Reading Burroughs at this particular moment in my own life, it is interesting to consider Burroughs's attraction-revulsion to the written word through the lens of attachment styles, a subject that has become of great interest to me since recently discovering I have a fearful-avoidant attachment style myself. It is clear from the anecdotes revealed by his friends that Burroughs was profoundly emotionally avoidant in his personal life, most likely a highly avoidant variation of fearful avoidance. Fearful-avoidant attachment style, which is often caused by an unstable and/or traumatic childhood (which Burroughs was no stranger to, as he once revealed to a psychoanalyst that he had been forced to perform oral sex on his nanny's boyfriend at the age of four), is characterized by an intense desire for, yet also aversion to, intimacy, leading to a hallmark push-pull dynamic.

It is also strongly associated with a number of reoccurring themes appearing in Burroughs's work and life: his extreme fear of and resistance towards systems of authoritarianism and control; his proneness to addiction; his fear of women as "sexual enslavers of men"; his affection for animals but difficulty connecting with humans; his alienation from connecting sex with love and view of sex as a "biological weapon"; his tendency to observe humans through clinical detachment, which revealed itself in myriad ways ranging from his choice to study anthropology at Harvard, to his fascination with psychoanalysis, to the characteristically jaded tone he used to describe the "perversion" and "deviance" in the underworld he inhabited; his morbid fascination with death; and his attraction to all things transgressive and compulsion to subvert social norms. In addition to being a pariah in the wider society, these traits made him queer even among the iconoclasts, the outcasts, the junkies, and the queer community itself. Even as he was being worshiped by his fellow artists in the cult of coolness, Burroughs himself always cut a lonely, misfit figure.

Based on the image he projected, it would be tempting to classify Burroughs as being as emotionally detached as he appeared. Yet, there is strong indication that much of his avoidance was a wall he used to protect a vulnerable heart. If there is any doubt of Burroughs's intense emotionality, one need look no farther than his youthful Van Gogh moment, in which he cut off part of his own finger in order to prove his love to a man. Over time, however, Burroughs, who was described by his friends in the 2010 documentary *A Man Within* as "very physically and romantically awkward, lonely", increasingly kept his heart more and more remote. Sexually promiscuous with the hustlers he picked up, he rarely fell in love and was deeply hurt when he did, leading to increasing emotional withdrawal in his later years. While Burroughs walled himself off from humans (one friend described trying to tell Burroughs he was in love with him, only for Burroughs to respond by patting his arm and saying, "Oh, that's okay," and then rolling over and going to sleep), his love for non-human animals, particularly cats and lemurs, was unrestrained. Friends recall the only time they ever saw him cry was the moment he thought of nuclear war and realized he might not survive to take care of his cats. "He was always talking about endangered species and other animals," reminisced one friend. "It was a safe place for his love to flow."

Yet, as is characteristic of all fearful avoidants, Burroughs was a paradox, constantly pulled in two opposing directions at once. He loved and was fascinated by animals, yet he hunted them. He abhorred war and capital punishment, but was obsessed with firearms and never left home without them. He was a junkie, yet he hated drugs. He was the literary King of Sexual Deviance, yet a recent Salon.com article described him as "an asexual Tiresias-like seer". He was a free love advocate, yet was uncomfortable with that in his own life. He had great friendships with women, yet his writing reveals his fear and revulsion towards them, classifying them as "sex enemies" and "another species". He was queer, yet he loathed the gay male scene. He embraced communications technology, yet railed against its power to manipulate. He was a nihilist, yet also a humanist. He was a prolific writer, yet considered the written word to be a virus.

One could argue that writing literature is a sort of sexual act, a form of intercourse between the writer and countless readers. If the literary word is a virus, it is surely a venereal disease. In order for writers to write, they must *nakedly* expose their internal reality for all to see, while the readers receive that without ever needing to expose themselves in return. If we consider Burroughs as paradoxically both fearing and desiring human connection, his ambivalence about the written word becomes more comprehensible. For an avoidant, the prospect of writing is in many ways a nightmare, for avoidance stems from overwhelming shame which compels the avoidant to hide, and writing is all about revealing. As a homosexual at a time when that was looked upon with horror and disgust, a man who had killed his own wife, an addict, a victim of child molestation, and a neglectful father of the son he abandoned after his wife's death, it's no mystery why Burroughs might have internalized shame. Yet, the other side of this duality is the need to express, to be seen, heard, and understood. In Burroughs's case, that which drove his shame may have also impelled him to reveal those aspects of himself in the hopes of (self) acceptance—and in the case of his terrible guilt over his wife, and later over their son, who died as a young man from alcoholism after years of neglect from his father, some sort of absolution.

Viruses are both created and spread through contact, whether that's through a confined feedlot or slaughterhouse, a crowded slum or prison, or a globalized, colonized, hyper-connected world. It is for this reason that we socially distance to protect ourselves from them, whether that's to #stayhome or stay offline. Yet, developing antibodies ironically requires exposure to either the virus itself, or else some part or simulation of it. Perhaps this is why Burroughs often simultaneously avoided and reached toward that which he considered to be a virus. The question of how best to handle a virus is a potent one in an era in which we are constantly re-evaluating whether it is better to expose ourselves to or shield ourselves from potential infection. Exposure means risking the spread of all kinds of pathogens, not just Corona but also the viral threats of white nationalism, conspiracy theorism, copycat shootings, and stochastic terrorism. If any type of word is a highly contagious and deadly virus, it's hate speech. Yet, cloistering ourselves too much can weaken our immunity in all forms, including our tolerance for the unfamiliar and for dangerous ideas. And since sequestering also involves confinement, it can lead to new viruses forming, including word virus phenomena like public shaming campaigns (e.g. #calloutculture) and forms of exclusion (e.g. #cancelculture), which appear in different forms throughout history and which ironically lead into new forms of xenophobia, moral panics and other reactionary manifestations of mass conformity and fear of difference. It's a delicate balance, one that Burroughs, who both warned us of word viruses and simultaneously pushed the outermost limits of what was acceptable to say, was keenly aware of. Perhaps this is why he felt compelled to cut up words and put them back together in new and unexpected ways, as a method of exposing people to just enough of the virus to develop the antibodies to it, but not to enough of it that it might fully infect them and spread in uncontrollable ways. By taking control of the virus' himself rather than avoiding it and thus leaving it to naturally mutate or else be harnessed by others as a way of gaining power through seizing the means of infection, Burroughs sought to guide the process of exposure in a way that was both safe and liberatory—both for the society at large, and for those afflicted.

As a queer, outlaw artist whose life spanned almost the entire twentieth century, Burroughs witnessed and experienced many viruses in his lifetime—the Spanish flu in childhood, the tail end of the Industrial Revolution, hyper-inflation followed by Great Depression, the rise of Nazism, two world wars, fascist, anarchist and Communist movements and revolutions, McCarthyism, the rise of mass media, the spread of both right-wing and left-wing authoritarianism, the sexual and political revolutions, Watergate, AIDS, the drug and mass incarceration epidemic, and the collapse of statist Communism and rapid global spread of deregulated capitalism in the neoliberal era. It was through these events, and his own complicated life, that Burroughs realized the way to treat a word virus was the way you would treat any virus—through exposure to a harmless form of that virus. And what is narrative media but a simulation of real world viruses, able to prime the readers'/viewers' minds to create antibodies for when they are exposed to the real thing? Just as Burroughs himself was in many ways the embodiment of a walking contradiction, he intuitively realized that words can be both the virus and the cure.

"THERE WAS A KIND OF PERMISSION HE GAVE ME": AN INTERVIEW WITH TONY KUSHNER

BRIAN ALESSANDRO

With the release of Angels in America, Millennium Approaches, *and* Perestroika *almost thirty years ago, Tony Kushner's cultural, artistic, and sociological impact continues to be unparalleled and immeasurable. His doleful, lyrical interrogations of race, religion, sexuality, gender, nationalism, politics, and AIDS remain groundbreaking and unprecedented, in a voice that is disarmingly compassionate, breathtakingly perceptive, and qualified in its many provocations.*

Kushner discusses what makes a work of literature like Naked Lunch *or* Junky *enduring and iconic, the power of Burroughs's uncompromising, dark vision, the sociocultural influence Burroughs has had through his work, which also focused with candor and without maudlin guile on homosexuality and disease, and the political contexts of both.*

BRIAN ALESSANDRO: Why do you think that *Naked Lunch* and *Angels in America* are both so enduring, so timeless? What are the common qualities?

TONY KUSHNER: That's hard to answer because I can't think of two things that are less alike.

(*We both laugh.*)

KUSHNER: That's an interesting question, though. I'll be completely honest about it: I was horrified and completely hooked by *Naked Lunch* and by *Junky* when I read them years ago. Burroughs has always, for me, represented a kind of writing specifically about sexuality and in a certain sense about life in general that I've felt somewhat chagrined by not being willing or able to do. When I read *Junky* in the Seventies when I was in college, I was already twenty years old. It seemed even at the moment—I came to Columbia from Louisiana in 1974, so it was only five years after Stonewall—and I was completely in the closet growing up in a small Southern town. The book seemed so transgressive, but not in any kind of stupid or vulgar way, but kind of like reaching beneath the surface of things and exposing in this kind of stunningly comfortless way the raw truths about life and about desire and about compulsion. I've always been somebody who is fascinated by law and by attempts to rationalize and better organize existence by progressive politics, and while there is certainly something progressive in a sense in Burroughs's insistence that pretty much anything can be said, and it's a very dark view of existence that is at its best anarchic and at its darkest kind of nihilist. It's endured mostly because it's really great writing. It wasn't like Henry Miller, somebody I was never able to stand. It didn't feel pornographic although sometimes it was disturbingly erotic. It was among the first explicit stuff I read about homosexuality ever, except *Everything You Always Wanted to Know About Sex* or something German.

(*We both laugh.*)

ALESSANDRO: Like Fassbinder.

KUSHNER: Well, Fassbinder was afterward. Burroughs was one of
the first people, and in the sense of *Naked Lunch*, Fassbinder felt slightly
tame. The first thing I ever read that acknowledged the existence of
homosexuality was that horrible book (*Everything You Always Wanted
to Know About Sex*) and my mother had a marriage manual that was
like 800 pages long and it had a little chapter in it about homosexuality
written by some German, and it was something that her mother had
given her, and it was incredibly technical and sort of a tedious Freud-
ian, Kraft-Ebbing version of sexuality. Burroughs is a very great writer.
Whether or not you like this vision of the world or whether you could
completely own it or whether you thought it was a distorted vision,
there's something kind of inarguable and true about it, which is always
the case with great art. Unlike a lot of great artists who are peddling visions of the world I can't quite share like Wagner, for instance, or Saul
Bellow. Those people ... there's always someplace in Bellow even when
you think you have greatness, and then he will always at some point
become nervous about asserting his kind of reactionary vision of things
and he'll do something stupid that's easy to dismiss so you can love his
writing as I do but then still say "But..."Or on a much higher plane,
Dostoyevsky does this, and he's a little bit more like Burroughs when he
does this. Sometimes he tips his hand, and you can breathe a sigh of relief and you can say, "Okay, here's where he's wrong about this and I can
get off this nightmare for a little while." Burroughs doesn't really do that,
and that's part of his power. There's a kind of coherence, and he's not
peddling an agenda ever. It's just this fever dream, which is maybe the
one way ... there are some writers who just give you a kind of permission to write what you want to write. Usually, I talk about the enormous
impact Herman Melville had on me. Another writer whose vision of the
world is kind of progressive and kind of reactionary. Hopeless and air-

less. In *Cities of The Red Night* and *Naked Lunch* and in *Junky*, this kind of permission to write a kind of a dream state or a vision that doesn't have any kind of context-setting apparatus around it to sort of attach it to this or that political program. I have frequently found that I have wanted to attach my art to a program, so I didn't follow it exactly, but in *Angels*, one of the things I think works and has made it last as long as it's lasted, one of the critics who saw an early production of Part I called it a "fever dream," which I sort of like. And Burroughs is very much one of those writers that I admire as much as his acolytes like Kathy Acker or Dennis Cooper, people who kind of dig into the polysemous body, the flesh as a way of exploring meaning in the way that the world has sort of inscribed on the body and the way their body is at war with the world around it and the costs of that and I think that's sort of one of his legacies. I can enjoy the sense of dread and horror movie feeling of some of the work but temperamentally, I think I'm a different kind of person.

ALESSANDRO: Your answer is wonderful and maybe suggests that Burroughs transcended concrete politics and moved into something eternal or elemental. To that point, what makes a work of art—or literature—iconic?

KUSHNER: Define iconic.

ALESSANDRO: Something that can have a lasting cultural impact that can recur throughout generations.

KUSHNER: It can come from any number of places. It can be something that hits the zeitgeist on the head of a particular moment or comes to stand for something or effortlessly evokes a particular moment in time or it can be something that is just really groundbreaking, the first sonnet, the first genuinely tragic musical ... the first of its kind.

A kind of a radical work of art … a work of art that essentially performs a radical break from the past and the energy of that is trapped inside. A lot of Stravinsky like *Firebird* or *Rite of Spring*. Sometimes it's just as simple as that it's very, very great. *Middlemarch* in my opinion is the greatest novel ever written because it's the greatest novel ever written. Or *War and Peace* or *The Brothers Karamazov*. Or *Moby Dick*. These vast kind of miraculous works. Every time you read them, you discover something new. And I never reread any of Burroughs, so I can't say that this is true of him, but my guess is that in some sense it might be. The mystery of Chekov, the four big plays, they're all somewhat similar and they have different stories, and the character types get repeated, the monster mother, you know, and it's sometimes hard to keep track of which one is in which play, and if you like theater you've seen the plays many times. I mean I think I've seen 100 different productions of *The Cherry Orchard*. Every fucking time I see it I hear something new that I would swear was not there before. The same thing with Shakespeare. It's inexhaustible.

ALESSANDRO: Dense with layers.

KUSHNER: And that I think is one reason why something begins to ascend in the pantheon. At different times it changes. At different … I read *Middlemarch* now three times. And I always thought that Rosamond Vincy was one of the greatest portraits of a pathological narcissist in all of literature. And I never realized it until the very last time I read it and I think it was because I read it during the Trump era …

(*We both laugh.*)

ALESSANDRO: Context.

KUSHNER: And I was thinking a lot about borderline pathology and psychotic levels of narcissism, and I went back to this old Otto Kernberg, who was one of the articulators of psychoanalytic theories about narcissism in the Fifties and Sixties and he's completely despairing of it and did not think it was treatable and when you look at someone like Trump you think, "Okay, so they're right."

ALESSANDRO: Right, it's malignant.

KUSHNER: Right. Kernberg called it a version of moral evil and you think that and at the end of *Middlemarch* because I didn't need to notice it before. You find that in a work of art, something that opens up new vistas. It becomes worth revisiting over and over again and if you make art, you sit there staring at it, and you think, "How the fuck did she [Eliot] do that?" And I've certainly found that in the Burroughs I've read. It has a Beckett quality. It's so bleak, and it's so unsentimental and sort of very, very funny, but it's so scary, the vision of the world, and yet because of the magnificence of the writing, it's got incredible vitality. You could talk about how ugly people are so that the ugliness becomes beautiful. That's a paradox. I think we're drawn to that. I have absolutely found that in Burroughs. It's like the way Burroughs growls in Laurie Anderson's *Sharkey's Night*. I love the way his voice sounds in that—exactly as you want it to sound like.

ALESSANDRO: Or like *The "Priest" They Called Him*, when he collaborated with Kurt Cobain in the early Nineties. Yeah, Burroughs was close with Laurie Anderson and with Lou Reed.Changing gears a bit, how central is homosexuality to Burrough's work?

TONY KUSHNER: Absolutely central, it seems to me. Certainly, the books I've been drawn to, and that's part of the reason I was drawn to them. It's a queer sensibility. It's an absolute embrace. There's a great faith there that the real truth about life is to be found in the margins and not at the center. He shares that with one of my favorite writers, Tennessee Williams, in that knowledge flows from the bottom up rather than from the top down. There's an artificiality and a degree of fabulizing and invention and artifice in human existence that comes from being sort of born wrong. Having genitalia that you sort of want to do things with that aren't what the obvious biological functions might be or what the world's opinions are telling you are the proper usages of them, the genitalia. Something a little more dated, and here I am not on very safe ground, because I sometimes get memories of Burroughs and Genet confused. The notion of Leo Bersani, whom I can't stand. The kind of solipsism and narcissism of homosexuality, the mirroring of same sex attraction is a sort of a fundamentally a narcissistic thing and that if it's not sentimentalized it leads you to core truths about human disconnection and loneliness and where that leads, I don't know. It's not a view that I subscribe to or have a lot of patience with it. I think it, like with Genet, there are traces of Burroughs, a degree of this kind of underworld sexuality that's become a neurotic defense of criminality and degeneracy that is understandable given the world these guys came of age in, but it needs to be problematized maybe more than these guys were capable of doing.

ALESSANDRO: The primary aim of our anthology is to reclaim Burroughs as a queer writer. Why do you think for so many years he has not been acknowledged by the community and accepted into the gay literary canon?

KUSHNER: I don't know how I knew this but when I first moved to New York City and started going to old used bookstores and looking for the Grove Atlantic paperbacks of his books, I was led, in that mysterious way when you get led, to the right part of the library. Something led me to him. I was in the closet, and I was looking for gay writing or maybe someone I read like Edmund White might have mentioned him. I always thought he was part of the gay canon and there is a certain part of the gay canon that is … canons are always tricky because of the keepers of the canons. And there is a certain desire to … somebody like Burroughs who really wants to dig into the claim and make art out of it and dig into darker feelings and things that make people squeamish and to be very specific about drugs and also fucking and there are people who just think it's like … sort of like the old thing, "Why are all these drag queens marching in Gay Pride or these leather queens, we need to put on a better face," you know, "or it's bad for the Jews, so don't say these things in public." There's some of that. Also, we are among other things, the civil rights movement so there is a kind of … I didn't do this to make *Angels* more popular among gay people, but since it was a gay play and it had this large reach, I wrote the epilogue with Walter Prior talking to the audience, saying things like "We'll be citizens," and it is almost an unapologetically political statement at the end of a seven hour play if you've been enjoying it also has a priestly function but it also has a political thing. It's hard to know how to fit and there are times when the negative imagination has enormous power. For instance, ACT UP, the beginning of the play, "Silence Equals Death." I mean, that poster was terrifying. I remember it very well. A black poster with pink, Weimar lettering and triangle. And in LA, the LA chapter of ACT UP had "Action Equals Life." And it was bright lettering with the triangle pointing up and it was, of course, kind of lame and wimpy. The thing that really made your blood pulse and made you want to act was this terrifying thing that had the word "Death" in it and sometimes that is … that kind of darkness is galvanic, but it's hard with somebody like Burroughs to say exactly how … I mean, I absolutely believe that there is a political function of all great art and I think he's a great artist. Anything that deepens our understanding, anything that broadens our sense of what the human is, anything that liberates our voices, even when they are in lamentation, is of importance politically but it's not quite as clear how to use it in the immediate moment.

ALESSANDRO: Is it fair to say that Burroughs had an influence on you as a young writer?

KUSHNER: I'm sure in some ways, probably, yeah. I think there was a kind of permission that he gave me that I was getting from other places, as well. A kind of recklessness. Although he is a very disciplined writer. I tend to write from a place of panic, and his stuff has a feeling of incredible polish and precision, which is part of his power. I wouldn't say that stylistically he had an influence on me. But there are things in *Angels* about the body and during the epidemic [the AIDS crisis] the meaning of the human body became something that everybody started talking about, the battleground was the body, and I think that some of the way of talking about this is feminist writing and some of it is, at least my first awareness of that, of thinking about the body, came from Burroughs.

ALESSANDRO: I was thinking just that! And to that point, if you had to interpret Burroughs's themes, what does his work say about homosexuality and disease?

KUSHNER: Oof! I re-read *Junky* recently, because of *West Side Story*. I just adapted it for Spielberg. Everyone is down on Arthur Laurents's rather brilliant original book because of things like hip beatnickisms that sound very corny now and I was searching around for different kinds of Fifties slang that would make it a little bit different, fill my ears with something different from the original book, so I read *Junky* again. The main themes are disgust and shame and vulnerability and fragility. I think importantly an overall theme of a kind of an embrace of disease as an expression of life. It's "nothing human is alien to me." In his very dry way that he has of describing things it's stripped of ... the narrator ... the person who is taking you into these dark places is not sanctioning your feelings of revulsion. He is demanding that you scrutinize them and do an inventory of what their compound parts are. What components of loving or disgust or horror are ... what's compounded into those feeling. They are not simple feelings. They involve forms of ecstasy and erotica and sometimes spiritual ecstasy and terrible yearning for companionship and sympathy and pity. And the most disturbing things are how in the midst of these kind of nightmarish narratives there are moments of a kind of ordinary morality and decency sort of bubbling up and catching you unawares and there is a sense of a kind of an ethical being operating throughout these works that is not always in charge but is present. It's not the Marquis De Sade or something. It's not pornography.

ALESSANDRO: What are your thoughts about Burroughs's idea of "language as a virus, words as a virus, speaking as viral evolution"? It makes me think a bit about the end of *Angels* when you wrote that "the world only spins forward" and that there is a necessary anguish we sometimes must endure in pursuit of progress.

KUSHNER: Yeah, but that's more from Walter Benjamin than anything else, but I'm sure that Benjamin would have very much enjoyed Burroughs. There's some kind of genealogical connection between people like Robert Walser and Heinrich von Kleist and Kafka, certainly, and Burroughs. And in a lot of French theorists, the notion of language as a virus. And Althusser, and *The Prison-House of Language*. You're fucked before you could even get started. You're called in this symbolic order and your tools of comprehending it and even changing it are so completely of it that it's very hard to imagine how escape is even possible, which is problematic. In the Eighties, the Left took over the academy and the Right took over the White House and both houses of Congress. There is a political price to pay. It doesn't mean I revere Althusser. I think he's an extraordinary thinker. I think what we're going through right now is a sort of extraordinary moment where a generation of people have learned a language of a kind of a microanalysis of the way that oppression functions—

ALESSANDRO: Structurally.

KUSHNER: Structurally, yes. And in incredibly subtle ways as well as in large gross legal ways. We're now in a kind of a paroxysm, trying to figure out how to create new standards that address a deeper level of awareness than is usually permitted into political discourse or into the way that we organize our interactions with one another and that's imponderably difficult and also often necessary. Writing like William S. Burroughs lives very much ... that's sort of part of the challenge that it's constantly making to us, that it's how do you assimilate what this book has to tell you into your sense of how to create a better and more just world because it's not entirely saying it's impossible to do that and even if it were, it's great enough. Dostoyevsky is literally telling you that, and yet progressive people have been obsessed with Dostoyevsky since he first started writing even though he hates progressive people! It poses a tremendous challenge. Can you conceive of a justice large enough, of a legal system broad and generous and supple enough, of a notion of progress that's human enough and non-mechanical enough to incorporate the truths that are contained on the philosophical side of things, like Derrida, and on the aesthetic side, somebody like Burroughs.

ALESSANDRO: Does this suggest that writers or artists have a moral responsibility?

KUSHNER: Well, I feel that artists and writers do. And in one sense I think we do. And in another sense, someone like Burroughs reminds us, the primary responsibility is to find out a way to tell the truth. Which is the hardest thing of all, and the biggest enemy of the truth is yourself always. To circumvent that and what happened to him, sometimes you run into a wall, but for most of us, it's simply not letting the internalized police state tell us that we can't say this, or we can't say that. I do feel that you can feel a social responsibility at work in somebody like Burroughs in that it's not primary process, it's not just undigested crap spit up by his id. It's not psychotic. It's really organized. It's really coherent. The rhythms and syntax of his speech and the purity of his writing, there's something very powerfully sort of organized there and I feel that there is a morality operative in that kind of … You have to decide, depending on what your vision of the world is … I've said elsewhere that I think that hope is a moral obligation. I feel that that's true for me because of the enormous comforts and privileges I've enjoyed. Despair would feel like an act of ingratitude and abrogation of a moral responsibility. There's something paradoxical in all of great art because even if it is completely despairing like Beckett it's still so gorgeous it makes you feel happy to be a human being. But if your vision of the world is such that you don't feel … I mean, we all are going to be facing this now with climate change. I mean, at what point are you talking about hope and at what point are you talking about delusion. And if we decided that we really are doomed then is there any point in making … I mean, "No poetry after Auschwitz," … is there any point in making art? Again, when you read something like *Cities of The Red Night* or *Naked Lunch*, Burroughs is sort of directly asking you this question. There is no point in doing this and yet here I am doing it. And here you are reading it.

BIRTHDAY ODE: A POEM FOR ALLEN GINSBERG ON HIS BIRTHDAY.

JAMES GRAUERHOLZ

O Allen,
O hairy Bard, jumping liberator,
I remember you today,
On your birthday, again.

I remember you in New York City
In your apartment on East 12th Street
In '73 when I first pilgrim'd to you—
When I drove an old Mercury
With my friends from college Kansas,
Twenty-six hours straight through
From the Vortex to the Lower East Side.

Stopping only to fuel our car and change
Drivers, or eat at truck stop diners,
Omelets with meat chili and red beans
Heaped on top—we were young, and we rolled down
The Merc's rear sliding window to ventilate
Our boyish gas.

Then at dawn we saw
The windowéd cliffs of the West Side Highway,
Rolling up old I-95 past the tank farms
Of Elizabeth, Linden, past Bayonne's great smoking
Moloch refineries, through an oily haze
Past Newark and Secaucus, Weehawken,
The Indian names, Moonachie and Hackensack ...

But now turn East, to Fort Lee, go to the Bridge!
George Washington first? Not in the hearts of those tribes, but
Our young hearts pounded on trucker whites, our grimy
Windshield was greasy from cigarettes and Jersey's acid rain.

The rising Sun over canyons of built Mannahatta,
The stays and cables of the singing Bridge,
Glistened to welcome us, *You* were welcoming Us
(Did you even know it?) to your City ...

Where you stood in your beard with Leg in plaster Cast,
Brushing your teeth quietly by Tompkins Square,
Not waking Denise, Peter up all night anyway,
The tenement tap water brown going down
Porcelain pedestal sink bathroom drain.

We were voyagers, crossers of prairie, in our wagon
Filled with dreams then.

Happy Birthday, Allen!

You're 94 now, "safe in Heaven dead,"
Your cock shriveled and black, my dreams a bit

Shriveled now, and my cock now too, not
The prodigious fleshy pink telescope
That your thoughts may have fondled for a moment
When you sat at your plywood desk, opened
Your calendar, and saw the words:

"James Grauerholtz arrives."

AUNTIE BILL

NANDI LASOPHIA

Salacious, gross, exploitative giggles.
Illegal fags adopting boyfriends as sons.
Fucked up, imprisoned, morphine fever dreams
Fueled by jack-off cut-ups,
Hyped-up trash- Treasured, revered, Auntie Bill.
Handgun at the ready.
Antigay, profag, hard-on, dirty, dirty street trash, Mexican border hang-
over.
Mexico City, Murder city, booze-fuck American bliss,
Punk rock grand daddy takes it in the ass and mouth with fervent joy.
No place in respectable company-
Pick its nose!
Flick a finger, dead cold and "Fuck you"
Rebel rebel, pretender. Coy smiles are too clean.
Pull back the hammer and shoot spunk sideways in webs
On the bourgeoisie, make their clothes sticky and filthy
Break the upturned noses of pretty homosexuals at their cocained par-
ties
Bloated with cheese dip and pricey vermouth.

Button up shirts get dirty too.

Buttoned up boys get dirty too.

Buttonfly jeans get crumpled on the dirty floor

In Hot, loud, shameless moans

Fucked deep in paracetamol, valium, opioid constipation shitdick.

Respectability politics blasted in the face,

Hot cum dribbling from its every bullet hole,

Seared in disgust and shame for its own wanting.

Wanting so bad it dies.

Bill don't give a reverent fuck.

Bill fucks bullet holes like buttholes

Creamy skin rent deep with slashes

Lathered with passion like shampoo and dirty wet

Like truck stop showers or a busted hydrant on side streets.

Lawrence Kansas summer fucks like a good boy.

I first heard of William S. Burroughs when I was a teenager. I'd picked up a Psychic TV album, and it was the weirdest shit I'd ever heard. It felt dark and ceremonial and disjointed yet also had a flow to it that worked somehow. Listening to their music brought me a lot of conflict and joy because there was no structure to it. I'd never heard of music that didn't follow a precise formula! They led to Einstürzende Neubauten and all sorts of other weird, noisy shit that spooked me. Genesis Breyer P-Orridge spoke at length about Burroughs's influence over them and told stories of looking him up in the actual fucking phone book when both Burroughs and P-Orridge lived in London in the Sixties or Seventies. They talked about cut-ups and making new words, creating new forms. They began to approach music that way and so finally Psychic TV made sense. The flow made sense. I created a handful of cut-up poems and although I liked them, I felt like a poseur since

I wasn't of that generation, so I trashed them and found my own way around words being a filthy degenerate too sick for gay respectability. I had nothing to be ashamed of, now that I knew I was just a link in a long, twisted chain of iconoclastic freaks.

This was in the Eighties when gay porno mags were often shared between teenage boys, and having no interest in hetero porn, I had nobody to share this with. I once met an older man (he was probably twenty-five to my fourteen) in a wheelchair at a punk show staged in a decrepit squat full of crushed beer cans, cigarette butts, and hot, angry bodies jumping about, thrashing, punching walls and each other, male, female, me, us, all the fucking disposable garbage asshole kids doing this ridiculous, ceremonial, primordial screaming of lyrics that made no sense and ultimately no difference to anything but our servile affectations at the altar of hyperbolic masculinity espoused by androgynous looks that sadly dove headlong into heteronormativity as soon as the veiny, pink phantom of cocksucking reared its tumescent head.

This guy was a friend of a friend. He was a fucking pervert: a real nice guy in stained jeans who whispered, "Psst! Hey, I know you're a fag and me too. You want this porno mag? It's really hot. Lots of young guys like you getting fucked real hard. You can have it if you want it." I took it gladly and pored over it as soon as I got home, unfazed by the crisp, used pages and sour smell of it. I was fueled deeply by a night of being ground down to nothing by the loud music and sweaty bodies of guys in their twenties with dark, thick eyebrows and bleached hair wearing sleeveless shirts. I got crazy over armpit hair or the peek at a treasure trail I would have waded through literal gallons of shitty, bloody piss to just smell those guys.

When I read Burroughs at that age, I felt like my world and his were ultimately the same, save the broad discrepancy between his wealth and my poverty. I didn't care much for the company of regular gay people. They were banal and unimaginative, sniveling assholes. I lived in the part of the gay world where all the abandoned, dying kids and junkies slept, ate, and fucked and shit. It was cool to look like a girl so long as you didn't feel like one, and it was okay to act like a girl so long as you also fucked them. I hung out at cafes and wrote my first angsty, politically queer poems and would talk to other people about poetry, plays, music, and civil rights mostly. Whenever Burroughs came up in conversation, nobody ever talked about his queerness. They focused on his addiction or his wild past rather than what may have driven him so fuckin' bonkers creatively. I pretended maybe he and I were banging our heads against the same wall that keeps the nascent part of you invisible and projects outward to others, the parts that are commodity. In his case, a tremendous talent for words, rhythms, and vision. In my case, well, nothing yet. I was like a tiny jester on acid asking inane questions about existential crises and beating down the demons of being raised Catholic with a baseball bat made of cotton candy.

Burroughs seemed to have this veneer of "tough shit, baby" whilst also donning a visage of stoic, tender fragility, and this romance with street life, like a curator's eye lusting after a rusty iron nail because it was rumored to have been touched by Jesus. He was revolutionary quite literally, and also tongue-in-cheek Let's give them what they want because if they want a sick, gun-wielding faggot gacked out on methamphetamines or down for days on Dilaudid, well then all right... that suits me just fine because the American dream is dead anyhow and I get to ride on the crest of this explosive wave with the forerunners of reinventing the English language and bringing all you fuckers with me and you're going to want to come with me to prove how tough you are, oh yes, you're so tough but can you take it in the ass? Didn't think so. Take a seat, milquetoast. I'm driving the goddamned bus now, and we're going to Mexico for a while to stew in the ghastly juice of intolerable memories, accidental murders, and boozepuke. We're gonna look ourselves straight in the eye and wretch out a long "Fuck you" deeper than the pull of a laced joint and hallucinate forgiveness, transcendence and kindness. We're gonna slough off former skins and embrace our dependence and burn like the hills of Pompeii.

My vision of him may be deeply flawed, and that's okay with me—legends and iconoclasts are often misread and plagiarized to the point of giving identity crises to those admiring them. I'm okay with that. In the fall of 2000, I moved to Lawrence, Kansas, partly to advance my knowledge in the field of massage therapy and partly to explore the dynamics in building traditional sweat lodges from an insane, part-indigenous woman that took a shine to me. I also knew that Burroughs had lived there and found the prospect of meeting any of his clan exhilarating. I accomplished all of the above and found his fleeting influence there still palpable in small writer's circles and poetry exhibitions. I could see how a man like him could end up there and be happy in a double-wide. The town is small but open with plenty of weirdos hiding in plain sight with nothing to feel ashamed for. The town is insular, youthful, and an oasis amidst the Republican, Westboro Baptist vibes permeating the vast remains of the state. I lived there happily for a year and moved on equally as pleased to have experienced it. Now a woman in my late forties, I can say that Burroughs's influence has been a placid and daring one that often pushes me to fuck with words and structures as often as I fuck with politics and society at large. I don't carry a gun or threaten a revolution, but I do fuck with ideas and allow the slim figure of him to whisper in my dirty ear, "Fuck 'em up, kiddo. Let 'em have it raw".

WILLIAM S. BURROUGHS
AND ALBERT EINSTEIN,
THE ENTANGLEMENT OF TWO
COMPLEMENTARY GENIUSES

IOANNIS PAPPOS

Questioning everything is at the core of science; yet questioning science itself by challenging its foundations may lead one to be condemned and ostracized as an extremist. Still, it is the non-complacent, non-consensus oriented thinkers who have provided the most profound paradigm shifts, redefining science itself. Of course, this takes courage or having nothing to lose. For two hundred years, the brightest minds believed Newton's concepts of space and time were absolute—or perhaps they kept their mouths shut. Then came Albert Einstein, a patent clerk with minimal career prospects, who engrossed himself in thought experiments seeded in fictive and counterfactual settings (*Gedankenexperimente*). It's safe to say that Einstein's mind lived in an eloquent, all-encompassing, consistent, and magical world, in which as a kid (he was sixteen when he began his thought experiments at his gymnasium in Aarau) he could run as fast as, and parallel with, a beam of light in the vacuum of the universe, and thus like a surfer riding a wave observe the light wave at rest. (But the experience of frozen light eludes us...

Bam!—Einstein's first paradox on the way to relativity).

William S. Burroughs lived in a magical world, too:

> "In the magical universe, there are no coincidences and there are
> no accidents. Nothing happens unless someone wills it to happen.
> The dogma of science is that the will cannot possibly affect external
> forces, and I think that's just ridiculous. It's as bad as the church.
> My viewpoint is the exact contrary of the scientific viewpoint. I be-
> lieve that if you run into somebody in the street it's for a reason ...
> Since the word 'magic' tends to cause confused thinking, I would like
> to say exactly what I mean by 'magic' and the magical interpreta-
> tion of so-called reality. The underlying assumption of magic is the
> assertion of 'will' as the primary moving force in this universe—the
> deep conviction that nothing happens unless somebody or some be-
> ing wills it to happen... There are no accidents in the world of
> magic. And will is another word for animate energy."
>
> "The Magical Universe of William S. Burroughs"
> Matthew Levi Stevens

Clearly the two men had things in common: the way in which they let
their imaginations run free in playgrounds without obstacle, as well
as their preoccupation with Parmenides's Principle of Sufficient Reason—all things that happen have a cause, for any fact, there is a reason why it is so, and why something else is not instead, if there is x,
then there is a y that explains the x. Einstein believed in strict causality,
something he suffered for in his quantum physics dispute with Niels
Bohr and the Copenhagen school, who were satisfied with the inconse-
quence of whether physical reality existed outside our ability to observe
it. To disprove them, Einstein naturally undertook yet another thought

experiment, which turned out to be his most controversial. He considered the collision of two particles resulting in a wave entangling them, i.e., correlating their properties. No matter how far apart they might fly in the universe, no matter how many light years away from each other, observing one ought to allow us to explain the position and momentum of the other.

Burroughs, too, was interested in space and in the concept of leaving earth, if only in the form of astral projection and/or human intelligence traveling. Influenced by a range of loud and divisive thinkers, including Timothy Leary, Brion Gysin, Bob Monroe, and J.W. Dunne, Burroughs's thought experiments focused on getting rid of physical constraints. On the back of a napkin as it were, he reverse-engineered NASA's body-centric and "Christian" (as he called it) space program and contemplated sending to outer space, by means of future transport or entangled technologies, preserved human intelligence in the form of dreams, say, which he aimed to control and link to consciousness. For Burroughs, dreams were not random thoughts played out in tangible scenarios, but definitive methods for gaining insight about the moment of awareness of future events. In other words, dreams were Burroughs's first step in artificial astral intelligence, a call to exploration more akin to Darwin's or Einstein's philosophical takes on reality than to the traditional ways of Columbus, Vasco da Gama, or Marco Polo.

But why the curiosity for the missing pieces of a grander puzzle? Why the whys? The reason why we care about the Principle of Sufficient Reason is entropy, the direction of time. At this juncture, the benign and articulate physicist and the sloppier, darker writer/artist part ways. Burroughs is open to non-unidirectional time. He combined Dunne's nested observer position (time takes time to pass: observing time's passing at "spacetime one," with its past, present, and future, can only truly happen from a different spacetime, i.e., "spacetime two," where time also takes time to pass, thus needs an outside observer, and so on, thus producing infinite series of observers and of spacetime universes) with Gysin's cut-ups (whereby a written text is cut up and rearranged to create a potentially revealing new text) and dream-manipulation, to arrive at the idea of divination ("When you cut into the present, the future leaks out"). This must have presented him with the biggest paradox he ever faced. Burroughs's non-unidirectional, nonlinear timelines of infinite existences (there was a William S. Burroughs living five years ahead of him, just as there was one living fifteen minutes behind him) introduce the idea of destiny, stripping away the notion of causality. Could it be that the will (a cornerstone of Burroughs's magical universe) is simply an illusion?

History has shown us that all scientists, even the geniuses, have biases. Einstein, possibly the greatest mind that ever lived, was no different. His feud with the Copenhagen school took on a life of its own. His quantum thought experiment on reality (the belief that the never-observed second particle, the entangled particle, had a position and momentum that was real at any time), and thus his belief about reality itself, was empirically proven to be deficient by experiments in the Seventies. Scientists can be sore losers in public arguments, too, refusing to admit their own errors; but ultimately Einstein was not one of these.

Artists and imaginists, on the other hand, question themselves fluently. Burroughs must have dared to doubt his mantras or at least accepted their limitations as he flirted with the concept of fate. In this way he was a quantumist, able to live with the uncertainty principle or with the idea of Schrödinger's Cat being both dead and alive, something Einstein never truly accepted. Through thought experiments, Burroughs challenged himself more than anyone else. What more could science ask for than a dose of this type of untroubled rationality?

PROTOPLASM

XAN PRICE

"*The Liquefaction program involves the eventual merging of every-one into One Man by a process of protoplasmic absorption.*"

"*The Divisionists… literally divide. They cut off tiny bits of their flesh and grow exact replicas of themselves in embryo jelly. It seems probable, unless the process of division is halted, that eventually there will be only one replica of one sex on the planet: that is one person in the world with millions of separate bodies*"

—*Naked Lunch*

July 20, Brooklyn

Dear Pappy,

I received your message years ago, but it took me a long time to get around to reading it. Your jokes always made me laugh, but honestly I thought you were a self-indulgent old junky. However, I finally began reading your message while on a quadruple dose of those very evil antihistamines you told me about. My head was full of mucus thick as yogurt a few weeks past the expiration date, very lumpy and partially hardened into a crust. The antihistamines did almost nothing to help with the yogurt, but under their influence, your words never made more sense.

Since you've been gone, the Liquefactionist agenda has progressed exponentially. Almost everyone is eagerly offering up all their protoplasm for total absorption by Control. I've even been guilty of doing this myself on occasion. And the Divisionists are unstoppable. The replicas are cutting replicas from replicas. Everything is getting pretty goddamn thin and worn out. Nobody has much juice left inside. They've farmed it all out.

But recently I did find a very rare holdout. Not long after I read your message, I met this guy, Gus. He's a stanky hot Crustie punk who lives on the streets. I stopped to listen to him sing, and he charmed and hypnotized me with his sweet, sour music. Then we ate out each other's pits right there on his blanket in front of the LensCrafters on 14th Street. After that we got to be buddies and pretty soon we were hanging out a lot. Boy are his flavors delicious. The Liquefactionists can't touch Gus, and he refuses to share his protoplasm, even with me unfortunately. I would happily merge, as you say, Pappy, into one "gweat big blob" with him. It would be booful. But Gus is wary and suspicious, and I can't blame him. He's got what they used to call scruples. Sharing our sweat and oil and jissom is one thing, but whenever he feels my protoplasm reaching out, those ghostly fingers "straining with a blind worm hunger to enter his body, to breathe with his lungs, see with his eyes, learn the feel of his viscera" then he twitches and recoils. Does he think I'm an agent of Control? Or does he think I'm unwittingly being used by Control, and that the Liquefactionists will absorb him through me by proxy?

I have to admit that it's an unsettling possibility. And so I've been forced to take a serious look-see at all the ways I may have been co-opted by the Liquefactionists. For one thing, some years ago I gave up fighting and now carry one of their control boxes that allows them to eat my sentences. All of my words, written or spoken, are invisibly whisked away and absorbed and churned in whatever diabolical blender they use to split language apart and reassemble it into strange talismans they use to taunt and entice me. Usually, I assume that I'm strong enough to resist their titillations and temptations. But when Gus looked in my eyes, I saw what he saw, and I knew that something was not right. Part of me was not me.

What pulled me toward Gus was that he's all himself. He seemed to have sidestepped the intrusion of all forms of Control, and that was exhilarating. But then we had an experience that revealed something unexpected. During the Super Blood Moon, we went back to his tent under the BQE overpass and initiated a powerful sex magick ritual. As we labored and toiled upon each other, we were flung from the outer cosmos to the deepest maw of Tartarus, and in that frenzy, a new persona looked out through the heat in Gus's eyes. A fierce and ancient voice spoke from his mouth and told me I must bow down and prolapse my entrails before him. "I will teach you," the voice said.

Unable to move, I felt a hidden crustacean speak through my lips, "There is no room here. I am already using this body."

But Gus did not give up. We grappled and fought and pleasured each other's flesh, and trails of spit and shit stretched between our open mouths. Fire peeled us away from all the infernal jitterbugs of infection and Control. And as we teetered between chaos and self-knowledge, we found a strange and almost impossible balance, so raw and intimate it quivered on the edge of destruction, like we were wrestling on the rim of a magma chamber. I saw millions of faces in his face. That was when I felt a *sshlupp!* of something heavy squirm through him into me. Was he giving birth? Then I felt that we were being watched. The hosts and rulers, the powers and principalities of the universe crowded around us and shook their heads. "This shouldn't be possible," they said to each other. "And yet it is happening. And now it is unstoppable."

We tussled and probed for many more hours until we finally collapsed. When we unstuck our eyelids around noon, Gus said, "Wow. I don't know whether I went to outer space or Nottingham Forest."

"I think you had a baby last night."

I reached out and touched Gus's hand, but he shoved me away.

My blood stopped moving. "What's wrong?"

"So it's all come to this has it?"

"Huh?"

"I know what you were trying to do." His voice was flat and dead. I could tell he had the horrors.

Then he told me to leave, and the force of his protoplasmic core reached out and pushed me away and out of the tent. I shrank down into myself and stumbled off through the piles of garbage under the BQE overpass.

The next day I went back, but his tent was gone. So I went to the LensCrafters. He and his blanket were not there either. At home in my apartment, I paced and mooned around. My brain stopped working. Everything I heard and saw during our ritual faded out of my memory. All I knew was that I had to see Gus again. I was too jittery to stay in bed and too tired to get out of bed. It was just like what you said, Pappy, about junk sickness: "A man might die simply because he could not stand to stay in his body."

I don't fit in my own body anymore. There's too much open space inside. And it's funny how much that hurts. Gus went in there and threw out all the old useless junk and all the hitchhikers and bossy crustaceans, and now there are rooms and rooms that are clear and free. But Gus never planned to stay around for that. He doesn't stay in any place. I always knew that. It's absurd for me to want him to stay. Gus doesn't stay inside rooms. For him, that feels like Control.

He is far away by now, probably very happy on his blanket in front of a Popeye's in Topeka or Louisville or Minneapolis. Nothing makes him smile like fried chicken. But wherever he is, I still feel his hot ectoplasmic fingers pushing deep inside me and my skin still has his sickly sweet, rancid stink. I found his crusty t-shirt and tie it around my eyes when I sleep. Days and nights and days and nights, I've been speaking his name to the walls.

xoxo,
Xan

August 11, Brooklyn

Dear Pappy,

A month has passed now since Gus disappeared. A few days ago, as I was picking through a jumble of discarded books on the sidewalk, I felt a presence behind me. I stood up and a blank faced man was watching me. He was so hazy I could hardly see him. His body almost seemed to reject being seen. My antenna isn't as finely tuned as yours, Pappy, but it definitely twitched when I saw this guy. I knew exactly who he was. He was the man you told me about, the one with "the obsolete and unthinkable trade."

He stared at me, and his eyes did not blink.

"Can I help you?" I asked.

"I know what you're looking for."

"Oh yeah?"

"Yes. I can show you."

I followed him into the back of a bodega and through an alley and down a narrow staircase into a basement. He took off his shirt and unraveled a long tube from a plastic box that seemed to be fused to his flesh.

"They'll kill me if they find out I gave this to you," he said. "But you deserve to know."

The man pushed a button on top of the plastic box and a thick substance inched down the transparent tube. So, I took the tube into my mouth and drank. The walls fell away and I was thrown into great darkness where I floated in silence. Then I was surrounded by the smell of fried chicken. A smacking sound got closer and closer and there he was, gnawing on a crunchy drumstick.

"Oh Gus, I missed you."

He grinned his crafty cat-dog grin. "I never left you."

"You did. It's been awful."

"No. You don't understand. You see, I conjured you. You didn't exist before we met."

"I'm pretty sure I did."

"It's true. I created you. Don't you remember?"

I could remember lots of stuff. I remembered learning to swim as a child in an electric blue pool. I remembered chocolate mint ice cream and my sweet grandmother's rose-scented cheeks. I remembered drunk driving on Alabama turnrows and failing chemistry two years in a row. I remembered living on Saltines for a year in a New York basement and stealing cauliflower at midnight with friends in the Italian Alps.

"Gus, I'm a real person. You didn't invent me. That's got to be the most extreme gaslighting thing anybody ever said."

"I know you feel lonely, but that's not you. It's me. You only exist because of me, and I'm alone. So you feel alone too."

"Um, have you ever heard of self-other confusion?"

Gus opened his mouth and bared his teeth and, like something happening far away, I felt his fist slam up through my colon meat. "You WILL remember!" he shouted.

Thousands of voices burbled through my lips, and I saw ancient cities and abandoned planets and steaming oceans filled with waving kelp. I saw military parades and moon rockets and conquistadors and covered wagons. I saw cave men and cinnamon buns and burning buildings and happy children laughing. Somehow Gus and I were in all those places. And always looking for each other. But we never ever recognized each other. All down the ages, through every permutation of everything, we were both always around but never together. And then, in front of the LensCrafters on 14th Street, we met. And finally, for one night in his tent under the BQE, we totally bumslopped each other until we punched a hole through the Protoplasm Daddy and the Mother Cell right out into the fiery beyond. And that was when Gus gave birth to me.

I looked at him, and our eyes connected like an impossible puzzle clicking into its final position. "Yes. I remember now. You're right. I've been around for a long, long time. But I didn't finally wake up until I met you, Gus."

He leaned into me and took my lips into his mouth and his core connected to mine until our protoplasm merged. A spiral nebula exploded, and clouds of interstellar dust expanded out through the universe. So much room. So many possibilities. Who knows where insides and outsides begin and where they end?

I woke up on the pavement beside the jumble of books. My shirt was dripping with sweat and my pits were rank with that stink Gus liked so much. *If you were here, I think you would be happy,* I thought to him.

The book nearest me had a picture of a beaming, red-haired woman on the cover, holding up a drink like a toast. I didn't even look at the title. I picked up the book and took it back to my apartment.

Xoxo,
Xan

THE GREAT DEFIER

J. DANIEL STONE

I stumbled upon the work of William S. Burroughs in my early teens, a time when my reading brain was still budding, and also a time when I realized, subconsciously, that I needed more variety in books. Even at the rudimentary stages of reading for pleasure, I knew that I'd been fed books with marketed tropes and cliches targeted at an audience that I was not part of. I was bored, frustrated, and craving change. There had to be books out there that did daring things, but I'd no clue how to find them. That inspired me to change my shopping habits from commercial bookstores to mom & pop, rattrap, hole-in-the wall booksellers around New York City. St. Mark's Bookshop (closed for good), was home to every hue of punk, goth and, queerdo, where one could shop for books that reflected the counterculture, anti-establishment sentiment that was born in that part of town. Then there was The Strand, a towering tenement-like space that proffers eighteen miles worth of books, used and new. I easily got lost in its dust-laden, creaky haunted house aisles for hours, reading and learning and thriving. Argosy, Book Culture and Gryphon Bookshop (now called Westsider Rare & Used Books) spring to mind, but there are many more that have since closed for good as well.

I came across a copy of *Queer* in a used bookshop somewhere in the East Village. It was a battered, thin noodle of a book sandwiched between two mammoth titles long since erased from memory. I found myself magnetized by that title: *Queer*. Book titles and cover art are the first indicators of any book's contents, and being that I knew I was queer even at that age, in many a way other than just sexuality—fourteen years old and coming to terms with it—I very much felt like Gatsby reaching for the green light when I found this book. Like most queer boys in America, you can't just come out of the closet and find acceptance (maybe in 2021 you can more so than in 2001). I was born, bred, and raised in a working-class neighborhood of Queens, NY. Touted as the most diverse borough within all of New York City, Queens did nothing to foster a thriving gay community, at least from what I remember. It's a squat piece of land polluted by smog and ridden with swamp right beneath its uneven blacktop. But Queens also had a hidden secret, at least in the part of town where I grew up in the late Nineties and early Aughts. It was a budding source of artists and creators and thinkers, young kids (like me) who saw beyond the nine-to-five lifestyle; who dreamed loud like The Ramones in the Seventies and Eighties. Despite being the world's melting pot, Queens was a place that did not make gay people feel welcome, specifically because there had been many gay bashings and hate crimes against LGBT people. This would give any homosexual (or one figuring it out) a complex about themselves, and so when a book like *Queer* is presented, you don't just ignore it. I held the book in my hands, taking in its secret power, and opened to a random page. As a reader this is my personal test to see if an author's voice will catch my attention at any part of their book. Burroughs transported me into his personal madness without remorse. I still remember the quote that kidnapped my mind:

Death was in every cell of his body. He gave off a faint, greenish steam of decay. Lee imagined he would glow in the dark.

Until that point in my short reading career, I'd never read a charac-

ter descriptor in fiction that sucker punched me like that. Something
changed instantly within me. I felt my soul melt into those pages. *Queer*
was not only the renegade novel I'd been surreptitiously seeking in terms
of content, but it was the novel that showed me that word play was in an
author's power and prowess. Words are an author's weapon. Burroughs
proved to me that language could be altered, rearranged, and used like
a scalpel across the eyes and mind, while at the same time keeping the
reader's attention. Curious floodgates opened. From prose style, to
drugs, to keeping your enemies close, dream sequences, and the infamous cut-up method, I found myself questioning art, life, and existence
in ways that I never knew was allowed. I'd been spoon-fed a rhetoric of
how life should be lived, how books should look and read, and that boys
should be attracted to girls, et al. Burroughs helped me throw that brain
wash out the window. And thus began my infatuation and admiration
of a man who I felt matched my daredevil spirit, but also answered my
literary prayers that putting words on a page didn't have to be bound to
linear laws and tropes. Burroughs was a game-changer, proving to me
that fiction does not need to follow any sort of precedent.

They can be the beasts you always intended them to be.

From novels to screenplays, essays, and spoken word, Burroughs made
sure his readers knew that language was central to existence. Reading his fiction is like a surreal game of exquisite corpse via his myriad
worlds of drugs, prostitution, boys fucking on Ferris wheels, criminals,
jism squirting over the moon, peyote nightmares, death, and sex. Death
by sex and sexy death, plague horrors, radioactive mutants, and unim-
ageable prose styles that still dumbfound critics and readers to this day.
The beauty of Burroughs's work is that just when you think you've read
it all, you still find yourself fascinated by his gall, his passion, his ability
to "go there" at a time when it was impossible to do such. His books are

not the type you read once and never come back to; there's always some-thing to take away, no matter how many times you read them. That's a rare talent and something I try to emulate in my own work. I don't want to be pigeon-holed into the "good read" category of books where people read a book one time and never come back to it. I prefer to produce books that readers return to later in life for comfort or nostalgia or just to visit old friends. Whatever it may be.

Being the Great Defier, it only makes sense everything from his life outside of his writing to the writing itself was his way of expressing a preferred reality. It starts with how Burroughs rejected the linear. Ho-mosexuality alone betrays the laws of accepted society. But what most people don't realize is that while we may conduct our lives in a rote fashion, life is anything but linear. So why must books be? Burroughs certainly thought about that when writing. Imagine what goes through our heads from the minute we wake up to the minute we hit the sheets. We go from thinking about breakfast to suddenly being transported back into a memory because something as simple as a sound or smell can trigger that for us. Burroughs not only sought to put that brand of chaos on paper, but he succeeded more than anyone in his literary circle. Consequently, this dark divination demonstrates his influence on the horror genre. A lot of his subject matter is horrific; he wrote about cannibal mutants, centipedes, viruses ravaging society, alien invaders and much more. While there may not be many horror authors, we can speak of who have publicly admitted to being directly influenced by Burroughs (maybe not the ones I pay attention to), a few come to mind immediately, Kathe Koja (*Skin*, 1993, Dell Abyss), Caitlin R. Kiernan (*Silk*, 1998, ROC), Clive Barker (*Books of Blood*, 1984, Ace/Putnam) and Gemma Files (*Kissing Carrion*, 2003, Prime Books). These authors all have taken influence whether they know it or not from Burroughs's visceral corporeality. Horror auteur David Cronenberg is an obvious Burroughs disciple. *The Fly* and *Videodrome* bubble with Burroughs's badass, almost impossible imagination. And then there's Cronenberg's insane adaption of *Naked Lunch*, which doesn't get called horror enough.

What really is horror? Is it gore? Is it psychological? Is it a decayed romance? Horror is every genre encompassed in one. Burroughs worked and expanded this horror without even knowing it. Not in the supernatural sense, but in a *horrific* sense. He's penned some of the most grotesque scenes in the history of literature. Gaping jaw, bug-eyed, terrifying descriptions that still fill me with shock and envy when I read them. Most people will pass it off as gore for gore's sake, or nonsensically explicit, but Burroughs put every single word down with purpose.

Take this scene from *Naked Lunch*:

"The hypochondriac lassoes the passer-by and administers a straitjacket and starts talking about his rotting septum: 'An awful purulent discharge is subject to flow out…just wait 'til you see it.'"

Or this scene from the lunacy that is his final novel, *The Western Lands*:

"At dinner there is this mealy-assed Bible fart with his hunched-over fat lump of a son, looks like he is sculpted out of rancid lard."

William S. Burroughs was the most innovative and influential author of his time (and maybe even today). His work was published before the hippie culture was prevalent, before the summer of love came and went. Much has been written about Burroughs's influence in rock music. He coined the phrase "heavy metal", a genre of music created by Black Sabbath. It's possible Sabbath didn't have any interest in Burroughs. They were more of a Lovecraftian band, but they might not have had a name for the musical genre they created if Burroughs had not written about "Uranian Willy, The Heavy Metal Kid." I would consider myself a disciple of heavy metal and rock n' roll. Much like Burroughs's fiction, heavy metal was a genre of music that flipped the bird to more widely accepted forms of music. Bands like Tool, King Crimson, Rush, and Pink Floyd (known for unconventional time signatures and lyrical content) are the actual sound of Burroughs's words. Heavier bands such as Black Sabbath, Nine Inch Nails, and Ministry (our Great Defier has a cameo in the "Just One Fix" video) are filled with a dark mystery that keeps people wanting more, and the same goes for our unsung queer hero.

Lastly, when I was in my early twenties, I decided to tattoo WSB on to the backside of my wrist, my writing hand, because I knew that Burroughs would keep changing/inspiring my life until the day I take my own dirt nap. Whenever I look at those three little letters, I can't help but to think how many lives he's influenced, how many worlds he created; he showed us queers the way. I dared to follow. You should too.

Rest in Perversion.

"How I hate those who are dedicated to producing conformity."
—William S. Burroughs

NAKED LUNCH AS INITIATION RITE

JUSTIN ADDEO

> *I can feel the heat closing in, feel them out there making their moves,*
> *setting up their devil doll stool pigeons, crooning over my spoon and*
> *dropper I throw away at Washington Square Station, vault a turn-*
> *stile and two flights down the iron stares, catch an uptown A train..*
> —Naked Lunch

The moment you open the pages of *Naked Lunch*, you are submerged in the world of Burroughs. You are already a fugitive on the run in a laboratory rat maze amidst a bewildering claustrophobic architecture. Burroughs is at once the guide and the designer. No sooner do you narrowly evade undercover agents in one urban cul-de-sac then you are in flight again. You are led directly into the surgical hands of some fresh new hell of dystopian social engineering. The occasional, sinister soliloquy by the enigmatic Dr. Benway is all you have to guide you. He explains in the driest of irony possible the monstrous logic of it all. It is by no means an uplifting read, but you do feel honored to be among the elect initiated into the hip gnosis of this underworld/otherworld—this interzone—that only the permanent outsider of the junky or the queer could be privy to.

At the time I first dipped my very stoned, twenty-one-year-old brain into this maze back in the early Nineties, I was very much not among the elect. I just thought it sounded cool to read aloud to my other stoned compatriots in the crummy, off-campus housing. My roommates and I sat around blasting Cypress Hill and ripping hits from a bong concocted ad hoc from beakers and tubes. My friend and housemate, an environmental science major, had lifted the hardware from the university laboratory. Also, I had been fascinated by the Beats since high school. There was something of a renaissance in an interest in their literary antics and experiments that influenced so much of the culture at the time. It was also the last decade any of the original Beat trio were alive, Burroughs, the oldest, being the last to pass away after Ginsberg. I knew something was going on as its influence, and more specifically his influence, was once again slithering its tentacles outward from the sphere of literature to music as it had done cyclically since the Sixties. Every alt rock band on the planet wanted a photo op with Burroughs. The height of the absurdist eruption of Burroughs into Gen X consciousness though was his appearance in a Nike commercial doing his "word virus" spiel. He skipped no beats nor was he flummoxed by the irony. Burroughs was ever the master of deadpan cool in all situations.

The summer just before I dropped out of college for a few years I was living alone in a cramped, sweatbox of an upstairs apartment in the upstate New York college town of Plattsburgh that bordered Canada. I had a few select books by Hesse, Joyce, and Burroughs, and CDs by P.J. Harvey, Nirvana, My Bloody Valentine, the *Pulp Fiction* soundtrack, and *Spare Ass Annie*, Burroughs's collaboration with the experimental rap band, The Disposable Heroes of Hiphoprisy. This media kept me company as my mind drifted into the void that I crammed full of scribblings. I thought these scribblings had made me a writer. What a conceit! As I said before I was not among the elect yet. I was not possessed of the "Ugly Spirit" as Burroughs. That would come later in the next decade and a half during my descent into addiction to speedballs. The

addiction emerged after my divorce. It at once fueled and ultimately ruined a musical project with a friend of mine. I had farther sunk into the
world of the junky. It was indeed like another dimension, one hidden
in plain sight. One decipherable to the elect to gain access through the
magical language and "open sesames" of the slang that only we trafficked
in and knew the code to. For the time being, though, I was just a stoner
student English major with no direction in life and a headful of racing
emotions and pretentious longings to be an artist of some kind.

But to return to the world of Burroughs, as I said before, it is a
realm only the elect gain access to, which is not just the junky on the run
but also the queer. Outside of one kink that has blossomed in my life in
the last few years—the desire to watch my woman have sex with other
men—my sexuality has been for most of my life fairly conventional. I
am straight, not gay. Gay men, however, have always been among my
most revered literary and artistic heroes. Besides Burroughs, Jean Genet
comes in at the top of the list. John Waters and Pasolini in film. Rimbaud, Oscar Wilde, Basho... the list goes on. However, I almost feel that
this point is somewhat moot. Yes, Burroughs was a gay man in a society institutionally hostile to homosexuals, but the fundamental insight
one gleans from reading him is that *all* sexuality is queer sexuality. That
is, in the original sense of the word of being strange or odd. (Is this
the genesis of that famous Kurt Cobain lyric?). We aren't simply alienated from our sexuality because of societal repression, although there
are plenty of examples of that in *Naked Lunch*, but that sexuality and
to a greater extent our flesh in general is essentially alien to us, an alien
force undermining the rational, conscious mind, always mutating and
treacherous to the individual will in its futile attempts at controlling its
errant impulses and fantasies. It has a life of its own, its own agenda and
aspirations. In these sections from a particularly infamous passage from
Naked Lunch, the insurgent nature of the flesh is laid bare in a hilari-
ously surreal anecdote by the loopy Dr. Benway:

After a while the ass started talking on its own. He would go in without anything prepared and his ass would ad-lib and toss the gags back at him every time.

Then it developed sort of teeth-like little raspy incurving hooks and started eating. He thought this was cute at first and built an act around it, but the asshole would eat its way through his pants and start talking on the street, shouting out it wanted equal rights. It would get drunk, too, and have crying jags nobody loved it and it wanted to be kissed the same as any other mouth. Finally it talked all the time day and night, you could hear him for blocks screaming at it to shut up, and beating it with his fist, and sticking candles up it, but nothing did any good and the asshole said to him: 'It's you who will shut up in the end. Not me. Because we don't need you around here any more. I can talk and eat and shit.

That's the sex that passes the censor, squeezes through between bureaus, because there's a space between. In popular songs and Grade B movies, giving away the basic American rottenness, spurting out like breaking boils, throwing out globs of that un-D.T. to fall anywhere and grow into some degenerate cancerous life-form, reproducing a hideous random image. Some would be entirely made of penis-like erectile tissue, others viscera barely covered over with skin, clusters of three and four eyes together, crisscross of mouths and assholes, human parts shaken around and poured out any way they fell.

This a perfect parody of the plight of the minority, the worker, or the oppressed in a liberal democracy, the literal bottom demanding equal rights and the brain representing the unbending bourgeoisie incapable of containing the uprising and overthrown in the end, its neural

supremacy quarantined in the gulag of the skull. It is also a potent metaphor for the internal struggle of a closeted gay man when confronted
with his homosexual desires that won't go away, no matter how much
he tries to contain or conceal them. They just literally eat through his
clothes—his façade of normality and self-control—to out him to the
world. In the end, we see the whole corpus becomes mutable, gelati-
nous, and even amorphous. It takes on the ever-transforming, formless-
ness of what the philosopher Deleuze envisioned the body without or-
gans to be. Total anarchy is the true nature of sexual desire. And yet for
this very reason, we also see in *Naked Lunch* that primal chaos of the
libido that evades all sorts of control both individual and bureaucratic.
It makes it paradoxically susceptible to the infinite manipulations of the
skilled technocrat such as Dr. Benway, who no doubt is a stand-in for
the psychiatrists of Burroughs's days, those who espoused with clinical optimism that homosexuality could be cured through electroshock
therapy.

For the human organism isn't just a sack of ooze that slips through
your fingers only to absorb you amoeba-like in the end. It is a machine
that can be tweaked and tinkered with. What McLuhan or Deleuze
would reiterate later, Burroughs speaks of presciently here in 1959:
"The study of thinking machines teaches us more about the brain than
we can learn by introspective methods. Western man is externalizing
himself in the form of gadgets." And truly throughout *Naked Lunch*,
bodies are found writhing in uncontrollable orgasms as they are probed
by electrodes at the base of the spine in laboratories run by shady governmental and corporate agencies. These shadowy and nefarious agents
are bent on totalitarian control through operant conditioning of the
sexual responses of the imprisoned. These poor saps become the guinea
pigs on the first step of fashioning a new humanity by a scientific elite.
And we drift unknowingly amidst a particular social order in our nightmarish cruise through the many terrifying, vistas, cities, and nations

that populate the bewildering, complex geography of Interzone.

Between the Scylla of intrinsic biological anarchy and the Charybdis of extrinsic sexual control by the experts, the Ulysses of the initiated elect must proceed ever so cautiously through the world of Burroughs. Burroughs protected himself on this journey by using an Orgone box to recharge his life force. The Orgone box was a contraption that William Reich, the vanguard leader of the sexual revolution, purported to be able to trap and harness a cosmic energy known as Orgone that supposedly revitalized the user. The ravings of a crank or a persecuted genius? Only the initiated elect can deign to say as they navigate this frontier. Maybe we will even get to the cheese at the end of that maze one day and be able to say to the nosy Philistine who would moralize to us one of their trite, ineffectual solutions to any of the social or existential ills that plague us, those who lack any and all experience on the matter and therefore who are incapable of seeing who they are and what they do that is the essence of that *Naked Lunch*: "You were not there for the beginning. You will not be there for the end. Your knowledge of what is going on can only be superficial and relative."

"I FELT I WAS ALMOST CHANNELING HIM WHEN I WAS WRITING": AN INTERVIEW WITH DAVID CRONENBERG

BRIAN ALESSANDRO

Filmmaker David Cronenberg relives the experience of befriending Burroughs as he reconceptualized Naked Lunch *into a film.*

David Cronenberg adapted Naked Lunch *into a feature film in 1991. I first saw his unique cinematic interpretation the year it was released when I was only fourteen years old. I never could have imagined as I exited the theater that thirty years later, I would be interviewing Cronenberg as a pandemic raged. It all felt too constructed, as though the universe had assembled various themes and preoccupations from his corpus for this surreal moment.*

Like Burroughs, Cronenberg's creations focus intensely on what it means to be stuck in a body. His entire oeuvre consists of close dissections of mortality, injury, disease, decay, disfigurement, modification, and death. It's not surprising that he would ultimately end up making Naked Lunch *into a movie. And a quite corporeal one at that. In many ways, both Burroughs and Cronenberg have captured better than most of their contemporaries in literature and cinema the bittersweet sensation of being alive. Perhaps in their cases more bitter than sweet.*

BRIAN ALESSANDRO: What initially drew you to *Naked Lunch?*

DAVID CRONENBERG: It was basically the English producer Jeremy Thomas who suggested that we do a movie of *Naked Lunch*. He said he knew William Burroughs, and he could introduce us, and so on and so on. And so, I started to think about it, because I was a Burroughs fan, but of course I hadn't thought about turning anything he had written into a movie, really. But Jeremy really had the vision that it could be done. That was the basis of it.

ALESSANDRO: Had you read other works by Burroughs at the time?

CRONENBERG: Yes, I had read a few things, yeah.

ALESSANDRO: Many people said the novel was "unfilmable," famously, of course. Were you ever concerned that they might be right?

CRONENBERG: No, because my understanding, especially since my first adaptation had been Stephen King's *Dead Zone*, and I realized pretty immediately—and of course I had seen many, many movies that were adaptations of books—and I realized very early on that you can't really adapt a book. All adaptations are unfilmable, basically. You just don't have to worry about it. What you're really doing is recreating something in a different medium that will automatically alter everything. What you hope for is that it will convey the feeling, the tone, perhaps, the ambiance of the novel, without necessarily being faithful to any of the details, particularly, and with *The Dead Zone*, for example, people thought it was very faithful to the book, but actually it was not very faithful to the book in terms of details, but the tone, it resonated, it felt right, it looked like New England, it felt like America, even though it was all shot in Canada, so I wasn't really worried about that because to me it's going to be a project that involves original creation and you don't really have to worry about it. Of course, there are always going to be fans of the book that hate what you've done and there will be people who've never read the books who like what you've done, so it's not really something I worried about at all, ultimately.

ALESSANDRO: You mentioned that while writing the screenplay, you felt a moment of synergy between your screenwriting style and Burroughs's prose style, and you even joked, "I'll just write his next book." Can you say more about that moment, that synergy?

CRONENBERG: Yeah, it's interesting. I always assumed I was going to be a novelist, not a filmmaker. Two of the writers who had a strong influence on me in terms of style were very different writers. One was Vladimir Nabokov and the other was William Burroughs, and of course, they both come from very different places. Their approach to writing couldn't be more different, but I still felt somehow that I was influenced by both of them in terms of my writing. I could easily fall into the mindset of Burroughs as he wrote, the sort of flow of his writing. The vernacular. It's, of course, very, very American. I felt very connected to it, and when I was writing, after I had figured out how I was going to approach the structure of the movie, and I can tell you about that soon, I felt that I was almost channeling Burroughs when I was writing. A lot of the dialogue is directly from his novels, not all of them *Naked Lunch*, and he had such a great grasp of American vernacular. He gave it its own tone and yet was true to American speech. I really felt that once I had figured out the structure everything would flow, and it did. When I first met Burroughs and we chatted, and I liked him very much, I didn't know what to expect, because I had seen him performing in Toronto and his stage presence is very kind of sarcastic and cynical and kind of mean and kind of scary, you know. But when I met him, I found that he was incredibly sweet and kind, and that's my experience of him. And so, eventually I ended up traveling with him to Tangier, and I found him to be consistently like that, with me, anyway, he was very polite and warm and interested and friendly and sweet, so I hadn't expected that. The main moment for me was when I said to him, "William," you know his close friends called him "Bill," but I called him "William," as others younger than him tended to do. I said, "William, the only way I can make this movie is if I can include the writing of the book in the movie and also use some material from some of your other books, particularly, the book *Queer*, and I said, in particular, I need to address the killing of your wife. If you don't want me to do that I would completely understand, but I can't really do the movie otherwise." And he said, "I don't really separate my work from my life, go ahead." So, at that point I had my structure and from there it was not that difficult to write the screenplay, but I have to say, I did a lot of reading around it, I mean by the time I was writing it, I had inundated my brain with "Burroughsiana." I still have an entire bookshelf that is just filled with stuff about all the people around Burroughs, you know, Jane and Paul Bowles, Ginsberg, Kerouac, everybody, and I just read voluminously about them and also their work, so I was really very familiar with that whole generation and that movement in literature, and so I was very prepared, I mean extremely prepared for the writing of the screenplay, and a lot of it, of course, went into that because it deals with his adventures in Tangier at Interzone and so on.

ALESSANDRO: I was just going to ask you about how you went about incorporating aspects of Burroughs's life as well as components from his other fiction and turning it into an adaptation as well as a biopic. And to that point, many people have called the film metatextual? What does that mean to you?

CRONENBERG: It means nothing to me.

(*We both laugh.*)

CRONENBERG: It means nothing. I mean basically you can examine it from an academic, literary point of view, and honestly there is value in that and as a former academic I have a lot of respect for that approach, but it does not factor into the way I wrote it. The writing was all image and emotion and basically getting inside the creativity of Burroughs and the people around him, as well, and trying to find a way to embody that in physical things on screen. Tell me, what does it mean to you?

ALESSANDRO: I think it sort of means what you had explained previously, about how you drew from his other texts like *Queer* and some of the episodes in his life, biographical detail that you pulled into the adaptation. It went beyond *Naked Lunch* as a text.

CRONENBERG: Okay, yes! Meta ... beyond! So, yes! And as I said because as vast as the world within the book *Naked Lunch* is, it wasn't enough for me to make a structure, and I really did need to expand outside the book in order to encompass the book.

ALESSANDRO: The characters of Hank and Martin are based on Jack Kerouac and Allen Ginsberg. Is this correct?

CRONENBERG: Yes.

ALESSANDRO: What did Ginsberg say about your portrayal of him?

CRONENBERG: No, no, I never met him. I think I read somewhere that he and another, I'm trying to remember the name of this very seminal figure in the Beat and post-Beat movement. Ginsberg and this man had seen the movie and were discussing it.

ALESSANDRO: Was it Herbert Huncke?

CRONENBERG: No.

ALESSANDRO: Ferlinghetti? Lawrence Ferlinghetti?

CRONENBERG: Nope. It wasn't Ferlinghetti. You know, the Merry Pranksters guy.

ALESSANDRO: Oh, Ken Kesey!

CRONENBERG: I think it was Ken Kesey, yeah. I had sort of heard ... You know, I have no idea what they would think. I must tell you, I found that the novelists of the time were not very tuned into cinema, at all. I mean they were not movie people. They didn't have movie references in their work. Their references were all literary. And to me they really didn't have—I mean, of course, they could respond to the movie, emotionally. But I felt that they didn't have the equipment to make a truly interesting critical appraisal of the movie because they knew nothing about film technique, film history, I mean they seemed to be pretty ignorant about that.

ALESSANDRO: The characters of Tom and Joan Frost are based on Paul Bowles and his wife, Jane. What did Paul Bowles say about his portrayal?

CRONENBERG: See, that's the thing, I met Paul in Tangier with Burroughs and that was fantastic. We were at the El Minzah Hotel, and we went and had dinner with Paul Bowles and to see him and Burroughs see each other, they probably hadn't seen each other in fifteen or seventeen years, or something like that, because Bowles would never leave Tangier, and Burroughs hadn't been there since then. It was kind of like two old gunfighters. They were kind of friendly but wary of each other, you know, and it was very exciting to see these two legendary guys and I really had great affection for both of them. Of course, I didn't know Bowles other than that, but we did go to his apartment for some drinks and stuff. This was before we made the movie. I went to Tangier with my production designer Carol Spier and with Jeremy Thomas and with Burroughs and James Grauerholz, William's personal assistant, and it was really exciting to go there and walking the streets and reacquainting himself with Tangier and we were hoping to shoot there and we were actually looking at locations and finding places that would work for Interzone and, in fact, I'm looking at a photo right now that my cinematographer Peter Suschitzky took of the very room and apparently the very table that Burroughs sat at when he was in the apartment he had written some of *Naked Lunch*. It's a beautiful photo. I can't vouch for its total authenticity, but Burroughs said, "Yeah, yeah, that's where I was." Then the Gulf War happened, and we almost had to cancel the movie because suddenly you couldn't fly over the Mediterranean at all, and the bombs were falling. And that's when I said to Jeremy, "We could do this in my city of Toronto. We could do the whole movie in Canada." Interzone is, of course, an invented place. It's not really Tangier, so we got some camels and we created Interzone in Toronto, and I think successfully because there is a hallucinatory element in the film as there is in the novel, so it didn't have to be a documentary on Tangier. It had to be Interzone. I never then went back to Tangier, and never met Paul Bowles again and did not hear if he even saw the movie or if he had, what he thought of it. I have no idea.

ALESSANDRO: You mentioned that you had asked William if it would be okay to integrate aspects of his life, including the killing of his wife, Joan Vollmer. Did he ever have any reservations about including that particular aspect?

CRONENBERG: Not at all. And of course, in *Queer*, he discusses it at length and so it's not as though he hadn't addressed it in his novels, like it was something that was always repressed in his life. I mean, you can play psychologist and suggest all kinds of things, but you can't accuse him of not talking about it. So, obviously by the time I was talking to him about it he was quite cool about it. He never expressed any regrets about ... also once he saw the movie, he never expressed any regrets about allowing me to do that.

ALESSANDRO: What did he say about the film?

CRONENBERG: Well, he was very positive about it. To me! Now, there is a gentlemanly aspect to William. It's possible that he was just being polite. But you know he did come to the film set as we were shooting and he loved the insect typewriters, which I invented, because he wasn't really an insect kind of guy. And he said he liked it. Now I have heard that he has expressed to some people that I didn't really understand the queer culture of the time. Who am I to deny that? I have to say that in *Queer*, he does discuss his ambivalence to his gayness at the time of writing *Naked Lunch*, and I felt that I have to say that I was pretty accurate in focusing on that particular moment of time in his life when he still had ambivalence about his own gayness. Other than that, I can't say very much.

ALESSANDRO: I just want to go a bit deeper into that. *Naked Lunch* explores queer themes, implicitly. You followed it up with *M Butterfly*, which explores queer themes explicitly. Was it difficult tackling queer themes cinematically in the early Nineties? What was the response like by both gay and straight audiences and critics?

CRONENBERG: It's never been a problem for me. Thinking about it or dealing with it. In fact, in my first two underground films, *Stereo* and *Crimes of The Future*, there's all kinds of gender sort of blurring and so on, and part of that was because I was improvising with an actor, a couple of actors, who were gay, and I wanted that in the movies, so, in fact, I remember having a screening of *Stereo*, my first movie, and I think I was screening it in Montreal, and a young man came up to me, and he's flirting with me, and he said, "Well, you're gay, aren't you? It's obvious from this movie that you're gay." And I said, "Well, actually, I'm not, but you know, I'm flattered that you think I'm attractive." Obviously, there is that element in a lot of the things I was doing, and also the New York underground cinema, because of Andy Warhol and Kenneth Anger, there was a lot of gay imagery and stuff, and in Toronto, we are very influenced by the New York underground, and so you couldn't really play in that field of art if you were sort of freaked out by gayness, so I never had a problem with it. And of course, that continued with all of my work, because I find it a part of human sexuality, and I find human sexuality to be fascinating and complex.

ALESSANDRO: And I do have to credit you, throughout your entire oeuvre, I feel like you've explored the fluidity of sexuality before it became trendy. You were like twenty years ahead of the curve there, maybe even thirty years ahead.

CRONENBERG: Well, thank you. Is there a way I can monetize that?

(*We both laugh.*)

ALESSANDRO: Well, I'll definitely keep it in the interview in the book. For whatever my opinion is worth!

CRONENBERG: Well, it's true. It's worth a lot, I'm sure.

ALESSANDRO: Thank you. You directed Debbie Harry in *Videodrome* in 1983. She and Chris Stein were also close with Burroughs. Did she ever discuss their friendship?

CRONENBERG: I knew that they knew each other, that they were friends with each other, that they had respect for each other. And I know that Burroughs liked the way that Debbie Harry looked and performed. Other than that, we didn't really, there wasn't a lot there. She had a whole life involved with him that I don't know anything about.

ALESSANDRO: *eXistenZ* feels inspired by both Burroughs and Philip K. Dick, but it's an original screenplay. Were they influences?

CRONENBERG: It could well be. It's really impossible for me to say because I had been reading tons of science fiction as a kid, and ironically, I had not ever read Philip K. Dick. I came to Philip K. Dick late in life, even though I used to read *Galaxy Magazine* and *Fantasy and Science Fiction Magazine* and *Astounding Science Fiction Magazine*, and for some reason I never read anything of Philip K. Dick, even though he was so prolific, and eventually [after *eXistenz*] I sort of fell into it and read a million of his books. It makes sense that one could see similarities to themes and stuff, but I was really thinking of video games because I was also a computer nerd from an early age and the whole video game, and even in *Videodrome*, and even when I made *Videodrome*, I had not read any of Philip K. Dick. I don't feel it was a direct influence from Burroughs or Dick.

ALESSANDRO: Influence is a tricky subject, and I have one more question about it. Your debut novel, *Consumed*, has been favorably compared to the work of Burroughs. Did he influence you as a novelist?

CRONENBERG: I really don't think so. I would say [the novel is] maybe even a little more Nabokov than Burroughs. Because it's a little academic. But once again, you absorb these things and they're in your DNA now and we know now that your DNA can be changed and altered, so who knows. I certainly wasn't thinking consciously of Burroughs when I was writing it.

ALESSANDRO: If you could adapt one more Burroughs book which one would it be and why?

CRONENBERG: You know, I am so far away from my days of intense Burroughs research, that I can't really honestly, accurately answer that question. I'd have to go back and think about, you know, I'd have to look at my bookshelf and look at the books I've read and say wait a minute was it *Cities of the Red Night*? No, I just don't know. I do like the title, *Cities of The Red Night*, though.

"HE WAS VERY SEDUCTIVE": AN INTERVIEW WITH DEBBIE HARRY AND CHRIS STEIN

BRIAN ALESSANDRO

Debbie Harry and Chris Stein share intimate moments with Burroughs, revealing the breadth of his influence on the music world.

Like Burroughs, Debbie Harry and Chris Stein, the founding members of Blondie, of course, were icons and iconoclasts. Creating their own myths while busting up the molds set by their forebears. The trio were close friends throughout the Eighties and the Nineties.

BRIAN ALESSANDRO: When and how did you both meet William S. Burroughs?

CHRIS STEIN: From Victor! There was a period where Victor was making a lot of introductions with Bill and everybody else. (Victor Bockris is a biographer who wrote primarily about Burroughs, Andy Warhol, and Muhammad Ali, and who also between 1977-1983 worked with Burroughs at The Bunker.)

ALESSANDRO: Was this during the early Eighties?

STEIN: Yes, early Eighties. Yeah.

ALESSANDRO: Had you read Burroughs's work before meeting him? What did you think of his writing?

STEIN: Yeah, I was always a fan. I had read *Naked Lunch* earlier. I had one of those copies of *Junky* that was reversible. You know, there was one book on one side and another book on the other side. I had bought it at a thrift store. I had read it a bunch of times.

ALESSANDRO: How often did you all see each other?

STEIN: Intermittently. Not a lot. I hung out with him quite a bit after a while.

ALESSANDRO: You had seen him more regularly than Debbie, right?

DEBBIE HARRY: Oh yeah, absolutely. Yeah.

STEIN: When we were living on The Bowery, I don't think we knew him. We lived like a block away from where the Bunker is.

HARRY: Yeah.

STEIN: I don't think we met him until after that, but we might have run into him. Not sure.

ALESSANDRO: Did his literature influence any aspect of Blondie?

STEIN: Maybe some of the surrealist elements, you know, but I'm not sure.

ALESSANDRO: These sorts of things sometimes find themselves in the subconscious.

HARRY: Absolutely. That's what I was going to say. His influence spreads much further than a direct ... it's indirect, but it's all encompassing somehow.

ALESSANDRO: Had you read his work, Debbie, before you formed Blondie?

HARRY: I think I had, you know, probably looked at *Naked Lunch*. And I had a funny connection with *Naked Lunch* because of David Cronenberg writing the screenplay. So, there was sort of a link for me in that respect.

ALESSANDRO: Did Bill ever tell you what he thought of Blondie? Was he a fan? Did he ever come to a show?

(We all laugh.)

STEIN: I guess he must have. I don't know if he came to a Blondie show. I feel like he must have. I'm not sure.

ALESSANDRO: I just interviewed David Cronenberg about adapting *Naked Lunch*.

HARRY: Really?!

ALESSANDRO: Yes. Debbie, he told me that Burroughs had a great respect for your artistry and that you two had a long history before he'd met him in the early Nineties. Why do you suppose Burroughs had such appeal with filmmakers, artists, and musicians? Maybe even more so than with other writers?

STEIN: It's kind of intangible, you know. Something about his mindset that was far reaching and maybe he was always writing screenplays. Who the fuck knows? Maybe there are things that can't be made for another twenty years yet, you know.

ALESSANDRO: That would be amazing.

HARRY: In a way his visual images were, you know, especially for a director, it would sort of be very juicy but yet it would leave a lot of room for you to create your own images as well, and it's very sort of seductive. Very seductive.

ALESSANDRO: I can see that. David [Cronenberg] said—

STEIN: There's a rhythm, too! There was a musical underpinning to the writing.

ALESSANDRO: David actually said the same thing. He said that when he was adapting *Naked Lunch*, he was thinking in terms of images and feelings rather than a literal adaptation.

HARRY: Yes, absolutely. Yes.

ALESSANDRO: I've read that he was something of a mentor to you both. Can you tell me about that?

STEIN: Yeah, for sure! We had a bunch of stuff in common. I was on methadone for many years, so we kind of shared that and I was also a big knife fanatic. I collect knives. Have you ever seen that picture of Bill where his eyes are half closed and he's wielding a gigantic sword?

ALESSANDRO: *(Through laughter)* Yes, yeah, I have!

(Harry laughs heartily.)

STEIN: That's at our house!

ALESSANDRO: Very cool.

STEIN: That's a sword by a guy named Tom Maringer who was a great knife maker and that was at our place on 72nd street, when we had a big, fancy townhouse at one point.

ALESSANDRO: Debbie, can you tell me a little bit about how he might have been a mentor to you?

HARRY: Other than the fact that, you know, I respected him and his ... I don't know ...the awe with which people spoke of him and how the artistic community or world held him. I think that that sort of magical reputation was very, very exciting and attractive to me. Plus, you know in terms of just in the flesh practical experience, I had a great fondness for John Giorno, and John and he were old friends, old compatriots, and whatever, and so I think ... John was a lot easier for me to understand and to sort of get close to. He was a ... I don't know ... he was a totally different personality, but he was part of the way that we got to hang out with Bill, initially. It was at John's Bunker. And so, you know, I don't feel ... unfortunately, I'm a woman, and I don't know that I ever felt completely ... I don't know. I don't know if I ever really understood him, completely.

ALESSANDRO: Interesting.

HARRY: I do remember once that we were at this dinner party, and he was holding my little dog and I—

ALESSANDRO: I just read about that in *Face It*.

HARRY: Yeah. So, you know, he really loved my little dog, so I felt that that must mean that he really liked me.

(*Harry laughs.*)

STEIN: For me, he was a very positive guy.

HARRY: Oh, absolutely, I'm not saying that he was negative, at all.

STEIN: No, no, I'm just saying, I just mean that that was part of the attraction and the mentor aspect. His positivity. He's been through so much shit. And he always had this sort of sparkle about him and forward, upward motion.

HARRY: Yeah, I never felt that he was being judgmental in any way.

STEIN: No, no!

HARRY: I didn't have a lot to share with him, experience-wise, you know. The other thing that I remember clearly was that he and Chris have a way of speaking where they don't move their lips.

(*Everyone laughs.*)

HARRY: They speak with very minimal mouth movements, and Bill would also [imitating Burroughs's gravelly voice] "talk kind of like this" ... and I never really understood much of what he was saying!

ALESSANDRO: Okay, oh wow, that's interesting.

HARRY: So that was a problem, you know. A physical problem for, you know, having been in a rock band for so many years.

ALESSANDRO: Oh sure. I love that you both said he was positive! I think the perception of him in pop culture is that he was misanthropic and nihilistic, maybe, and we ...

STEIN: No, no, he was totally, you know, ploughing ahead at all times.

ALESSANDRO: That's a great insight. Can you tell me more about what it was like in The Bunker?

STEIN: It was a little formal.

HARRY: I think they were well aware of ... that their sort of innocence had long gone and so the Bunker, you'd say, "we're going to the Bunker," and everybody in the world knew what that meant, you know.

ALESSANDRO: Sure. What was it like spending time at his Lawrence, Kansas house?

STEIN: Well, we were on tour and we went to what they called the Stone House first, and then I had that long fucking illness where I didn't leave Manhattan for like four years or something crazy like that. I don't think I even went to Brooklyn. The first place I went ... I asked

Bill if I could come and stay with him, and so I went down there. And stayed for about two weeks. That was a great experience.

ALESSANDRO: Had you gone, too, Debbie?

HARRY: I went once, I think.

STEIN: Yeah, we have pictures of us shooting with him, but that was at the Stone House, which was some old Civil War mill or something.

HARRY: Yeah, I remember going and shooting in the barn—

STEIN: Yeah!

HARRY: You know, he hung up these targets—the targets were great—and we took some targets away with us.

ALESSANDRO: Do you still have them?

STEIN: Yeah! Sure!

ALESSANDRO: Were they the basic targets, the standard ones, or did he put up something eccentric?

STEIN: I know of several other people who have targets from Bill. It was kind of this rite of passage thing.

ALESSANDRO: Chris, you and Burroughs discussed war and weapons quite a bit. Can you distill the essence of your conversations regarding those topics?

STEIN: I interviewed him for Andy's [Warhol] little TV show, he used to do this TV show called *Andy Warhol's 15 Minutes*, and you could find it on YouTube.

ALESSANDRO: It was on MTV, I think.

HARRY: Yeah, it was MTV. MTV!

STEIN: There's a clip of me and Bill on there discussing war, and he compares war to almost a natural phenomenon which is just a sort of cleansing, the universe cleansing, like the waves, the waves coming on shore, that was kind of what he thought warfare is.

ALESSANDRO: Debbie, I just finished your memoir, *Face It*, which was compelling, direct, and moving, by the way, and in it you mention a tribute to Burroughs that you played in Lawrence, Kansas, alongside Patti Smith, Philip Glass, and Laurie Anderson. Can you tell me more about that show?

STEIN: The Nova Convention. We played at the Nova Convention. We had Gary [Lachman, AKA Valentine] at that, if I remember correctly.

HARRY: That was such a long time ago.

ALESSANDRO: Do you remember when?

STEIN: It was before we put the band back together. [1996].

ALESSANDRO: Debbie, in *Face It*, there's a great photo of you with Burroughs and his quote, "Love? What is it? Most natural painkiller that there is." I just had an essay about coming out of the closet, *Naked Lunch*, and experimenting with hallucinogens published in *Lambda Literary*. In *Face It*, you wrote that you and Chris, like Burroughs, had done heroin. Did you and Burroughs ever discuss your experiences?

HARRY: I don't remember doing that, no.

STEIN: Not directly, you know. Indirectly. I definitely talked with him about methadone. He was a proponent of it at that time. Up until the end, you know.

HARRY: I think that … just as a major overall statement, you could probably talk with Bill about anything.

ALESSANDRO: He was very open, huh?

HARRY: Yeah.

ALESSANDRO: And he had experienced so much.

HARRY: Yeah! He certainly was not judgmental.

ALESSANDRO: That's great to hear. At one point, in *Face It*, you share that you thought Chris in the early Eighties might have had AIDS when he was very sick with pemphigus vulgaris.

STEIN: [*Correcting my pronunciation of the illness and then:*] It's Latin for blisters.

ALESSANDRO: Burroughs wrote thematically about disease and decay for decades. Since the bulk of your friendship with him was in the Eighties, did he ever discuss AIDS with you? In so many ways, he seemed to have predicted it in his work.

STEIN: I can't really remember discussing with him things that were in the books and his philosophy so much. Conversations were probably a little more mundane and about weapons and stuff like that.

HARRY: I think it was more about daily lives and not so much about theory or philosophy but in respect to you know … daily living and things we were experiencing, that would reflect the basic philosophical position, but not so directly put, you know.

ALESSANDRO: Debbie, regarding *Videodrome* [Cronenberg's 1983 film in which she starred], did you and David ever discuss Burroughs?

HARRY: No, but I presented David with the New York Film Critics Award for his screenplay of *Naked Lunch*.

ALESSANDRO: Oh, how nice.

HARRY: Yeah, and I felt particularly honored to do that. I have no idea how it happened, but I remember going to the ceremony and presenting the award and I had total respect for both of these people and to be the presenter I felt, "Wow, this is really hot shit," [laughter] but it's a great screenplay.

STEIN: Did you read Cronenberg's novel [*Consumed*]? It's pretty great!

ALESSANDRO: I asked him about that, as well, if Burroughs had inspired him at all, and he said probably subconsciously, but he said it felt like Nabokov was even more of a direct inspiration

HARRY: Oh wow, that's one of Chris's favorite writers!

ALESSANDRO: Mine, too! Thank you both for doing this.

STEIN: Of course, we love Bill!

THE GIFT OF THE TORTURED SPECTER

SAM DESMOND

John F. Kennedy was one of the most profound high school crushes I had. I feverishly watched A&E and History Channel documentaries on him (as an elder millennial, I had to rely on VHS tapes for my historical fix). It was from there I vowed to marry a great man, but in making my fantasy realistic, I thought that meant I'd have to sacrifice marrying a good man. Admittedly, the whispered affairs of the Kennedy men intrigued me as my steady reading diet of Theodore Dreiser had me dead set on being an ingénue to middle-aged men.

In winter of 2001, when I was fifteen, a made-for-TV movie version of J. Randy Taraborelli's *Jackie, Ethel, Joan: Women of Camelot* came out and to this day, remains one of my lift-me-out-of-a-depressive episode go-to DVDs. Perhaps it was a lack of feminism, or perhaps just my love of all things vintage, but I found happiness in the existence of being the glamorous woman married to the powerful man. The era certainly made itself a picture frame for the devoted wife, or the eclipsed wife.

For me, there was a freedom in that role, to be admired and sought after, talked about constantly in the press just for buying a dress. Never in direct power, albeit powerful enough to direct where it would be wielded; it was the best of both the masculine and feminine world to be

the wife of a prestigious man. During my undergraduate and graduate
studies as a student of English Literature, I would always "treat" myself
to the biographical accounts of writers after finishing an analysis on a
piece and found a similarity in the women tied to the definitive men of
genres.

Joan Vollmer, born only six years before Jacqueline Kennedy, was
one of those women. The wife of William S. Burroughs, she was both
an ornament and gravitational pull of the Beat Generation. Dying at
twenty-eight, under the horrific circumstances of a botched William
Tell endeavor by Burroughs, a story he would go back and forth on, he
cemented her place as a tragic Ophelia of the generation because she
wouldn't be able to go on to create her own story. Between being introduced to benzedrine in 1945 and to Burroughs in 1946 by Ginsberg,
Joan would be both a launching pad and a punching bag for what fueled
the destructive, chaotic beauty of the Beat Generation. Even with Allen
Ginsberg stepping in to convince Burroughs to end the affair, Joan remained and gave birth to their child in 1947, perhaps the most tangible
of Burroughs's legacy to the general public.In *Kentucky Ham*, William,
Jr.'s novel published in 1973, we get an homage to a caring, but tragically
self-destructive mother who is a pawn to the machinations and whims
of her equally drug-addled husband. But despite the chaotic, unstruc-
tured life of Joan, she was still a woman I wanted to be.

Born into an upper middle-class family and eschewing the comfortable life that would have been her fate, much like Jackie Kennedy, she
became a muse, a siren, and the genesis of the greatest counterculture
art movements of the twentieth century. During one of her affairs, Joan
wrote term papers for her baby-faced, nineteen-year-old lover who at-
tended Columbia University. An essay she wrote for him on Dryden
and eighteenth century literature imitated Dryden's distinctive style and
was so admired by a professor for its clever wit and understanding of
Dryden that her young lover was afraid of being expelled for plagiariz-

ing her work.

Muses, especially to men, often remain on a pedestal because they do not tell their own tales and have to wait for someone else to discover their own innate talents separate from inspiring a grand man. Similar to Laurence Leamer's treatment of the alluring wives and daughters in *The Kennedy Women: The Saga of an American Family*, Barry Miles's *Call Me Burroughs* tries to tell the story of Joan as a force on her own, but she still cannot escape the male gaze that pigeonholes women to nurturing origin points for men's accomplishments.

But if the Beat Generation was captured from Joan's perspective, in a treatment like Joyce Carol Oates's 2000 novel *Blonde*, would she be any better off than in descriptions by a man? Or would she just lose the patina of grace afforded to her by authors who didn't condemn her for her lack of responsible motherhood? Male writers will focus on beauty and youthful exuberance, and forgive all if this is maintained, but women will not forgive a "bad mother."

One of Jackie Kennedy's idols was Evangeline Bruce, who in C. David Heymann's *The Georgetown Ladies' Social Club*, is described as a bit of a femme fatale with hostessing skills that the State Department relied upon for the most delicate situations with foreign diplomats, but what has held her back from being heralded as a brilliant women ahead of her time is that she was also an absent mother, whose first daughter was so distraught and disconnected from her, she died by suicide before thirty.

Joan was a woman I saw myself in, a maddening mind and uncontrollable compulsions to self-medicate, all the while trying to anchor herself in a traditional relationship with a man whose own genius was beyond control.

In his journal during his years in Latin America, roughly two years after the death of Joan, Burroughs wrote, "What persistent pimps in Panama. One stopped me chewing my ear off about a 15-year-old girl. I told him, 'She's middle-aged already. I want that 6-year-old ass. Don't try palming you old 14-year-old bats off on me.'"

More than anything else I've read from Burroughs this line has stayed with me. Was it just his sense of humor? Was it just for the shock value? Was it for real? And then my thoughts went back to Joan. To what extent did she endure this type of cruelty to the flesh and the psyche? How much did this contribute to her instability?

But then we get to Burroughs's statement in *Queer*:

"I am forced to the appalling conclusion that I would have never become a writer but for Joan's death ... I live with the constant threat of possession, and a constant need to escape from possession, from Control. So the death of Joan brought me in contact with the invader, the Ugly Spirit, and maneuvered me into a life long struggle, in which I have had no choice except to write my way out."

Perhaps, in the end, she did prevail in her long-standing influence on the men of the Beat Generation, as the Dorian Gray portrait that took on the consequences of death and degradation that they escaped to write their works.

PARALLEL SYSTEM

MICHAEL CARROLL

What happens when there is no limit? What is the fate of the Land of Where Anything Goes? Men changing into centipedes . . . centipedes besieging the houses . . . a man tied to a couch and a centipede ten feet long rearing up over him. Is this literal? Did some hideous metamorphosis occur? What is the meaning of the centipede symbol?

I'll kill the suspense ahead of time: the theme of this essay and the theme of my personal gayness is that queerness means *Mind your own business—and don't go around trying to correct others. Have some context.*

Genius fusion duo Steely Dan, hipsters or hipster wannabes from the suburbs who met at Bard College, borrowed everything they could from the jazz and Beat life—riffs, sentiments, street scenes, nighttime romantic souvenirs—and took their name from Burroughs, who had a compositional habit of forming his own comic and improbable narrative riffs which he called Routines. "Steely Dan" was chosen by Walter Becker and Donald Fagen for their novel jazz-rock-pop act from a satiro-surreal Routine in *Naked Lunch* about violently deployed dildos.

But the idea for the Routines began when Burroughs was writing the earlier *Queer.* I see the Routines as a plot device, a blowing-up of the

key need in fiction for dialogue and characterization. The Routines appear throughout *Queer*, and in *Queer* serve as diversions or deflections
from the main conflict, which is about the protagonist's leaning into his
own queerness and, in doing so, trying to impress a younger lover, to seduce this younger lover by dazzling him with his wit and inventiveness.
The Routines are all pointedly outrageous, even disgusting. "Disgusting" is an interesting choice for a depicted act of seduction:

> *"Got an idea for a new dish. Take a live pig and throw it into a very*
> *hot oven so the pig is roasted outside and, when you can cut into*
> *it, still alive and twitching inside. Or, if we run a dramatic joint, a*
> *screaming pig covered with burning brandy rushes out of the kitchen*
> *and dies right by your chair. You can reach down and pull off the*
> *crispy, crackly ears and eat them with your cocktails."*

The notion in *Queer* for the Routines differs from Burroughs's use
of it in *Naked Lunch*, where Burroughs seems to be seducing the reader,
dazzling the reader with his wit, socially transgressive feralness, and
horny imaginative candor.

In *Queer*, the character Lee is in love with Allerton and haunted by
his dark past. An expatriate in Mexico City who lives in a glass closet,
Lee desires someone clearly not in love with him. The grandiosity and
morbidity of the Routines here are psychologically motivated, making
Queer the second (after *Junky*) and final novel of realism Burroughs
wrote. Here the only fantasy element, the Routines, being not phantas-
magorically drug-related kookiness. His first, previous novel, *Junky*, he
described as a novel of addiction, while *Queer* is a novel of withdrawal,
but stylistically and content-wise they are related time-sequentially in
the life of Burroughs's early Mexico City period. About *Queer*, which he
wrote in tandem with *Junky* and tried to fuse the two, Burroughs wrote
about his self-subject: "during withdrawal he may feel the compulsive

need for an audience, and this is clearly what Lee seeks . . . So, he invents a frantic attention-getting format which he calls the Routine."

It is enough for a single modern narrative that gay erotic feelings drive Lee listlessly across Mexico City in an abject search for—what? The entire novel is a listless search through Latin America. In the 1985 introduction to *Queer*, Burroughs wrote that Lee is "disintegrated" and "desperately in need of contact, completely unsure of himself and of his purpose." The unrevealed autobiographical character motive never mentioned on any page, Burroughs said, is what in fact made him a writer: Burroughs's dissolute reeling from his accidental shooting and killing of his wife.

Here we depart from the author's 1985 assertion that he hadn't written a "queer novel." If being a queer isn't the theme of queer, and the other motive the main character Lee is submerged, then what is *Queer* about? *Queer* is about self-exploration and moral reckoning, and it takes place in a sequence of voyages—into the night, into the existential postwar, American-haunted experience, and into the despoiled world of Latin America whose only treasure for Burroughs is the mythic, hallucinogenic, and spiritually significant plant, yage. The novel is short, but takes its time arriving at the meaningless, unfulfilled wreckage of a white man searching for the unattainable.

Queer may seem to have desultory movement, but that is because the character of Lee is directionless after so many rejections by the younger man. It bears a light structure but this loose frame suffices not only because there is wise realism in its findings but also because it is one of the first frank depictions of an underground gay life. At the time, the worst things you could be were a Communist, a heroin addict, or a homosexual. And in *Queer* we encounter the scathing observational critique wrought by capital back home and abroad. He is depicting and describing the world that hates him. And yet, problematically, he has contempt for the natives.

But not as much hatred as he reserves for himself. The germ of this midcentury time capsule is the self-loathing that came from what most considered deviancy. The Routines are meant to help relieve and deflect away from this hatred. Object relations psychology would call this stylistic recourse to sarcasm—this includes the facile use of racist stereotypes—*grandiosity*. Something meant to keep Lee from looking into his true self and facing the authentic nature of guilt, loss, yearning, and disappointment as facts of every existence. Later Burroughs characters in his more way-out novels have space alien mental powers, but in the realism-driven *Queer*, Lee is paranoid, sad, and full of love-hankering enough to imagine the thoughts of others, or overhear conversations, knowing that he's being held in contempt:

> "*I like the guy, Tom, but I can't stand to be alone with him. He keeps trying to go to bed with me. That's what I don't like about queers. You can't keep it on a basis of friendship . . . .*" Yes, Lee could hear that conversation.

I first read this novel when I was twenty-one. I was in college, living with my first boyfriend, the year it was first published—thirty-three years after it was written. The original Fifties editor had warned Burroughs that he might end up in jail. Later he would be embroiled in an obscenity trial for *Naked Lunch*, but by then the stuffy puritanical fifties were winding down.

I remember my two reactions: the humor and sour inventiveness of the Routines, and, as a fiction writing student, the wan, minimalist, and powerfully simple effectiveness of the prose. I had not expected tenderness and honesty from an author of his reputation.

Thirty-six years after that, I am struck mostly by the sadness yet-still admirable the style of an internalized homophobia. I have read it twice in recent weeks and the sadness does not go away. I understand that we have been living, appropriately to the topic at hand, through warped, deceiving, and edging-on-dystopian times—and this may color my mood.But this late to me, *Queer* is cringingly poignant, and bleeding raw with frankness:

I don't remember feeling sadness when I originally read lines like these:

> *Lee was deeply hurt. He could hear Moor saying, "Thanks for running interference, Tom. Well, I hope he got the idea. Lee is an interesting guy and all that . . . but this queer situation is just more than I can take."*

I don't remember the hurt.

Maybe the pain of similar personal memories had me looking away, seeking the comic entertainments of the Routines. I remember a junior high yearbook candid of me with my hands on the hips of a hot guy I stood behind. He was bent over, and it looked like I was positioning him to drop his pants and let me stick my dick inside him, in a classroom full of gifted students. I have no idea the context, but even miming buggery at that age would have been unthinkable to me. I sought protection from girlfriends. In any event, besides confronting my hidden sexuality all that time before, as someone who'd always wanted to write, I was also searching for the ways the sentences were strung together:

> *Actually, Moor's brush-off was calculated to inflict the maximum hurt possible under the circumstances. It put Lee in the position of a detestably insistent queer, too stupid to realize that his attentions were not wanted, forcing Moor to the distasteful necessity of drawing a diagram.*

The self-loathing not only continues, but demonstrates Burroughs's courage in tearing the scab off:

> *As Lee stood aside to bow in his dignified old-world greeting, there emerged instead a leer of naked lust, wrenched in the pain and hate of his deprived body and, in simultaneous double exposure, a sweet child's smile of liking and trust, shockingly out of time and place, mutilated and hopeless.*

That observed leer suggests to me that the author is standing both inside and outside Lee's queer self. Creative writing workshops would likely insist that Lee be looking in a mirror to judge his expression a leer. But what grabbed me originally still holds me today: this is very cinematic writing at the same time that it's psychological and cerebral. You can see Mexico City, and when the action shifts to South America, you *feel* the blue-green canopy of bush and jungle. Ruined villages and abandoned corporate towns owned by international companies like Shell slide by. The newness of the obviously despoiled lands takes us by surprise.

Every once in a while, the narrative sensor leaps into the mind of Allerton, the beloved:

Allerton was appalled. "Perhaps he has some sort of a tic," he thought. He decided to remove himself from contact with Lee before the man did something even more distasteful. The effect was like a cut connection. Allerton was not cold or hostile; Lee simply wasn't there so far as he was concerned. Lee looked at him helplessly for a moment, then turned back to the bar, defeated and shaken.

Queer among other things is a novel of voyage and discovery, so much of the drama, not to say the backstory or background drama, is submerged, effaced. It takes us geographically south, just as it takes Lee emotionally and psychologically south.

At nineteen, I was still living at home. I'd dropped out of a college and skipped out on a local scholarship. I'd watched a movie on Cinemax called *Heart Beat*, a romantic depiction of the Beats that focused on the Cassady/Kerouac ménage and did not have a Burroughs. The lesson I obtained from it was that the Beats loved and wrote passionately and travelled to places like Mexico, where I wanted to go and write a travel journal. Someone at my job as a handyman at an apartment complex spread the word that I was gay, and so I left my house in the middle of the night and took a Greyhound bus to Miami. On that trip I met a guy six years older. He was taking a cross-country bus tour from his home in Los Angeles to celebrate his twenty-fifth birthday, and so then I learned what freedom tastes like—it tastes like cock and mouth and asshole, and it begins in Mexico with beer in sunshine.

Lee ordered a drink at the bar and looked around. Three Mexican fags were posturing in front of the jukebox. One of them slithered over to where Lee was standing, with the stylized gestures of a temple dancer, and asked for a cigarette. Lee watched them from an inner silence. He registered something archaic in the stylized movements, a depraved animal grace at once beautiful and repulsive. He could see them moving in the light of campfires, the ambiguous gestures shadowed into the dark. Sodomy is as old as the human species.

I'm sharing my apartment with a man less than half my age. He isn't a sexual interest. He's just an interesting guy going through an important death anniversary and some relationship problems. He is beautiful, but thank God I don't lust after him. We met through my husband, who's in Italy with his much younger lover. Quinn is the gay nephew who exists inside the gay utopia of my mind. I try not to admonish him, except when I think I can be supportive and remind him that he's both valid and talented. It is important that he writes on a level, at his tender age, far beyond mine. I know that this kind of relationship has always existed, but it's 2021 and gay men of his generation are afforded the privileges and assumptions neither I nor Burroughs could ever have imagined. And as I write this, he's out on a hookup, what he called in a text a Grindr rando. To be so cavalier about casual sex when the rest of us had to meet and smile and get to know someone in person! I envy him. And I wonder if Burroughs would, or if Burroughs was so old-fashioned, he would have found it alien?

Here's a sentence I never envisioned myself saying, that young gay men like Quinn can say: "Yeah, whenever my friends and I get together, we always make sure we're squeaky clean."

When I was his age, we didn't anticipate anal sex, and the possible sudden shit-dirtiness.

Yesterday we talked about the difference between objectification, Othering, and abuse. I said that I think, from having lived a longer time than Quinn: "First in my lifetime, the lingo was that people were objectified. Then they were exoticized, then they were Othered. Finally, they have been abused. It doesn't matter that they weren't touched, it's how they were they looked at. That's abuse."

Quinn seemed to be a little embarrassed by my analysis, but from my point of view, it's true: What used to be called looking at someone wrong, or touching them, now constitutes abuse.

In Mexico, Greg and I met a German named Walter who was constantly stoned. He worked at a Volkswagen plant in Saxony for half the year, and had the other half of the year off. It was the Reagan era, and this is what many of us, including Greg I think, called socialism. Too much leisure, too much slacking off. How could a society afford such indulgence?

Greg and I were staying in the same cement block hostel as Walter in Cancun, and Greg and I'd pass Walter's room and smell the ganja. He was listening to reggae, and when we talked to him outside of his room in a cafe, he'd say, "This is all just Babylon System."

We asked him to explain, and he mentioned something about Rosicrucianism, and then explained it when our expressions dulled by beginning again by talking about Rastafarianism. More nonconformist, drug-induced fantasy and rebellion.

Anyway, Babylon System meant not-reality. And yet he was touring Babylon System.

Walter believed in this parallel world, and was happy. I hope he still is, in Saxony.

What is the place of literature now? It used to have so much import. Don't write about a gay man hating himself. And don't show him being vulnerable or else imperfect. That's bad for the cause. That's not revolutionary.

I say this truly: if a writer can't be honest to his experience, that society doesn't deserve him. Nor does he need that readership.

Why does literature need to be revolutionary when the author's honesty, and yes, even self-scrutiny, is sufficient to the call of art? You doubt yourself? By all means, confess.

PHALLIC SHADOW ON A DISTANT WALL

GREGORY WOODS

Young boys need it special

I was once accused in print of having assassinated William S. Burroughs. This surprised me because even if I'd had the means and the opportunity, I doubt if I could have worked up a motive. His books had played an important role in my life—indeed, in the beginnings of my sex life—for years.

I was a bookish boy, and my bookishness and I were gay. We were in dialogue about our gayness. Most of the books I loved most were accounts of first love, some of first sex. They told me about boy-loving boys and man-loving men. David and Joey in James Baldwin's *Giovanni's Room* ("It seemed, then, that a lifetime would not be long enough for me to act with Joey the act of love" ... "*But Joey is a boy*"). Eric and Yves in Baldwin's *Another Country* ("Yves' body shook and he called Eric's name as no one had ever called his name before"). Jim and Bob in Gore Vidal's *The City and the Pillar* ("Now they were complete, each became the other, as their bodies collided with a primal violence, like to like, metal to magnet, half to half and the whole restored"). Georges and Alexander in Roger Peyrefitte's *Special Friendships*, Fielding and Christopher in Simon Raven's *Fielding Gray*, Yuichi and Minoru in Yukio Mishima's *Forbidden Colours*...They all had their part to play in my adolescent explorations of my own body and mind. They were pioneering books, but their representations of sex were as restrained as was required by their times.

That's kid stuff. I wanta

It is hard now to reconstruct the viewpoint from which even Thomas Mann's *Death in Venice* ("the truly god-like beauty of this human creature") was, in a positive sense, pornographic: masturbatable-to. Yet it's only by reconstructing that viewpoint that I can convey how mind-blowingly the novels of Jean Genet and William Burroughs started making things new. To find yourself, suddenly, in the throes of *Naked Lunch*, with an overwhelming feeling of being abducted to multiple unknown destinations by multiple unknown narrators... What a book! Nothing by Peyrefitte or Mann had prepared me for what happens in Hassan's Rumpus Room or at any of A.J.'s insane parties, where it's hard to avoid being spliced into one of the Great Slashtubitch's blue movies. In turning to Genet and Burroughs, I had—as E.M. Forster said when he had, at last, made love with another man—*parted with respectability*.

Pack up your ermines Mary!

"I say this: any writer who hasn't jacked off with his characters, those characters will not come alive in a sexual context. I certainly jack off with my characters." You would reasonably infer from his having said this, that Burroughs expected his readers to do the same. That would be the apt confirmation, in "the flash bulb of orgasm", that his characters had "come alive" beyond the confines of the book.

From early in my teens, I thought of masturbation as a narrative art. I was nerdily interested in the ways in which my own fantasies both varied and remained the same, repeating their obligatory tropes. The stories I told myself had to feel always both reliably predictable and yet, even if only in some apparently insignificant fetishistic detail, thrillingly updated and refreshed. Favourite details had to be manipulated to occur or recur at the right moment. If any detail didn't work, it could quickly be abandoned and replaced.

In a not-unrelated development, during my last few terms at school, I had become a fan of the broken unities of Modernism—*The Waste Land* ("the first great cut-up collage", according to Burroughs), *The Waves, Ulysses*, a few of Pound's *Cantos*—so the cut-ups of Burroughs held few terrors for me. I associated these experimental texts with sex. (I associated anything with sex.) How sexual fantasy harnesses repetition and fragmentation—of desired bodies as of the narrative itself—and how favoured aspects of past experience might be cherry-picked to be turned into future aspirations... These are still preoccupations in my poetry.

As soon as I found a secondhand copy of the paperback—there were a lot of them around in those days—I read each of the Burroughs novels in turn, but it was *The Wild Boys* that brought all the sexual themes together in a coherent narrative of erotic fragmentation and metamorphosis.

Boys laughing comparing sepia pictures

I always thought his novels were as much nostalgic pastorals as they were futuristic speculations. Most of his positive scenes of affectionate sexual intimacy have a retrospective glow. Many of their images are explicitly sepia-tinted. As an undergrad, I had done a lot of work on pastoral elegy—work which has had a continuous resonance for me ever since, in both my critical writing and my poetry. My first scholarly publication was a group edition of Milton's *Lycidas* for Cambridge University Press. Many of the moods and themes I'd read in Theocritus and Virgil, Gray and Tennyson, seemed present, though transformed and made new, in Burroughs. Even his futuristic erotic scenarios are essentially nostalgic. Not only that, but they are often rural, bucolic— although not located on rolling greenswards beside gurgling rills, set at least on bare mudflats or urban wastelands already half-reclaimed by nature: "distant smell of weeds in vacant lots"; "slow pressure of semen rectal smell of flowers two naked bodies bathed in smoky rose of the dying sun phantom bed from an old movie set long since abandoned to weeds and vines"; "sunlight in pubic hairs". *The Wild Boys* is a pastoral elegy.

Nothing is true. Everything is permitted

As an undergraduate, I'd grown tired of being told my interventions on aspects of gay texts were irrelevant to the focus of the discussion, whether on paper or around the seminar table, and even that they were irrelevant to the focus of the given book or the motivation of its author. So, when it came to devising a dissertation topic for my MA, I chose *Functions of Sex in the Novels of William Burroughs*, so that there could be no doubt. In its way, the proposal alone was a fuck-you to my department. For a short while, it looked as if no one would agree to supervise me, but then Professor Guido Almansi stepped up to the plate. Guido had just published his book *L'estetica dell'osceno* (*The Aesthetics of the Obscene*), with chapters on G.G. Belli, Henry Miller, Charles Baudelaire, and others, and he was about to publish his book on Boccaccio, *The Writer As Liar*. He was also an authority on nonsense poetry and on literary parodies.

The title alone of Guido's Boccaccio book was a revelation to me—

or a welcome confirmation of something I had already intuited but not felt able or allowed to express—since I had internalised, when younger, all that Hemingway bullshit about writers and the Truth. Yes, writers lie, and good lies often make good literature. Also, heterosexually skeptical, Guido proved adept at ensuring I didn't allow myself to be uncritically taken in by what turned me on. He would later play this role again while supervising my PhD thesis on homo-eroticism in gay men's poetry, which eventually became my book *Articulate Flesh*.

Writhing in orgasms of prurience

I had encountered homophobic literary assessments before—in class as well as in print—but this dissertation gave me my first opportunity for a systematic critique of homophobic litcrit. This was in the days when serious literary magazines could publish essays with titles like "Jean Genet and the Indefensibility of Sexual Deviation" (Philip Thody in *20th Century Studies*). Rather than allow themselves to seem shocked by obscenity, critics often pretended haughtily to find it all just too, too boring: "*Naked Lunch*, whatever else it may be, is a very indecent book, and *Nova Express*, whatever else it may be, is a very tedious book" (David Lodge). "*Naked Lunch* strikes me as a strident bore, illiterate and self-satisfied right to its heart of pulp" (George Steiner).

At a time when writers were expected to sublimate and/or conceal their and their characters' same-sex desires by writing of them, if at all, only obliquely, metaphorically, Jeffrey Meyers (*Homosexuality and Literature, 1890-1930*) summed up a prevailing view: the novels of Genet, Burroughs, John Rechy, and Hubert Selby "concern the homosexual's acts and not his mind, and appeal to sensation rather than to imagination". Therefore: "the emancipation of the homosexual has led, paradoxically, to the decline of his art." My job—in my dissertation, then in my published literary criticism, then in my published poetry—was to show otherwise. Taking Burroughs seriously was a step in this process.

Relax Johnny. It happens

Two decades later, in 1993, I contributed the item on Burroughs in Emmanuel S. Nelson's *Contemporary Gay American Novelists*. It was this that later (2001) drew the accusation of an "assassination of Burroughs" (Jamie Russell, *Queer Burroughs*). I think Russell was referring to this passage in my essay:

> Whether one should unhesitatingly describe William S. Burroughs as a 'gay novelist' is open to debate. Of his homosexuality there is no doubt. That it is a crucial element in the shaping of his fiction, where it plays a major and explicit role, is also certain. There are many readers who would argue that Burroughs is not gay at all, but a rather old-fashioned kind of homosexual who has never contributed, or sought to contribute, to the momentum of social change. His few representations of adult gay couples, as of lesbians, tend to combine unsympathetic humor with real contempt.

I would have said much the same about Jean Genet. I allow myself to be critical of those I admire. My high opinion of Genet was never undermined by his declaration, "I did not write my books for the liberation of the homosexual."

A room full of fags gives me the horrors

While I was happy to hunt down and expose the homophobia of literary critics, I was far less certain of my ground when dealing with that of the author himself. You don't have to read much of *Naked Lunch* before you encounter fags, queers, fruits, fairies, old queens, and "simpering blond catamites". Then, of course, there are "homosexuals", born to be case studies, forever under scrutiny from figures of pseudo-scientific authority. Plenty of the hostile language, including the racism and at least some of the sexism was attributable to characters or narrators, often implicitly distanced from the author, but that did not account for it all. "The live human being has moved out of these bodies long ago. But something moved in when the original tenant moved out. Fags are ventriloquists' dummies who have moved in and taken over the ventriloquist." Isn't that the author's own voice in *Junky*?

Burroughs is not interested in gay identity or gay politics. He is not even interested in the symbolic bedrock of gay liberationism: gay love. "I think that what we call love is a fraud perpetrated by the female sex, and that the point of sexual relations between men is nothing that we would call love, but rather what we might call *recognition*." Like Genet, he despises the bourgeoisification of desire—queerness declining into gayness, the domesticated gay couple, lasting relationship, cushions and drapes. That's why I declined to call Burroughs a gay writer. If I had been writing a few years later, I suppose I would have called him queer and Jamie Russell might not have complained.

The positive effect of reading this homophobic stuff was to give me a certain level of immunity to it. I have tended to anticipate such hostility to gay love and gay lovers, whatever its source, but not to court it. Burroughs and Genet taught me not to repudiate indiscriminately all sources of homophobic pain: for the language, the virus if you prefer, of homophobic speech plays a substantial part in our experience of the world. We need to build up our resistance.

This bad place Meester

"I think love is a virus. I think love is a con put down by the female sex". "The word is now a virus ... Modern man has lost the option of silence". "Poverty, hatred, war, police-criminals, bureaucracy, insanity, all symptoms of The Human Virus". Burroughs took it on himself to speak as an authority on viral control. But when it came to HIV/AIDS... Despite his lifelong interest in viruses—as metaphor, perhaps, rather than as lived illness—and despite his status as a gay man, and despite his experience of intravenous drug use, as far as I'm aware, he had nothing useful or interesting to say about AIDS. I was disappointed. Similarly, I had been waiting to read excoriating essays from Gore Vidal on the Reagan administration's negligent response to the epidemic, but no such essays were written. It's not that I thought they *should* write about AIDS: it's more that I hoped they *would*.

"But that's dirty!" "Not dirty just alien."

Much later, on 16 June 2013, I announced on Facebook: 'I threw away my MA thesis this morning. Thirty-eight years seems long enough to appease my younger self with needless courtesy.' I hadn't even done myself the courtesy of re-reading it.

My often-re-read 1969 edition of *The Naked Lunch* is full of underlinings and marginal comments, many of which mean nothing to me anymore. Why did I underline "adolescent-nordic-sun-tan slacks"? Or "stark naked except for a badge pinned to his left nipple"? I must have imagined I would need, someday, to be reminded of these images, but duly reminded I'm at a loss. Yet, in the echoing corridors of my book-memory, *Naked Lunch* and *The Wild Boys* are as resonant with quotations as *Hamlet*: "No glot... C'lom Fliday"; "Fuck now talk later"; "the algebra of need"; "vile addictions and insect lusts"; "spectral janitors"; "smell of carbolic soap"; "smell of rectal mucous"; "atrophied boy-smell of dusty locker rooms"; "Wanta feel something nice Audrey?"; "K.Y. tubes squeezed dry as bonemeal in the summer sun"; "What happens between my legs is like a cold drink to me it is just a feeling… It is a feeling by which *I am* here at all."

QUEERING CHAOS

SVEN DAVISSON

"The Wild boys are always just out of sight in the colors they cannot see in the places they didn't go."
—*Port of Saints*

William Burroughs had a deeply rooted interest in the occult and fringe science. This fascination was kindled at an early age when his Irish nanny taught him the secret of calling toads and a simple curse to cause the target to fall down a flight of stairs. The latter would reoccur in his works all the way through his monumental final *Cities of the Red Night* trilogy. At age four, he describes how, while walking in a park, he saw a small green reindeer that he would later identify as a totem animal.

Burroughs and his literary alter egos were outspoken in their belief in the Magical Universe and the existence of an afterlife. For him, the world, as well as his novels, consisted of a universe populated by diverse gods, spirits, and ghosts. The threat of possession was very real and ever present. He personally felt himself stalked by an entity he termed the Ugly Spirit. He blamed his accidental shooting of his wife Joan during a William Tell act on possession by this malevolent spirit.

To Burroughs, the One God Universe, with its bearded benevolent father figure who yet lets bad things happen, was a logical impasse—

"irrevocably thermodynamic." For him the only cosmological model that made sense was a universe populated by numerous gods often operating from points of competing interest. Likewise, he viewed coincidence as a mechanism of control used to obscure the universe's true magical nature. In Burroughs view there are no accidents. "Nothing happens unless someone wills it to happen."

> "Like *The Great Gatsby*, Kim believes in the green light the orgiastic future. He believes in a magical universe, unpredictable, spontaneous, alive. A universe where anything is possible. A universe of many gods often in conflict. So the paradox of an all-knowing all-powerful god, who, nonetheless, permits suffering, evil and death, does not arise." (*The Best of William S. Burroughs*, Giorno Poetry Systems)

Burroughs's interest in writing and the occult intersected in the magical power of the written word. He first encountered this concept while in Morocco. When Brion Gyson operated his café, he discovered a cursed object presumably set against him. Inside was a written curse closing with the word mektoub, or "it is written." The act of writing itself is a magical one. William Lee, one of the author's many alter egos, is writing his way out of death—the very act of literary creation is a ritual in and of itself. For Burroughs, this carried through to an interest in occult grimoires and hidden books. Burroughs wrote evocatively of lost Mayan codices and even the dread *Necronomicon* of Lovecraftian fiction.

An interesting aside, the opening invocation of *Cities of the Red Night* includes calls to Kutulu, Humwawa, and Pazuzu. These clearly comes from the pages of the 1977 Schlangekraft edition of the *Necronomicon*. Attributed to the shadowy Simon, generally thought to be Peter Levenda, the inspiration for crafting this version of Lovecraft's tome grew out of late night discussions in the back the Magickal Childe occult shoppe on W. 19th Street. The Childe was the epicenter for occult New York during the 70s and 80s. The shop was operated by queer pagan pioneers and sometime provocateurs Herman Slater and Eddie Buczynski. Residing at his famous bunker at that time, Burroughs got wind that such a dangerous grimoire was in the neighborhood. According to its illustrator, Khem Caigan, he swung by the publisher and perused some production pages along with a couple of lines of "powder" declaring it "good shit."

In some respects, the act of writing may be viewed as a form of possession. Great writers often describe the process as less creative inspiration and more received dictation. Burroughs's later works, from *The Wild Boys* through *The Western Lands*, are akin to modern, or postmodern occult grimoires in the tradition of those that detail traversing other realms. The former is explicitly subtitled, "A Book of the Dead," linking it to Egyptian and Tibetan guides to surviving one's physical death. The latter is implicitly of the same domain telling the story of Joe the Dead's travels through the interstitial Du'at, the land of the dead, toward the Western Lands, the Egyptian eternity.

Burroughs's influence on alternative cultural movements, from heavy metal to punk to industrial music, has been well documented. His writings and mystical experimentations had similar impact on alternative spiritual movements. His work and philosophies had a profound influence on Throbbing Gristle/Psychic TV/Temple of Psychic Youth/Coil and their founders Genesis P-Orridge and Peter "Sleazy" Christopherson. The cut-up method and other experiments at disrupting reality were adopted by the early chaos magicians such as Peter Carroll, Douglas Grant, and Phil Hine. Burroughs contributed a forward and cover for Hine's *Prime Chaos*. These chaos psychonauts were frequent visitors to Burroughs's Lawrence, Kansas home. They, in turn, had an influence on the Old Man.

As demonstrated by his application of the cut-up technique and playback method, Burroughs was not simply an armchair occultist. He was indeed a practicing magician. In his later years, he would even take initiation in the chaos order founded by Peter J. Carroll, the Illuminates of Thanateros. No doubt Burroughs felt an affinity with the chaos magical approach focused as it is on results not dogma.

I view it as no coincidence that chaos magic and queer 'politics' arose at a similar time. They both exist in a space that is simultaneously transcultural and transtemporal. Each was in part a reactive alternative to pervading cultural ethos. Chaos magic pushed back at a headwind of rigid occult traditionalism based on a mostly fabricated historicity. Queer, on the other hand, was a determined cultural and political reaction to the pervading critical debate between essentialist and constructionist camps in analyzing expressions of same-sex desire. Burroughs's writing exists in a similar space apart from linear time with settings as varied as pirate enclaves, the Wild West, and ancient Egypt.

There has been much discussion and critical writing around certain aspects of Burroughs's occult interests: his use of the cut-up technique, rediscovered with his magical co-explorer Brion Gyson; his application of playback to control crowds and disturb cafés; and his interest in William Reich's orgone energy and the wishing machine. In contrast, comparatively little has been written about the male+male shamanism that weaves its way through his mythology of the space age.

The Grotta dell'Addaura in Sicily contains carvings dated to the late Paleolithic and Mesolithic periods. One of these depicts several males, some with erections, wearing bird headpieces circling around two males on the ground. The consensus among anthropologists is that the image is one of sacrifice, perhaps even self-strangulation through binding. Randy P. Conner, co-author of *Cassell's Encyclopedia of Queer Myth, Symbol and Spirit*, offers an alternative view. He sees the image as one of homoerotic ritual, a prehistoric hieros gamos, and not violence. To any gay man viewing the engraving, this interpretation is readily confirmed—the erect phallus of the upper central figure pointing at the buttocks of the bottom one while lines of raised magical energy swirl about them.

Similar images to that of Addaura reoccur throughout Burroughs's magical writings, especially in the material comprising *The Wild Boys* and *Port of Saints*. The wild boys often form magical circles around copulating central figures. As in the prehistoric imagery, animals play a key role in the wild boy rituals, and the participants are often masked. In *Port of Saints*, the boys come together in a circle where they are "fucked by Goat Gods." During their workings they feel "the hunters with reindeer heads." This naturally summons the famous image of the Sorcerer from Cave of the Trois-Frères in Ariège, France with his antlers, animal hides, and erection.

The wild boys are the recipients of occult knowledge as part of their training. They are taught the magical control of wind and rain as well as the "sex magic that turns flesh to light" alluding to Plato's 'body of light' adopted by fin de siècle occultists such as Aleister Crowley and Dion Fortune. As with shamans from various traditions, the wild boys are transformed, mutated into animals and magical entities. They experience the "sexual excitement of mutation." Becoming Pan Boys, Snake Boys, Shaman Boys, Seismic Boys, Lizard Boys, and Green Boys with foliage growing from their pores.

Shamanic practitioners, witches, and sorcerers have a long historical connection with alternative sexualities and approaches to gender.

Viking magical practice was divided into two forms: runic magic and seiðr. The former was considered the realm of men, while the latter was generally the domain of women. From the Icelandic sagas and tales, our earliest written records of Viking practices and culture, we know males who practiced seiðr were often called ergi, a term denoting effeminacy, and anally penetrated. While this term is often used derogatorily, it is hard to tell how of much that was true in the early Viking age and how much was the influence of early Christianization of Iceland. While it is entirely possible Viking culture held a negative opinion of same-sex eroticism, the matter is also complicated. Odin, the manly father of the Aesir gods, is known as the possibly shamanic magician who brought the runes to humankind. On the other hand, he is also known as the king of the seiðr practitioners. Tales tell of Odin practicing seiðr and even refer to him as ergi as a result.

Arthur Evans, author of the transformative *Witchcraft and the Gay Counterculture*, links the modern word "faggot" with the fuel used to burn witches and heretics. Evans was highly influenced by Margaret Murray's now generally discredited theories, so this etymology has to be taken with at least a grain of salt. On the other hand, Conner does propose a similar connection through a more circuitous yet probable linguistic route. Whether the connection exists or not, by the time of the anti-witch hysteria that swept Europe, known as the Burning Times, sexual and gender variants were grouped with witches, prostitutes, sorcerers, and other heretical criminals. One only need look at Joan of Arc.

Like shamans, sexual and gender variants walk in the liminal— existing at the edges of society, culture, criminality, and transgression. For much of our history, we have been literal lawbreakers. Burroughs pushes this farther into the domain of temporal and cosmic law. He describes his protagonist in *The Western Lands* thus:

> Joe the Dead belongs to a select breed of outlaws known as the NOs, natural outlaws dedicated to breaking so-called natural laws of the universe foisted upon us by physicists, biologists and, above all, the monumental fraud of cause and effect, to be replaced by the more pregnant concept of synchronicity... Or-

dinary outlaws break man-made laws. Laws against theft and murder are broken every second. You only break a natural law once. To the ordinary criminal, breaking a law is a means to an end: obtaining money, removing a source of danger or annoyance. To the NO, breaking a natural law is an end in itself: the end of that law. (William S. Burroughs, *The Western Lands*)

Despite these deep historical connections between homoeroticism and gender variance and metaphysical exploration, it is an unfortunate fact that gay culture moves us momentarily up and down, but not forward.

Neil Bartlett observes:

It is our commonest experience that after breaking the law we become law-abiding citizens.... We regularly watch ourselves turn into the most improbable creatures, transform back again, then set off to the office or the dole office just like anybody else.... Morning does not disrupt the night any more than the glamour, the ferocity and wickedness of the night challenges or abolishes the day.

He continues:

After the moments of harsh intimacy with ourselves or with others we like the world to fall back into place again. We acknowledge, with extraordinary calmness, given how much this all costs us, that there is no radical impulse beneath our radical acts. (Neil Bartlett, *Who Was That Man?*)

No matter how ecstatic Saturday night is, even if it continues late into Sunday, morning comes.

Like traditional shamans and historical spiritual explorers above, wild boys also exist in liminal space and are able to walk between worlds and realities where they interact with various entities and spirit guides. The wild boys make "frequent excursions" to the Blue Desert of Silence. Joe the Dead operates outside of natural laws as he travels the road to the Western Lands. One first makes contact with the wild boys in the dreamlands. There one's wild boy spirit guide makes first contact. There is some tonal linkage here with the theories of French critical theorist Michel Foucault who discussed moving through limit-experiences to expand consciousness. He espoused an askesis, an ascetic practice, a philosophy of life, where somaesthetic edging disrupts the perceived limits of ordered reality. Like the practices of Burroughs's wild boys, Foucault saw in rituals of the flesh a potential for sexual innovations to open new potentialities and invent "new possibilities of pleasure." He viewed homosexuality as, in his words, "an occasion to re-open effective and relational virtualities," since it has the potential to "introduce love where there's supposed to be only law, rule or habit."

In Western ceremonial magic, one makes contact with spirits through evocation rather than via the dreamscape or zoomorphic invocation. Burroughs's hardboiled detective Clem Snide employs one such technique in *Cities of the Red Night*. The section draws inspiration from the Egyptian rite contained in *The Occult Magic Primer* by David Conway, with whom Burroughs carried on a secret correspondence. In Burroughs's ritual, Snide and his partner attempt to invoke the Egyptian deity Set. Set is sometimes described as a "black god" and Burroughs describes this as a "dark ritual." He is the god of chaos, of unordered reality, of the lawless period between the death of the pharoah and the ascension of his successor. Set is also a queer god who makes advances on his nephew Horus only to be tricked by him into eating his semen on his divine salad. In some tellings, he subsequently gives birth to Thoth, the god of knowledge and writing, arising from this unique coupling.

This working echoes the 1913 "Paris Working" where Aleister Crowley and Victor Neuberg attempted to invoke the gods Mercury and Jupiter through an intense period of homoerotic sex magic.

These sojourns are not without risk. Indeed, for Burroughs, safety is antithetical to spiritual exploration. "The road to the Western Lands," Burroughs writes, "'is by definition the most dangerous road in the world, for it is a journey beyond Death, beyond the basic God standard of Fear and Danger. It is the most heavily guarded road in the world, for it gives access to the gift that supersedes all other gifts: Immortality. Every man starts the course. One in a million finishes."

Beware. We have been warned: "The wild boys take no prisoners."

CONCLUSION: MY HUNGRY INTERZONE OR: WHAT YOU CONSUME

BRIAN ALESSANDRO

In Agadir, a young woman tried to sell me her newborn. She was impoverished, I had been told by our tour guide, who'd translated her plea. She wanted a "better life" for her son in America. The perception held by most people in developing countries is that all Americans are rich, no matter their actual economic status, or at least had access to great wealth and opportunities. I had discovered William S. Burroughs at eighteen, in late 1995, just a few weeks before my trip to Morocco. An older friend from NYU, whose parents had been "close" with Allen Ginsberg, had turned me on to Burroughs. She insisted that my development as a writer depended on discovering Burroughs "right then, and not a moment later". She had a flair for heightened melodramatic pronouncements.

The timing of the uncovering was kismet as Burroughs, of course, wrote *Interzone* and *Naked Lunch* while living in Tangier International Zone in the mid Fifties. Closeted, paranoid, consumed with the idea of novelty and defector irreverence, fascinated by the forbidden fantasy of homosexuality, made sophisticated and sexy by *Naked Lunch*, I located Burroughs's magnum opus right on time. His disillusioned oddness spoke to my cloistered queerness.

I apologized in English to the young woman, and the tour guide translated into Arabic. I thought of Burroughs, perhaps not of *Naked Lunch* directly, and how he'd been born into an affluent family: his grandfather, William Seward Burroughs I, founded the Burroughs Adding Machine Company. Paul Bowles, who wrote *The Sheltering Sky*, while living in Morocco, was also "of means." Many of the famous, "rich" writers who settled in Morocco to write their masterpieces set a legacy of well-to-do expatriates claiming foreign lands for their own amusement, escape, and luxurious productivity. They had all gone for different reasons and during different eras, but Burroughs claimed that what brought him to the North African country was freedom and anonymity: "[Morocco] is one of the few places left in the world where, so long as you don't proceed to robbery, violence, or some form of crude, antisocial behavior, you can do exactly what you want." I couldn't blame anyone for believing we were all "rich" enough to buy their children. Any American who could afford a trip to somewhere like Morocco was.

In Casablanca, I met an actress from Chicago who looked like Sarah Jessica Parker. Her parents told me that she'd been miserable on the trip but lightened up once she met me. On this same tour, I befriended a political science doctoral candidate from Utah who possessed a wisdom beyond her years. She too had become enamored of me, telling me I looked like Tom Cruise, making me mix tapes of funky underground rock and jazz, and convincing me that I'd one day be famous. Though the young women made for comforting travel companions, I'd felt nothing sexual for them. The ubiquitous Moroccan, Italian, and Spanish men, on the other hand, commanded me. The Mediterranean gods appeared in kasbahs, restaurants, hotel lobbies, intent on drawing me out, I was convinced, to compel me to expose myself. I'd pictured myself in Burroughs's world, in the wild derelict fugue of secrets, intrigue, confusing sensations, illusory strolls, and intoxicating queer promise. The only thing missing were the drugs. I'd experiment with those years later, after graduate school.

In Rabat, I was invited into the backroom of a spice shop in a busy kasbah by a young Moroccan man, my age, the proprietor's son. He offered me dinner—couscous with lamb and vegetables—and shared a hookah. We discussed American exceptionalism, governmental over-reach, and thought control. We also covered Islam, terrorism, Salman Rushdie, and stereotyped media portrayals of Muslims. He thought I had the power to effectuate major change. That any single American was influential enough to reshape the political landscape or entertainment industry. His naivete was touching, and his sensitivity was almost erotic. He mesmerized me with his gentle touches and soft voice, his heavy eyelids and his sideways smirk. His intelligence also lit up my libido. The nature of our conversation was the stuff of Interzone mythology. The novel fresh in my mind, I imagined this scene as if written by Burroughs, and maybe even played through it harnessing his agency.

"Just tell your president that the world does not want any more war," the spice shopkeeper's son said before parting. (We'd only been four years removed from the first Gulf War in Iraq.)

In Tamri, goats balanced precariously on Argania tree branches. From a distance, it looked as if they hovered in staggered formation. I first saw them on the bus and then approached on foot. Mostly white and black, the beasts contrasted the shaggy green and brown trees, their twisted branches reaching out like gnarled fingers. The goats ignored me as they fed on the tree's fruit. Again, I was never altered in Morocco, but the dreamlike experience reminded me again of one of Burroughs's fantastic trips. Though heroin had always been his tonic, mushrooms would become mine.

In the years that followed the Moroccan holiday, I remained in platonic touch with the two women. They'd provide the basis for the diva worship of female friends that continues to this day. During this time, the desire to emerge from the shell of the straight man within which I'd been hibernating grew deeper. *Naked Lunch* would also find its way into my life throughout the next ten years, that period of potent hallucinogens, straight sex with gay visualizations, and literary aspirations. Like Genet, who I'd fall into years later, Burroughs made queer culture seem rebellious, cool, above morals and convention, impervious to ridicule and judgement. It was an artistic statement and a philosophy of spirit that no other writer or artist had provided me at that young age. The gay sex would come, though its arrival would be marked by tumult and humiliation, informed in large part by the musings of Burroughs. *Naked Lunch* was my default reference. No matter how lonely or scared or self-loathing, the novel served as a guidebook, an exit from the heteronormative theater that had become my life.

And yet even though the orientation had my respect—and covert identification—I'd not embrace it for another decade. As Burroughs asserted, "Exterminate all rational thought."

The strange zone between Morocco and coming out was marked by a teaching appointment at an at-risk school for troubled youth, teenagers grappling with emotional disorders, drug dependencies, truancy, and gang affiliations. I taught film, psychology, and health. Being a young teacher only five years older than the oldest "super" seniors, many of the students crossed blurry lines with me, and the job became a daily ethics test, one which I'm proud to say I never failed. As Burroughs asserted, "Confusion hath fuck his masterpiece."

The school, a refurbished car garage, hosted 120 pupils and had an unabating reek of mold and cigarette smoke. It was my Interzone, that untenable place of weird congregation, illicit substances, and the tension of inevitable violence. I disembodied like William Lee, a strange man in a stranger land. Forever on the run. And with several lovers who took on the projected representations of Joan Vollmer. I'd even named my first car—a hunter green jeep Cherokee—Joan. Maybe not enough has been written about how Burroughs murdered his common-law wife. Vollmer was shot by Burroughs in Mexico City during a drug-addled evening of re-enacting "the William Tell Act," in which Burroughs's attempt to shoot a liquor bottle off her head failed. He had stated that the incident had brought him into contact with his "invader, his Ugly Spirit."

I might not have physically killed my girlfriends—there were three back-to-back, two educators and a psychologist—but my deception was a kind of crime. I misled them, used them as either covers or tests, and during sex as warm bodies with which to get off, even as I imagined scenarios involving Dwayne Johnson, Mario Lopez, Brad Pitt, and at least half a dozen straight male porn stars and close straight friends. I, too, had been confronting an "Ugly Spirit." One of my girlfriends even asked me once if I would have climaxed harder with a man. She then said if she found out I was gay, she'd jump out a window. She survived my coming out and is now thriving as a therapist in a committed relationship with a male burlesque performer.

My heterosexual pageantry was mirrored by my priggish adolescence. I'd not touched a drug until I was in my twenties and even then, I'd begun softly with marijuana. Cocaine and psylocibin would follow. My first trip was frightening. The setting was an old empty house in Queens that belonged to an acquaintance whose family never moved in. One friend turned puke green. The other's face became a rectangular wall of teeth. The staircase lost dimension. The stucco ceiling moved in a wavelike formation. The terror of that evening was mitigated by thoughts of Burroughs and *Naked Lunch*, William Lee's pilgrimage across the Atlantic, his embrace of dark, absurd moments and dark, absurd people in places that were unwelcoming and deadly. I was a Burroughs disciple. I was not a common drug addict. I was not a kid trying to impress anyone. I was an intellectual on a journey, defying the strictures of polite society, of governmental rule. I was an artist standing up to his republic. Even that following morning when my heart fluttered so fast and hard, I thought it would stop and when I'd bore down on the toilet passing the fungal feces, I felt liberated and advanced. As Burroughs asserted, "If all pleasure is relief from tension, junk affords relief from the whole life process, in disconnecting the hypothalamus, which is the center of psychic energy and libido."

Much of the years between Morocco—the literary unearthing of Burroughs—and acceptance of my homosexuality were populated by students, associates, friends, lovers, and strangers that seemed to mirror the characters William Lee encounters at Interzone: Benway, Dr. Berger, Clem, Jody, County Clerk, Carl, Joselito. Bizarre figures presenting bizarre needs and neuroses.

At the school a nineteen-year-old male student passed out on his desk in a puddle of drool and vomit. His eyes rolled back in his skull, and his skin turned a deathly sallow. He'd overdosed on a cocktail of drugs he'd taken before my first period film class. An ambulance was called, and he was revived. None of the other pupils were spooked by the near-death would-be trauma, as such incidents had become common place. Later that academic year, another male student arrived for finals with small shards of glass embedded in his face. He'd been in a car accident the day before and hadn't gone to the hospital. He'd refused my insistence to go to the office to seek medical assistance and methodically pulled the glass shards out of his face while answering the essay questions I'd presented him in his psychology exam. The following week I learned that another student had shot himself dead while playing Russian roulette while high with friends. In the seven years I worked at the place that had become my Interzone, he was one of four students who would meet with premature, violent deaths. The other three were victims of murder in a gang fight, a car accident while traveling to Florida for a professional baseball opportunity, and a drug overdose. In another place and time, these passionate, wayward, haunted young people could have crossed paths with Burroughs and other Beats, leading romantic lives in remote locales with rarified company.

For me, Annexia, the totalitarian government in *Naked Lunch*, was an internal monitor. The fascist was inside. He overruled my appetite and negated my impulses. Burroughs served me well here, again. Many censors accused *Naked Lunch* of being obscene. It was indeed a celebration of the obscene, relished obscene amounts of creative freedom; Burroughs spat in the face of moral convention and issued a categorical rejection of bureaucracy. It was the defiance I needed at that age. Tapping the mettle that had been until then unfound. As Burroughs asserted, "The study of thinking machines teaches us more about the brain than we can learn by introspective methods. Western man is externalizing himself in the form of gadgets."

David Cronenberg's 1991 film adaptation, though a dramatic deviation from the text (really a marriage of the fiction with Burroughs's own life), only enhanced the renegade ferocity I longed for beyond theory, beyond speculation. Finding it soon after happening upon Burroughs's material helped with the nudge to kick open the closet door. As Burroughs asserted, "You see, control can never be a means to any practical end…It can never be a means to anything but more control…like junk."

I was twenty-eight when I first kissed a man, got naked with a man, had sex with a man. He was a photographer with a yen for much older lovers (being a year his senior rendered me "too young"). Our intimacy was at first awkward but then warm and temporarily even hot. More sensual than sexual, he preferred a deferential posture, revealed commitment issues that I'd learn would be common in the community, and after two months the affair ended as unceremoniously as it had begun. I was rid of presentiment. Free from clandestine fancies and exploited beards. The need for Burroughs dissipated in that encounter. *Naked Lunch* had satisfied its mission. As Burroughs asserted, "It is not the intensity but the duration of pain that breaks the will to resist."

My connection with Burroughs and his surreal work might have made me a more interesting person. For having remained in the shadows for as long as I had, for having endured, for having gone without, for having been a convincing liar. The modern world of gay rights and gay love is a beautiful reality, albeit not nearly as intriguing as the universe *Naked Lunch* had intimated. I'm grateful for the privileges we are now afforded, but also glamorously bored by them, too. As Burroughs asserted, "The broken image of Man moves in minute by minute and cell by cell.... Poverty, hatred, war, police-criminals, bureaucracy, insanity, all symptoms of The Human Virus."

At twenty, a year and change year after my introduction to *Naked Lunch* and Morocco, I read and was again reshaped by *Junky*. In fact, I endeavored to option the rights to the novel and even started—prematurely—adapting it into a screenplay. The Wylie Agency, who had managed Burroughs's estate, entertained my precocity as my bid reached $8,000, which was at the time all the money I had saved in the world. It being 1997, $8,000 was a respectful sum for temporary access to an obscure novella. My pursuit ended two months after it had begun when the agency informed me that I'd been outbid by the actor Steve Buscemi, who, twenty-four years later, has yet to realize the cinematic promise of the book.

In Marrakech, one of the young American women on our tour took a photo of two men, Tuareg Berbers, talking in front of a produce stand. Their heads and mouths were wrapped in blue and saffron cloth, indigo dyed. The men became enraged with the woman for sneaking a photo without permission and insisted upon payment for the infraction or the camera. I couldn't be sure as I didn't understand Arabic. It had not been in my nature to fight. I attempted apologies and reasons, explanation of cultural ignorance and monetary concession. The men were visibly confused and then annoyed by my entreaties, my hemming and hawing, my cowardly obsequiousness. They'd misread the display—I hadn't been frightened, rather diplomatic. Intent on resolving an issue in which they'd been wronged, albeit unintentionally. The women rushed back on to the tour bus and our guide settled the dispute with money at the threshold. Apparently, the men had brandished daggers. Even at that young age, I understood the dangerous entitlement of Westerners, taking what they wanted with impunity, no matter the harm, and leaving the resolution of that harm to others.

It's no secret that most teenagers feel alienated and put-upon by the adult world of establishments and arbitrary values. The institutions of heteronormativity, conformity, and capitalism had felt oppressive and imposing to my eighteen-year-old brain. Finding Burroughs in Morocco while being too spooked to exit the closet provided me strange solace. His own undercover explorations of alien sensations and territories gave me permission to remain concealed, to stay a spy, a queer in hetero clothing. All these years later, his literature has retained its resonance, a protest against social compacts I'd never signed, and an embrace of misanthropy, a cozying up to radical tenets. And yet his revolution is fought gently, as, dare I say, meekly, as a "priest." As I get increasingly acclimated to a quiet adulthood, to my own bourgeoise comforts—the comforts that kept me disingenuous all those years—I seek again a channel to sate a secretive, extremist hunger. To look again at the world and at myself, no matter how ugly, how un-appetizing, regardless of my metabolism.

"The frozen moment when one sees what is at the end of the fork."

CONTRIBUTOR BIOGRAPHIES

Brian Alessandro is a writer, artist, and filmmaker. His work has appeared in *Newsday, Interview Magazine, Bloom, PANK, Huffington Post*, Turtle Point Press, *Lambda Literary, Edmund White: By the Book*, and *(Re): An Ideas Journal*. He currently hosts live interviews with artists, writers, and filmmakers for Queens Public Library's *Culture Connection* series. He has also written and directed the feature film, *Afghan Hound*, founded the literary journal, *The New Engagement*, and wrote the novel, *The Unmentionable Mann*. He recently co-adapted Edmund White's *A Boy's Own Story* into a graphic novel for Top Shelf Productions. He holds an MA in clinical psychology from Columbia University and has taught the subject for twelve years.

Justin Addeo, a transplant from Long Island, lives with his fiancée in Grand Rapids, Michigan with their two dogs and her three children. When not working at a factory, he involves himself in the local Defund the Police campaign. Occasionally he musters the will to write and dreams of visiting family and friends back East when he finds the time.

Jason Napoli Brooks is a fiction writer living in Brooklyn, NY. His short stories have been featured in numerous publications. He is the author of the erotic crime serial *Cock of the Walk*, which is currently being translated into Spanish, and the play *Soundstage*, which was directed by Rob Roth and starred Roth and actor Rebecca Hall. Brooks recently completed the manuscript for his second novel, *Persona Non Grata*.

Tom Cardamone is the editor of *Crashing Cathedrals: Edmund White by the Book*, and is the author of the Lambda Literary Award-winning speculative novella *Green Thumb* as well as the erotic fantasy *The Lurid Sea* and other works of fiction, including two short story collections. Additionally, he has edited *The Lost Library: Gay Fiction Rediscovered*.

Michael Carroll's first collection, *Little Reef and Other Stories*, won the 2015 Sue Kaufman Prize for First Fiction from the American Academy of Arts and Letters. His second collection, *Stella Maris and Other Key West Stories*, was published in 2019 by Turtle Point Press and recently voiced for Audible by Michael Carroll. His stories and essays have appeared in the *Harvard Review*, *Yale Review*, *The New Engagement*, the *New York Times*, and others. He lives in New York with his husband, Edmund White.

Sven Davisson is a New Orleans based writer, photographer, and publisher. *The Desire Line: Memory and Impermanence*, his first full length collection of poetry, was released in 2017. His writing has appeared in the anthologies *Madder Love: Queer Men in the Precincts of Surrealism* and *Suffered from the Night: Queering Stoker's <u>Dracula</u>*. His story "Dim Star Descried" was selected for *Wilde Stories 2009: The Year's Best Gay Speculative Fiction*. Sven has a degree in Queer Theory from Hampshire College where his studies focused on a foucauldian analysis of the male+male askesis in Burroughs's writing.

Sam Desmond is a writer inspired by the intricacies of everyday life, as seen in her weekly articles celebrating the human spirit as a reporter for *The Long Island Advance* consortium of newspapers that have the highest local paper circulations in Suffolk County, New York. Her journalistic work has won awards from the New York Press Association and her short fiction has been published in literary magazines. Prior to becoming a journalist, Desmond was a legal writer for Top 100 law firms in corporate immigration law.

Peter Dubé is the author, co-author, or editor of a dozen books of fiction, non-fiction, and poetry. His most recent work, the novel-in-prose poems *The Headless Man*, was shortlisted for both the A. M. Klein Prize and the ReLit Award. In addition to his literary work, Dubé writes regularly on the visual arts and cultural issues; in this capacity he is a member of the editorial committee for the contemporary art magazine *ESPACE, art actuel*. He lives in his hometown of Montreal, where he teaches English Literature and Creative Writing.

James Grauerholz was William S. Burroughs's personal assistant and was largely responsible for helping him navigate his resurgence in American culture by getting him reading engagements, commercials (with Nike) and parts in films (Gus van Sant's *Drugstore Cowboy*). He also led Burroughs to Lawrence, Kansas, where he could find sufficient peace and quiet to write and make art. Grauerholz is currently Burroughs's bibliographer and literary executor. Though Grauerholz's poem, *Birthday Ode*, is about his meeting with Allen Ginsberg, that fateful encounter was life changing for Burroughs. Ginsberg is the one who recommended Grauerholz to Burroughs as a potential assistant. Grauerholz also helped Burroughs edit *Cities of the Red Night* (1981), *Place of Dead Roads* (1985), and *The Western Lands* (1987).

Recipient of a Lambda Literary award, two Publishing Triangle awards and a Violet Quill award, **Trebor Healey** is the author of the novels *A Horse Named Sorrow*, *Faun*, and *Through It Came Bright Colors*, as well as a poetry collection, *Sweet Son of Pan*, and three collections of stories—*A Perfect Scar*, *Eros & Dust*, and *Falling*. He co-edited (with Marci Blackman) *Beyond Definition: New Writing from Gay and Lesbian San*

Francisco and with Amie Evans) *Queer & Catholic*. He lives in Mexico City, where he works with refugee children. www.treborhealey.com

Dennis Leroy Kangalee is an African American writer, poet, actor, and guerrilla filmmaker from Queens, New York, born to a Black and Indian Trinidadian couple. In 1994, he was the youngest New York actor to et into the Juilliard Conservatory in over a decade, and the very first artist to establish a Black Theater Seminar in the winter of 1996 in Lincoln Center in the aftermath of the Robert Brustein-August Wilson debate. An eternal outlier, Kangalee—which literally means "the dispossessed"—was a theater director during NYC's final crumbling decade, the Nineties, leading Dionysus 2000 Theater Lab, one of the most dynamic and politically progressive theater groups in NYC in the final days before 9/11. Best known for his 2001 film *As an Act of Protest*, a powerful "line in the sand" against racism and police brutality and dedicated to the memory of Amadou Diallo, which has screened at colleges, universities, and activism forums across the United States and was well-received by the New York Times. He is a well-respected poet and author of *Lying Meat & Other Poems Beneath the Oil*, (2010) and experimental hybrid works such as his 'punk-performance' *Gentrified Minds*, a virulent poetic demonstration against the corporatization of NYC and globalization of the world and numerous screenplays. When not performing or writing, Dennis Leroy Kangalee teaches acting and works for and with Speller St. Films to promote new and old aesthetically or politically radical independent and "cult" films that have been otherwise neglected by the mainstream.

Nandi La Sophia is a transgender multidisciplinary artist, musician, author, award-winning playwright (*David's Dream*, Hilo Playhouse's best one-act play of 2003), creator of "Chochamilagros" vulva arts and Olorisha, currently residing in Portland, Oregon. Her fabric arts have been featured on IFC's *Portlandia*. She has had featured extra spots on *Grimm*, and she starred in the lead role of 2012 feature-length schlock B-horror flick *The Snatchers*. A world traveler and spiritist, she has lived in a Buddhist meditation retreat center, a Radical Faerie sanctuary, and tackled the themes and experiences born of youth homelessness, addiction, post-traumatic stress brain injury, living with bipolar 2 and life as a transwoman through the lens of a queer, spiritual journey navigating personal evolution, trials and tribulations as an initiate in the Afro-Cuban Lucumi tradition. She has engaged in performance art, spoken word, poetry, and musical performance for three decades. Her 2017 book, *Stagger: a collection of plays, short stories and trash*, can be found on Amazon. Her 2012 film, *The Snatchers*, can be found on You Tube, and her 2020 album, *Undone*, can be found on all music streaming platforms.

Ioannis Pappos is an electrical engineer, management consultant, and writer. He lives between New York City and Pelion, Greece. His novel, *Hotel Living*, was a finalist for the Lambda and Edmund White Debut Fiction awards.

Xan Price was born and raised in the Mississippi Delta and lives in Brooklyn. His films and videos have been exhibited internationally. He is currently finishing a novel.

Jerry Rosco is a New Yorker who has contributed to many journals and anthologies. He is the author of *Glenway Wescott Personally*, the ALA Stonewall Honor Book biography. He has also edited two volumes of Wescott journals, *Continual Lessons* and the Lambda Literary Award winning *A Heaven of Words*, as well as a collection of Wescott fiction, *A Visit to Priapus and Other Stories*.

Jessica Rowshandel (they/she) is a queer writer from Los Angles (via NYC). She has a fancy graduate degree from Columbia University and is currently studying geoscience as feminist performance art. Their art and writing have been published in various places, but they do not keep good track of these things. They are mainly a poet but sometimes Jessica writes fiction. Much of their work centers around death. Jessica is in love with Octavia Butler and should probably use divination to send her gay love poems, soon.

Paul Russell is the author of seven novels, including *The Unreal Life of Sergey Nabokov*, *The Coming Storm*, and *Immaculate Blue*. Two were awarded the Ferro-Grumley Award for Fiction, one was chosen as one of the 100 Best Gay and Lesbian Novels by the Triangle Publishing Group, and four were finalists for the Lambda Literary Award. His short stories, poems and essays have appeared in numerous publications. He has taught at Vassar College and the University of Exeter but is now retired and trying to finish his eighth novel, *The Angels Came to Sodom in the Evening*.

Laura Schleifer created the word 'artivist' to describe her vocation as an artist-activist. An NYU Tisch graduate (BFA, Drama), she's toured the Middle East, performing for Palestinian and Iraqi refugee children with the Boomchucka theater/circus troupe, taught in China, Nicaragua, and at Wesleyan University's Green Street Arts Center, performed off-Broadway, and arts-mentored homeless/targeted youth. Her screenplay, *The Feral Child*, was a Sundance Lab finalist. Her essays appear in *The Leftist Review*, *Project Intersect*, *Forca Vegan*, *The New Engagement*, *Kropotkin Now! Life, Freedom and Ethics*, published by Black Rose Books, and an upcoming anthology on neoliberalism in academia published by Peter Lang Publishing. Currently, she's writing a book, *Liberating Veganism*, for Vegan Publishers. Laura is also the Institute for Critical

Animal Studies Total Liberation Campaign Director, a Promoting Enduring Peace Board of Directors member, and co-founder of Plant the Land, a vegan food justice/community projects team in Gaza.

Christopher Stoddard's novel *At Night Only* from Itna Press was released in June 2018, and has been praised by *The Paris Review*, *Kirkus*, *Slate*, Lambda Literary, and celebrated authors Edmund White and Gary Indiana. Featured in *OUT Magazine*'s "Tastemakers" issue in 2015 for his contributions to literature and publishing as the founder of Itna Press, he's written two other novels: *Limiters* (Itna Press, 2014), and *White, Christian* (Spuyten Duyvil, 2010). A recent transplant from New York City, he lives in Los Angeles.

NYC born & raised **J. Daniel Stone** writes urban horror with a queer focus. He sold his first short story when he was twenty-two-years-old and has since published three novels, one collection of dark fiction, and one collaborative novella. His other lost children (short stories) are out there in the wild somewhere in many different online magazines and print books. He continues to write, read, dabble in magick, stargaze, and spend way too much money on books. He writes under a pseudonym to keep the wolves at bay. Visit him at www.SolitarySpiral.com.

Charlie Vázquez is the author of the novel *Contraband* (2010, Rebel Satori) and the story collection *Fantasmas: Puerto Rican Tales of the Dead* (CV Publishing, 2020). His writing appears in collections and anthologies such as *San Juan Noir* (Akashic, 2016) and *Crashing Cathedrals* (ITNA, 2019). He coedited the anthology *From Macho to Mariposa: New Gay Latino Fiction* (Lethe, 2011) and appears in the graphic novel collection *Ricanstruction* (Somos Arte, 2018), which donates proceeds to hurricane relief in Puerto Rico. Charlie is a founding member of Latino Rebels and a meditation instructor in the lineage of Chögyam

Trungpa Rinpoche, as taught by senior Buddhist teacher David Nichtern through Tibet House.

Jerry L. Wheeler is the editor of seven anthologies of gay erotica for Bold Strokes Books, Wilde City Press, and other publishers. His own collection of short fiction and essays, *Strawberries and Other Erotic Fruits* was shortlisted for the Lambda Literary Award in 2012 and has recently been re-published. He has also been Lammy-shortlisted for *Tented: Gay Erotic Tales From Under the Big Top* (2010) and *The Bears of Winter* (2014). He lives and writes in Denver CO, maintaining his review blog, *Out In Print: Queer Book Reviews* (https://outinprintblog.wordpress.com/) and his own editing business, Write And Shine (https://jerrywheelerblog.wordpress.com/). *Pangs* (2021, Queer Space/Rebel Satori) is his first novel.

Edmund White is the author of 30 books and is a professor emeritus of creative writing at Princeton. Among his novels are: *A Boy's Own Story*, *Hotel de Dream*, *A Saint from Texas* and most recently, *A Previous Life*. He received the 2019 medal for Distinguished Contribution to American Letters from the National Book Foundation.

Gregory Woods is the author of *Articulate Flesh: Male Homoeroticism and Modern Poetry* (1987), *A History of Gay Literature: The Male Tradition* (1998), and *Homintern: How Gay Culture Liberated the Modern World* (2016), all from Yale University Press. His poetry includes *We Have the Melon* (1992), *May I Say Nothing* (1998), *The District Commissioner's Dreams* (2002), *Quidnunc* (2007), *An Ordinary Dog* (2011), and *Records of an Incitement to Silence* (2021), all from Carcanet Press. He began his teaching career at the University of Salerno, Italy, in 1980. In 1998 he became the first Professor of Gay & Lesbian Studies in the UK, at Nottingham Trent University, where he is still Professor Emeritus.

Tim Young has been thinking and writing about the role of literature and music in the narrative of life for many decades. In addition to a series of essays on popular culture for *Design Observer*, he has contributed work for *The Yale Review*.

www.ingramcontent.com/pod-product-compliance
Lightning Source LLC
Chambersburg PA
CBHW021353090426
42742CB00009B/832